JAMES BOSWELL

JAMES BOSWELL Esqr.

of Auchinleck.

Publish'd by J.Sewell, Cornhill. 1787.

JAMES BOSWELL

By

C. E. VULLIAMY

GEOFFREY BLES
22 SUFFOLK STREET PALL MALL
LONDON S.W. 1

PRINTED BY
J. AND J. GRAY
EDINBURGH

FIRST PUBLISHED   OCTOBER 1932
REPRINTED   NOVEMBER 1932

JOHNSON: "Sir, you got into our club by doing what a man can do. Several of the members wished to keep you out. Burke told me, he doubted if you were fit for it: but, now you are in, none of them are sorry. Burke says, that you have so much good humour naturally, it is scarce a virtue." BOSWELL: "They were afraid of you, Sir, as it was you who proposed me." JOHNSON: "Sir, they knew, that if they refused you, they'd probably never have got in another. I'd have kept them all out. Beauclerk was very earnest for you." BOSWELL: "Beauclerk has a keenness of mind which is very uncommon."

NO one, no literary person at any rate, can be wholly incurious with regard to the life and character of James Boswell. The current idea of this peculiar man is influenced to a large extent by Macaulay's essay, in spite of later disclosures or defences. People are still inclined to think of Boswell as the uncouth and miserable sot, the toady, the lecher and the pompous fool who, by luck or by accident, wrote the finest biography in the world. Mr. Lytton Strachey certainly accepted this view. A brutal opinion may be a true opinion. The object of any enquiry should be to discover, not whether Macaulay was too harsh, but whether he was even moderately accurate. Every one knows the paradox of the Croker review: Boswell, to be sure, is the first of biographers, and yet he is a man of the feeblest intellect with absolutely none of the qualities which belong to literary skill; a man whose immortality is entirely due to the fact that he is a dunce, a parasite and a coxcomb.

Carlyle, in magnificently obscure utterances about the corruptible and the incorruptible, tried to show that Boswell truly revered Johnson, and had, indeed, a number of amiable qualities. But this hardly counteracted the blasting, passionate vituperation of Macaulay. As far as literary opinion was concerned, Macaulay probably held the field until 1878, when Dr. Birkbeck Hill, in the most decorous manner, suggested that Macaulay's estimate was wrong because he was altogether incapable of sympathy with erratic genius.

By far the greatest part of the material relating to Boswell comes from his own pen. In addition to the mass of his published writings we have letters, journals and note-books. No one ever wrote more copiously and more eagerly about himself, whether for private persons or for the public press. Indeed, when we consider how Boswell spent his time, the amount of energy which he devoted to writing is seen to be extraordinary. He was a born journalist, believing that his life was not lived properly unless it was written.

If Macaulay could have seen the papers which Boswell

scribbled so fast and so freely for his archives, he would doubtless have let loose a new fusillade. We are sure that he would have allowed no literary merit, either to the glittering facility of the dialogues or to the incredibly frank exhibition of a tortured or decaying mind; and he would certainly have found a new justification for the most violent of his passages. If it is necessary to take sides in reviewing a man's character, it may be admitted that the arguments for and against Boswell are equally strengthened by these documents. But the aim of biography should be to avoid taking sides, and to present, as far as such a thing may be presented, the true history of action, thought and circumstance which makes up the complex narrative of a human life.

The life of Boswell is not that of a hero. On the other hand, it is anything but the life of one whose thoughts and actions were ordinary. It is a life so varied, so pathetic and singular, so full of bewildering alternations and with so many flights and falls, that we know of none to compare with it. In this book an attempt has been made to find an explanation which need not be anticipated here.

For the benefit of those readers who are not Johnsonians or Scotchmen it is perhaps necessary to observe that Auchinleck is pronounced Affleck.

Italics in quoted passages are so written or printed in the originals.

In addition to the printed writings of Boswell himself, so admirably collated by Professor Pottle, and to the obvious contemporary sources, including letters, memoirs, newspapers and magazines, recent works on Boswell and Johnson have been freely consulted. Among the more important publications to which he is indebted the author would mention the following:

Letters of James Boswell, edited by C. B. Tinker; *The Hypochondriack,* edited by Dr. Margaret Bailey; *The Private Papers of James Boswell,* published by Lt.-Col. R. H. Isham, C.B.E., and edited by Geoffrey Scott and F. A. Pottle; the various collections, essays and editions of Dr. Birkbeck Hill; the essays of Professor Raleigh and of Leslie

Stephen; *Young Boswell*, by C. B. Tinker, and *The Literary Career of James Boswell*, by F. A. Pottle. The smaller popular works on Johnson and his circle, though competent, do not contain fresh information. Fitzgerald's *Life of Boswell*, published in 1891, contains much information, but is unfortunately marred by inaccuracies and by careless arrangement. Of the various editions of the *Life of Johnson*, that of Birkbeck Hill (which includes the *Hebrides*) is incomparably superior.

CONTENTS

CHAPTER I

GREEN GOOSE

ON the 21st of February 1766 William Pitt graciously received in audience a very strange young man. Although the occasion was extremely formal the young man was in fancy dress. His long hair was tied with a knot of blue ribbons. He was carrying a stiletto and a large pistol, and it is more than probable that he had a fusee or musket slung over his back. His coat was of dark cloth, his waistcoat and breeches were scarlet; black spatterdashes or gaiters were buttoned on each leg. On the left breast of the coat there was a fine embroidered badge of a Moor's head. It was the authentic dress of a Corsican chief, actually obtained, complete with all accoutrements, in the island of Corsica. The effect was astonishing. There was obviously no reasonable association between the clothes and the person who wore them. The soft amiable Scotch face of the young man was comically serious; it showed much good humour, severely controlled by a strong sense of importance.

William Pitt, looking up and seeing this grotesque fellow, could not refrain from smiling in his pompous manner. Yet he listened courteously and with interest while Corsica Boswell, discharging his mission, spoke earnestly in a rich northern voice about the brave islanders.

The astonishment of Pitt will be shared by those who study with attention the true portrait of James Boswell. He is, and he will remain, an astonishing person. His predilection for romantic disguises, his readiness to assume gravely the most unexpected characters, his rippling good nature, his extravagance and folly and weakness, his odd piety, his awful glooms, his alternations of revelry and solemnity, his prodigious literary success and his final melancholy abasement make him the most amusing and the most perplexing figure in our national biography.

If the heart of James Boswell's father had not been of the tough northern kind it might almost have been broken by the capricious nature of his child. Alexander Boswell, the father of James, was a judge in the Scotch Courts of Session, with the honorary title of Lord Auchinleck. He spoke with a broad homely accent, and seems to have been an aggressively virile type of Lowland Scot, with iron principles of duty and subordination. It seemed proper to him that young James (born in 1740) should become a lawyer. The interest of the family might have pushed him to respectable eminence. James himself, never openly resisting parental authority, and entirely agreeing with the principle of subordination, seemed willing enough to follow his prescribed course. But it was not long before the judge discovered that young James had a most unfortunate propensity for writing verses.

There is something in the spectacle of a boy writing verses which is profoundly offensive to people with a just idea of manliness or decorum: it is a spectacle which has often infuriated fathers. If the verses are good, there is something (though not much) to be said for them; but when they are only drivelling nonsense there is reasonable cause for dismay. And the verses of young James were unquestionably drivelling nonsense. He never succeeded in writing verses of any other kind. Lord Auchinleck growled and grumbled about duty and diligence, and still young James affected the airs of a literary personage, and showed a disposition for the profitless adventures of a literary career.

Little is known of Boswell's mother or of her views upon the education of a son. Her views, in any case, would not have made much difference. She was, before her marriage, Miss Euphemia Erskine; and we are told eagerly by her son James that she was descended in the line of Alva from the noble house of Mar. Although pious and respected, she lived in shadowy subjection to the rule of Alexander, and her only effect upon her children was that of setting before them an unobtrusive pattern of goodness.

Even less is known of the infancy of David, the younger brother of James, and of life in the Boswell household.

The family estate of Auchinleck in Ayrshire, with the "sullen dignity" of the old castle and the solid comfort of a fine new house, was always an inspiration to the feudal fancies of James Boswell. It was here that he learned about the planting of trees, the working of quarries, the liming of fields, the care of hedges and fences, and the proper management of the "tacksmen." Here were proudly preserved the Auchinleck pedigree and the "Auchinleck colours." And here he received his first lessons from Mr. John Dunn, the poetical minister.

But it was not until he got to Edinburgh that young James could really show what stuff he was made of. He went first to Mr. Mundell's academy, and then to the University of Edinburgh. When he had done with mere schooling, he began to study law; he also began to amuse himself, with energy but without discretion.

Among those who were studying Greek in the class of Robert Hunter there was a grave though amiable young man called William Johnson Temple, the son of William Temple of Allardean. Young William was a water-drinker, and he was also a Whig; Boswell, on the other hand, was a Tory and a toper. No two lads could have been more unlike; yet they became close friends, and to this friendship we owe the most astounding series of letters, written by a rake and addressed to a clergyman.

Temple was always a quiet, depressed man, sensitive and reserved, with a few discreet abilities. He had a good deal of literature, and wrote an essay on the clergy which was much admired by Bishop Horne. He was ordained in 1766 and obtained the living of Mamhead, about ten miles from Exeter, and afterwards that of St. Gluvias in Cornwall. His figure retires, as it probably did when he was alive, into blameless obscurity; he was not a man to make a noise in the world, or to show himself upon the stage. His friendship with James Boswell has preserved him from total oblivion, and it seems likely enough that the same friendship helped to preserve Boswell himself from total depravity.

The four ruling passions of Boswell's life were all strongly in evidence when he was eighteen. Of these passions, two are common enough—wine and women. But the other two are more remarkable: the burning desire for literary fame, and the desire to be acquainted, even momentarily, with those who were great or notorious. We find him, in 1758, already hob-nobbing with David Hume.

Now, it has to be remembered that Hume, in 1758, was forty-seven years old, and had produced all his great speculative and philosophical essays and the first volume of the *History*. Boswell describes him with easy condescension in one of his letters to Temple: "He is a most discreet, affable man as ever I met with, and has really a great deal of learning, and a choice collection of books . . . a very proper person for a young man to cultivate an acquaintance with, though he has not, perhaps, the most delicate taste." Even from a lad at the confident age of eighteen there is something in this which points to a more than ordinary degree of absurdity or of independence.

At the same period, and in his own words, he "was then very fond of the drama, and associated much with the players." He brought upon the stage a bad comedy, confided to him by Lady Houston with a strict injunction that he was not to reveal the author. In 1760 Francis Gentleman dedicated to him the feeble tragedy of *Oroonoko, or the Royal Slave*.

Although it is quite likely that Boswell had lent money to Francis Gentleman, who was Irish and plausible, this dedication certainly implies that Boswell, at twenty, was not unknown to the Edinburgh and Glasgow public. Even if he paid Gentleman for the dedication or accepted it in discharge of a debt (circumstances by no means improbable), the fact remains that his name was considered good enough to confer the benefits of patronage.

In the winter of 1759 Boswell matriculated at the University of Glasgow, where he studied moral philosophy and rhetoric under Adam Smith.

We do not possess many particulars in regard to his life during the period 1759-1762. The scandals of his flight from Glasgow with an actress and his adoption of the Roman Catholic faith do not rest upon a good circumstantial foundation. The actress has never been identified. He does appear to have been attracted by the Holy Church of Rome, and he may, for a little while, have become a Catholic; indeed, he himself admitted this to Rousseau in 1764; but the process of re-conversion, perhaps rather forcibly directed by Lord Auchinleck, must have been extremely rapid.

It is certain that he visited London in 1760, arriving in March and leaving in May. There was probably no serious intention in this visit, nor is it likely that it was undertaken with the knowledge and approval of his father. He had "an almost enthusiastic notion of the felicity of London," and he was not disappointed. Before he had been long in town he was aware of two distinct ambitions: to meet Samuel Johnson and to obtain a commission in the Foot Guards. For the introduction to Johnson he relied upon Samuel Derrick, a genial though futile fellow, who had been unsuccessful on the stage, and became Master of the Ceremonies at Bath in 1761. But Derrick was either afraid of approaching Johnson or of bringing to his notice such an odd creature. Yet he might safely have introduced Boswell, for the great Doctor declared, some years later, "I had a kindness for Derrick and am sorry he is dead."

Still, Derrick was worth knowing. He led Boswell gaily to the lighter and the lower amusements of London. He showed him the jolly world of coffee-houses and bagnios, the Ranelagh girls or the hardier beauties of Covent Garden. And when Boswell desired entertainment of a more elegant sort, he found it in the society of the Earl of Eglinton, who took him into the circles of "the great, the gay and the ingenious." With Eglinton he went to Newmarket, and there composed one of the most inane of his youthful poems. It was probably during this visit to London that he prodigiously amused the audience at Drury Lane by imitating the lowing of a cow, unrestrained by the insipid respectability of his companion, the Reverend Hugh Blair.

It was certainly at this time that he met Sterne, whose character and writings had an immediate effect upon his own. Professor Pottle has most ingeniously discovered the evidence of this meeting in a letter, obviously from Boswell, and presumably addressed to the Earl of Eglinton, in the *Scots Magazine* for September 1761. Sterne was then in his

B

5

forty-seventh year, and the publication of the first two volumes of *Tristram Shandy* had raised him giddily and rapidly to the front ranks of literature and had made him a famous man. He spent about three months in London. There seems to be little doubt that Boswell found his way to the sumptuous Pall Mall lodgings of Yorick. That he should not have made more of this meeting is a little strange; but we should remember the biting contempt with which Johnson spoke of "the man Sterne"—contempt more vigorously expressed by Goldsmith in his epithet of "bawdy blockhead."

After his return to Edinburgh, Boswell became exceedingly restive. He had got his mind filled, so he said, with the most gay ideas; he was dreaming of life in the Guards, of being about the Court, of enjoying all the felicities of the *beau monde* and the company of men of genius. Edinburgh, not yet Athenian, was horribly provincial. Homely voices, to which he now listened with a shrinking dismay, invited him to their homely festivities. The only alternative was the prim severity of the Auchinleck household. His flighty imagination was miserably choked by the dull and heartless bulk of the *Corpus Juris Civilis*. He compared himself, in his young rage, to a Newmarket courser tied to a dung-cart. Nor could the wandering ladies of the Castle Hill afford him more than a transient and sometimes perilous amusement.

But—thank goodness!—there was always literature. It is possible to write poetry in almost any place. It is equally possible to write letters, or critical essays. Young James had already printed some poems in the *Scots Magazine* (1758), and although they were bad, they might have been very considerably worse, and still printable. In 1760 he published a threepenny pamphlet of *Observations, Good or Bad, Stupid or Clever, Serious or Jocular, on Squire Foote's Dramatic Entertainment intitled The Minor. By a Genius*. This production was briefly but adequately described in the *Monthly Review* for December 1760: "All the humour of this lies in the title-page."

The *Observations* were followed by an *Elegy on the Death*

of an Amiable Young Lady, with an Epistle from Menalcas to Lycidas, price sixpence. We do not know of any notice of this performance, which is chiefly remarkable on account of the *Three Critical Recommendatory Letters* which introduce the poems, and which mark the beginning of the correspondence with Andrew Erskine, afterwards published.

Erskine was a sprightly boy in the 71st Regiment, quartered in Edinburgh. He joined one of those absurd facetious clubs in which Boswell invariably found a congenial atmosphere. If Boswell himself was not the founder of the Soaping Club he was the leading spirit, and he wrote, in memory of this association, a most astounding and most Boswellian song:

> "Boswell, of Soapers the king,
> On Tuesdays at Tom's does appear,
> And when he does talk or does sing,
> To him ne'er a one can come near;
> For he talks with such ease and such grace,
> That all charm'd to attention we sit,
> And he sings with so comic a face,
> That our sides are just ready to split.
>
> Boswell does women adore,
> And never once means to deceive;
> He's in love with at least half a score;
> If they're serious he smiles in his sleeve.
> He has all the bright fancy of youth
> With the judgment of forty and five.
> In short, to declare the plain truth,
> There is no better fellow alive."

Here you have that odd mixture of conscious buffoonery and of genuine self-approval which is one of the most perplexing and most subtle traits in Boswell's character. It is an invitation as well as an assertion. You may laugh at him or with him; from his point of view, you are perfectly welcome to do either. He sings with so comic a face, and yet he knows all the while there is no better fellow alive. Do please take notice of him—that is the main thing. If you can understand him in this, you are on the way to understanding the whole nature of the man. He printed the song in a volume of *Poems by Scotch Gentlemen* in 1762, and he reprinted parts of it, with unruffled complacency, in the *European Magazine* four years before his death.

And yet the king of the Soapers could be well received and well entertained by Lord Elibank, Lord Kaimes, Sir David Dalrymple (Lord Hailes), Robertson, Blair and Hume. He was admitted to the Select Society of Edinburgh—a choice association for curing gentlemen of the Scotch accent. His father was not ashamed to talk about him with the Duke of Argyll. In the calm apartments of the royal palace at Holyrood he talked sedately with Lord Somerville, who encouraged him in his literary ambitions. You might have thought that so young a man would be satisfied with so much attention. But still he was hankering after the dressed-up profession of the soldier, and still he longed for another and a deeper draught of London felicity.

Somehow or other, literature was not so easy as he thought. He wrote anonymously, but openly dedicated to himself, an *Ode to Tragedy* in 1761. He made a contribution of thirty-one poems, long and short, and all equally bad, to the second volume of the anthology of verse by Scotch Gentlemen. In 1762 Dodsley published in quarto *The Cub at Newmarket.*

The Cub is a thing which any intelligent schoolboy would be ashamed to own, but the Duke of York heard it with pleasure, and graciously allowed Boswell to dedicate it to him. It has no point and no story. Boswell describes himself sitting in the coffee-room at Newmarket and being laughed at by the sportsmen. He had tried to get it published before he left London in 1760, but had not succeeded—and no wonder.

A man who gets leave to dedicate to royalty must get his dedication printed somehow. Boswell therefore wrote to a London printer early in 1762 and told him to have *The Cub* printed immediately at the author's expense. "Let no expense be spared," he said, "to make it genteel. Let it be done on large quarto, and a good type." The *Monthly*

Review dismissed *The Cub* with a short though fair notice: "From the sprightly *Preface* we expected very high entertainment in reading the *Poem*; but the humour of the piece being chiefly confined to the occasion and the place, we were much disappointed, as the meaning was scarce intelligible to us."

In collaboration with Andrew Erskine and George Dempster, Boswell published the *Critical Strictures on Elvira*, a smart essay on Malloch's tragedy, towards the end of January 1763. About the same time he must have been preparing for the press the elegant volume of the *Correspondence with Erskine*.

Letters between The Honourable Andrew Erskine and James Boswell, Esq. appeared about the middle of April 1763: in boards for three shillings, or full-bound in calf for three-and-sixpence. This is the first book to bear Boswell's name in full upon the title-page. It is also, in the words of Professor Pottle, "the first considerable example of Boswell's life-long willingness to be indiscreet provided thereby he could be interesting." The letters are gay, topical, self-conscious and cheerfully impertinent; some are in prose and some in verse. The *London Chronicle* described the collection as "a Book of true Genius, from the Authors of which we may expect many future agreeable productions." But the *Monthly Review* (June 1763) was more discerning:

"Messrs. Erskine and Boswell are two juvenile Wits, who have chosen to exhibit themselves in a little octavo, for the entertainment of the public. . . . *Vive la bagatelle* is their maxim; and away they scribble, away they publish; freely abandoning their names, and their fame . . . to the morsure of criticism, and the mercy of the wide world. . . . We would not discourage them by any severity of animadversion on their light and airy labours. They are pretty fellows in literature; and must not be roughly dealt with."

Vive la bagatelle! The Newmarket courser is kicking and capering to a pretty tune, though Boswell pauses not infrequently to assure the scandalised onlookers that he is at bottom a sober and a grave man.

Sober and grave he may very well have been upon occasion. No man was ever more anxious to adapt himself, not only in behaviour but in actual mood, to place or company. If he was at home in "the mansions of gross sensuality" he was also at home (or thought he was) in a church. It was indeed this faculty of instant harmonisation which made him, in later life, equally congenial to the greatest or the meanest of characters. He was determined that nothing, and no one, should escape him. Whether pursuing a chambermaid up the creaking staircase of a wayside inn, or pursuing Rousseau in his retreat of Motiers, he was equally inflamed, equally sincere and persistent. Whatever charm or power he had lay in this faculty, the cause both of ruin and renown. He was an overbalanced character, swept away by a too voracious appetite for life in every conceivable form and a too ardent desire to feel the unmitigated force of every conceivable emotion.

Boswell's description of himself in the *Erskine Correspondence* is the best of his youthful portraits:

"The author of the *Ode to Tragedy* is a most excellent man: he is of an ancient family in the west of Scotland, upon which he values himself not a little. At his nativity there appeared omens of his future greatness. His parts are bright, and his education has been good. He has travelled in post-chaises miles without number. He is fond of seeing much of the world. He eats of every good dish, especially apple-pie. He drinks old Hock. He has a very fine temper. He is somewhat of an humourist and a little tinctured with pride. He has a good manly countenance, and he owns himself to be amorous. He has infinite vivacity, yet is observed at times to have a melancholy cast. He is rather fat than lean, rather short than tall, rather young than old. His shoes are neatly made, and he never wears spectacles. The length of his walking-stick is not yet ascertained; but we hope soon to favour the Republic of Letters with a solution of this difficulty,

as several able mathematicians are employed in its investigation, and for that purpose have posted themselves
at different given points in the Canongate. . . ."

At the age of twenty-two he was already watching himself
closely, most frequently with approval, but sometimes with
despair. He recorded vivaciously in private journals all the
foolish, amusing or nasty particulars of his life. He noted
that he was in a charming humour one day, very dull the day
after, and so on. And all the time he was dreaming of the
Guards. He was in raptures when he thought of his uniform;
he did not doubt that he would make a fine figure, and be
distinguished as a good officer and a gentleman of spirit.
He owned himself to be amorous. He certainly was.
Within a few minutes of meeting some pretty girl he was
quite ready to invite her to accompany him on one of his
"jaunts." He admitted that he had the most unaccountable,
the most veering, alert inclinations that could possibly be
imagined. The only antidote for one woman is another
woman; and so it goes on, literally, to the end of his days.
And yet conscience is always protesting, piety is always
reproving, in spite of comforting examples from the Old
Testament or desperate appeals to the customs of Asia.
Might he not be a patriarch on occasion, in view of these
respectable patterns?
On the 15th of November 1762 Boswell set out for
London again.
He was still hoping for his commission, and had with him
an introduction to the Duke of Queensberry. But his main
idea was to plunge once more into the joys—all the joys—of
London life. He was anxious to meet Johnson; but he was
anxious to meet every celebrity within his reach. It is im-
possible to follow in detail the course of his life between the
end of 1762 and his meeting with Johnson on the 16th of
May 1763. He met Goldsmith, apparently, before he met
Johnson, but we do not know precisely when. On his own
showing, however, we know that he was acquainted with
John Wilkes, Bonnell Thornton, Robert Lloyd and Charles
Churchill.

John Wilkes, one of the worst and most amusing men of his age, was then the member for Aylesbury and also a member of the Sublime Society of the Beef Steaks. He was thirty-six years old. Sir Francis Dashwood had enrolled him in the debauched company of the Medmenham Monks, together with Lloyd and Churchill. Wilkes had not yet published the famous Number 45 of the *North Briton*, which appeared on the 23rd of April 1763. He may very well have been engaged upon the obscene pages of his burlesque *Essay on Woman*. The Middlesex election, the liberty riots and the popular acclamation of Wilkes took place after his return from exile in 1768, but he was already recognised as a champion of the people against the crown. His diabolical squinting and grinning face, made yet more satanic by the horn-like central curls of his wig, presided over the tavern revels of those who were classically indecent and wittily blasphemous.

Charles Churchill, "the Bruiser," was the most profligate rogue who ever wore the dress of a clergyman. He married at seventeen, and at twenty-four he entered the church as a means of escaping poverty. After holding curacies in Wales and Somerset he came back to London in 1758. Here, in 1761, he began to let loose "a tempest of uncouth and vituperative verse." The best known of his foul satires are the *Rosciad*, the *Prophecy of Famine*, and the *Epistle to Hogarth*. The methods and the mind of Churchill may be observed, if anyone desires to observe them, in the *Epistle to Hogarth*, where a man who is known to be grievously ill is taunted with his approaching death. The *Rosciad*, however, made Churchill famous and raised him to a position of some eminence among men of letters. He died at Boulogne in 1764, burnt out by all the disorders of a vicious life, at the age of thirty-three. Hogarth died in the same year.

Robert Lloyd, the murky satellite of Churchill, fortunately extinguished himself when he was thirty-one. He had been the captain of Westminster school, and at one time was an usher there. His friendship with Churchill ruined him. He gave up his school appointment and tried to earn a living by literary hackwork. In 1763 he was confined to the debtors' prison of the Fleet. On hearing of Churchill's death in 1764 he fell into a fever and said, "I shall follow poor Charles." He died in prison soon after the first performance of his comic opera, *The Capricious Lovers*, and he is said to have been nursed with heroic devotion by Patty Churchill, the sister of Charles.

Bonnell Thornton, another member of this unpleasant group, managed to reach the comparatively advanced age of forty-four. He was a miscellaneous writer and a wit of some ability, chiefly known for his editorship of the *Connoisseur* with Colman. His burlesque *Ode on St. Cecilia's Day* amused Doctor Johnson, who was fond of quoting it.

If he had not been eventually held back by the gravitational pull of Johnson, Boswell might easily have gone the way of Churchill and Lloyd. It is true that Temple was then in London, where he had chambers in Farrar's Buildings; but the influence of Temple alone would hardly have been sufficient. And here is the young man, to whom the solemnities of public worship were so congenial, becoming the close friend of Jack Wilkes, who made a mockery of all religion and who composed an obscene parody of the *Veni Creator Spiritus*.

Goose though he was, we are not to regard Boswell as a goose of the ordinary kind. He was in bad company, but not the sort of bad company in which a mere cackling goose would naturally find himself. Wilkes, Churchill and the others had the supreme merit of being what Boswell himself would have termed *classick*. They would not have tolerated for one moment the conversation of a perfect fool. If we take the lowest estimate of Boswell we have to admit the fascination of his adaptability and cheerfulness. His humour and simple gaiety, his quick appreciation of a literary joke, the engaging drollery of his countenance, and above all his perfect readiness to admire, to listen and applaud, were qualities that would have made him welcome at Will's, the Cocoa Tree, or the Turk's Head, and perhaps even more welcome at Dolly's Chop House or the Mourning Bush. Moreover, his manly delight in bottle and brothel gave him the right to cut a passable figure among the bucks. There must have been something rather amusing in the fact of this freakish fellow being the son of a grave Scotch judge, and himself speaking with a whimsical Scotch accent.

And then you have to remember that Boswell, even at twenty-two, had some pretensions to be an author. What he had printed was certainly not the work of a genius; still, it was the work of a young man with some idea of writing, and with bounding vivacity.

Boswell had not come to town for the sole purpose of meeting Johnson or of getting into the Guards. London has had many lovers more worthy and more eloquent, but none more truly, more fatally enamoured than Boswell. London, to him, was the great emporium, offering to a civilised genteel man all the treasures of the earth. He could solemnly worship at St. Paul's, and he could run after the girls in the Piazza. He could sit, all beaming reverence, at Queensberry's table; or cut more lively capers at drum, festino and masquerade. He loved to see people hanged, and he could see them hanged nearly every morning. In Pall Mall he could look at the fops or beauties of the town, and the elegant books of Mr. Dodsley. When he was tired of Wilkes and his racketing crew, he found a change in the placid hospitality of Tom Davies the bookseller and his pretty wife. At his own rooms in Downing Street he was able to entertain company, to drink or gamble, talk philosophy or talk bawdy, or explain to his more serious acquaintances the privilege of being a Scotch landlord. Let it be remembered that his meeting with Johnson did not take place until he had been in London for six months. If he had really been desperately anxious for this meeting it seems incredible that it could not have been brought about sooner. Boswell, it is true, had been relying upon old Sheridan to introduce him, and Johnson had foolishly quarrelled with Sheridan; but Johnson had not yet risen to the great eminence of his later years, he was on familiar terms with a large number of people, most of them easy to approach, and he was a man who liked to meet a new friend every day and who prided himself on the amusing variety of his acquaintance. It is, indeed, a little remarkable that Boswell had avoided meeting Johnson for so long.

At the beginning of 1763 young Boswell was probably a good deal concerned with the publication and circulation of the *Critical Strictures*, which came out at the end of January, and the *Correspondence with Erskine*, advertised for the middle of April. The *Critical Strictures* was only a sixpenny octavo pamphlet of twenty-four pages, but the *Correspondence* was a book of some pretension; both were printed by Samuel Chandler, and sold by William Flexney near Gray's Inn Gate.

But these literary excursions were small affairs in comparison with what occurred on the 16th of May 1763. On that day Boswell saw for the first time the rolling, majestic frame of Mr. Samuel Johnson.

CHAPTER II

DICTIONARY JOHNSON

BOSWELL had been drinking tea with Tom Davies, when he looked up and beheld Mr. Johnson approaching the glass door between the shop and the parlour.

Johnson was then in his fifty-fourth year. His pension, only recently granted, had relieved him from the intolerable anxieties of the man who tries to live by writing. With the exception of the *Lives of the Poets*, not produced until 1781, he had written and published all his principal works. He had already become the grand perambulating social figure whose magnificent indolence and whose teasing melancholy led him to seek the entertainment of conversation and to visit with equal delight the gay company of a tavern or the quiet retreat of some learned friend. But it was not until Reynolds had founded the Club in 1764 that he grew to his full magnitude and exhibited all the richness and resource of his character. The great Johnsonian decade is unquestionably the period 1768-1778, and yet he produced no literary work in that period, except a few political tracts, and his *Journey to the Western Islands*. The publication of the *Dictionary* in 1755 had given him pre-eminence as a man of letters and raised him to the impregnable position of a literary dictator. His escape from mere drudgery was now permitting him to acquire pre-eminence of a more universal kind, and to become the huge impersonation of thundering common sense and of moral vigour. He was not yet Doctor Johnson. The degree of LL.D. was conferred upon him by Trinity College, Dublin, in 1765, and that of D.C.L. by Oxford (with customary tardiness) ten years later.

The figure that was now approaching the glass door threw Boswell into a state of agitation. It was to be his first meeting with a really great man, and he knew it. He was anxious to prove his worth, and afraid of making a fool of himself. Johnson, like every strong character, had strong prejudices, and the most notorious of these was a prejudice against the people of Scotland. It was, as Boswell himself described it in his serio-comic way, an "awful approach."

Johnson entered the parlour and saw dimly (for he could not see otherwise) Mr. and Mrs. Davies, and a plump, nervous young man, who was respectfully introduced to him by Mr. Davies. Before they had been together for many minutes Boswell had received two staggering blows from the great man: the first when he said, "I do indeed come from Scotland, but I cannot help it"; and the second after a foolish remark about Garrick.

Having reduced Boswell to a mortified silence, Johnson proceeded to talk about books and people in his usual emphatic style. He knew how to deal with Jack Wilkes; he would send half a dozen footmen and have him well ducked. The notion of liberty amuses the people of England. Oh yes! Derrick may do very well as long as he can outrun his character; but the moment his character gets up with him, it is all over. This book . . . deserves to be held in some estimation, though much of it is chimerical.

After he had listened to this facile talk for a little time, Boswell had to go; he had an engagement elsewhere. Tom Davies followed him to the door. Poor Boswell, though some of his observations had been civilly received, could not hope that Johnson would think it worth while to know him. "Don't be uneasy," said Mr. Davies. "I can see he likes you very well."

It is doubtful if Boswell himself, at the time, regarded this meeting as one of any great importance. When he wrote to Sir David Dalrymple on the 21st of May, and again on the 25th of June, he said nothing at all about Johnson. And yet, on the 25th of June he had met the Doctor at Clifton's eating-house and had arranged to sup with him at the Mitre.

The second of these two letters to Dalrymple is curiously despondent. All hopes of a career in the Guards had been abandoned, and Boswell had promised his father that he would study civil law, for one winter, at the University of Utrecht. After that, he was to have "the indulgence of travelling upon the Continent, provided that on his return he should become an advocate at the Scotch Bar."

"My great object," he wrote to Dalrymple, "is to attain a proper conduct in life. How sad will it be, if I turn out no better than I am; I have much vivacity, which leads to dissipation and folly. This, I think, I can restrain. But I will be moderate, and not aim at a stiff sageness and buckram correctness. I must, however, own to you, that I have at bottom a melancholy cast; which dissipation relieves by making me thoughtless, and therefore, an easier, tho' a more contemptible, animal. I dread a return of this malady. I am always apprehensive of it. Pray tell me if Utrecht be a place of a dull and severe cast, or if it be a place of decency and chearfull politeness? Tell me, too, if years do not strengthen the mind, and make it less susceptible of being hurt? and if having a rational object will not keep up my spirits? . . . Much depends on my doing well next winter. My future rout can be settled time enough. I hope my father has never thought of sending a travelling governour (as the phrase is) with me. That is surely a very bad plan for me, and what I could scarcely agree to. Pray keep him from thinking of that."

In a letter written to John Johnson of Grange five days later, he was again melancholy. He felt himself "indifferent to all pursuits," and the rainy weather had caused him "to view all things in the most disagreeable light." And still "many spirited gay ideas" came into his mind when he remembered that he was "a young man of fortune just going to set out on his travels." He had already to provide for the first of his illegitimate children, and the letter closed with instructions in regard to a maintenance allowance of ten pounds a year. He said nothing about his acquaintance with Johnson, although he had then enjoyed the supreme felicity of an evening at the Mitre.

Certainly Boswell never supposed, until Johnson himself had given him clear encouragement, that he was good enough to be the friend of such an eminent man. He did not pursue Mr. Johnson with swaggering confidence; he sought him with trepidation, and received, with astonishment and with gratitude, the first unmistakable signs of Johnson's approval.

Eight days after the meeting in the parlour, and then only after a consultation with Davies, Boswell ventured to call upon Johnson at Number 1 Inner Temple Lane. He found him, as he so often was, surrounded by a number of obscure but admiring gentlemen, whose names were not remembered. The sage himself was in his customary disarray: "His brown suit of cloaths looked very rusty: he had on a little old shrivelled unpowdered wig, which was too small for his head; his shirt-neck and the knees of his breeches were loose; his black worsted stockings ill drawn up; and he had a pair of unbuckled shoes by way of slippers." Presently the gentlemen rose to take their leave, and Boswell prepared to follow them. "Nay, don't go," said Johnson. "Sir," replied Boswell, "I am afraid that I intrude upon you. It is benevolent to allow me to sit and hear you." There was something in the plain sincerity of this utterance which made an immediate appeal. "Sir, I am obliged to any man who visits me."

So the friendship grew. Davies had not been wrong in supposing that Johnson had taken a liking to Boswell. There is no need to look far for the explanation. Hypocrisy in behaviour was never among the deplorable weaknesses of Boswell, and no man was less capable of hiding his thoughts or emotions. His very assiduity in pursuing great men, in spite of its more doubtful motives, does prove that he had a true reverence for greatness, at least in his earlier days, and, what is infinitely more rare, a true appreciation of greatness. His glorious record of Johnson's conversation displays, not only a degree of impressibility which is almost feminine, but also the most unerring perception of all those qualities that made his conversation so remarkable. In the art of recording dialogue he is without a rival, and he must there-fore have been an ideal listener. He was the proper comple-ment of Johnson, the perfect receiver of the Johnsonian transmission. He was more. He could set the transmission going. Just as there are some men who can wheedle out of others their property or wealth, so this peculiar man could wheedle out of them, and appropriate to himself, their riches of thought or fancy or wisdom. Whenever he found himself in the company of any remarkable man, that man seemed willing enough to display himself, to exert himself in conversation, for his particular benefit. His own part in conversation was generally negligible, and often contemptible, but his effect upon a good talker was to make him talk at his best. There is abundant proof of this in his dialogues with Rousseau, Voltaire, and Pascal Paoli.

He had also the supreme advantage of being an indestructible target: no broadside of wit or ridicule could ever sink him, and although he might be thrown into a little temporary disorder by the heavy fire of Johnson, he was cheerfully prepared to be shot at again and again. This obliging buoyancy must have been appreciated by the Doctor, who disliked equally those who ran away from him and those who opposed him with too much resolution.

Young Boswell had other recommendations. He was a lad of good birth, reasonably well educated. Although his Greek was uncertain, he had enough Latin to give him confidence when Latin quotations were produced—and without such confidence no one could then cut a figure in literary circles. He had an undeniable sense of what was good in literature. He believed himself to be pious. If he talked rather frequently about his own affairs, he talked with such pleasing frankness that he was nearly always forgiven, and was generally rewarded by interest or sympathy. His commonplace vices had not yet destroyed the natural gaiety and vigour of youth.

Johnson was fond of young men. When he was roused at three in the morning by the voices of Beauclerk and Langton, he cried, "What, is it you, you dogs! I'll have a frisk with you." He was always kind to youngsters; he liked to help or advise them, in a manner graciously paternal and with all the true benignity of his heart. In his own youth there had been few diversions and little ease. Nor had the bitter drudgery of his early manhood allowed him any time for amusement. He had therefore a latent capacity for juvenile frolic which he showed in mature age by sudden bellowings of hilarity and by a ponderous frisking with young people. Though he had no children, he was a man glowing with paternal sentiment. He could not refrain from slipping pennies into the hands of the children he found sleeping in the street, and he always felt the desire to guide or admonish those who were setting out upon the adventure of life. And there was another reason for his predilection for youth. Youthful society is generally a cure for gloom, and Johnson, left to himself, fell too often and too heavily into a gloom of tragic hopelessness. "Sir," he said, "I love the acquaintance of young people; because, in the first place, I don't like to think of myself growing old. In the next place, young acquaintances must last longest, if they do last; and then, Sir, young men have more virtue than old men; they have more generous sentiments in every respect. I love the young dogs of this age."

That Johnson immediately appreciated the society of Boswell is quite evident. Their fourth meeting took place near Temple Bar at one o'clock in the morning. Boswell, to whom opportunity was everything, at once proposed a visit to the Mitre. "Sir," replied Johnson, "it is too late; they won't let us in. But I'll go with you another night with all my heart."

The first evening at the Mitre raised Boswell to "a pleasing elevation of mind beyond what he had ever before experienced." The very name of the place, though it was only the name of a tavern, had an orthodox high-church sound which tickled his fancy. And there, before him, softened a little by the light of the wax candles, was the amiable gargantuan figure of Dictionary Johnson. Upon the table, after the remains of a good supper had been cleared away, stood a bottle of port—the most heartening and sociable of wines.

At first the conversation was literary. "Colley Cibber, Sir, was by no means a blockhead. . . . Sir, I do not think Gray a first-rate poet." But soon, expanding in the radiance of this majestic being, young Boswell ventured to give "a little sketch of his life." He had been educated in the principles of religion; but he had been misled for a while, not into anything very desperate, but certainly into "a certain degree of infidelity." In other words, he had been dazzled or confused by the grinning ribaldry of Wilkes. Now he had come to a better way of thinking. His contact with Johnson's colossal piety had already had an effect. On certain points of dogma he was not clear: perfect orthodoxy was beyond him. "Give me your hand," cried Johnson, honestly moved by the frankness of this avowal; "I have taken a liking to you." And then the great rumbling voice gave his views upon the force of testimony and our ignorance of final causes. Then he came to lighter and more personal things: "There is a good deal of Spain that has not been perambulated. I would have you go thither. A man of inferior talents to yours may furnish us with useful observations upon that country." It needed no more to make the young man fancy himself already a Spanish perambulator.

No one who has read carefully the early conversations in the *Life* can fail to have noticed how admirably Johnson talked when he was alone with Boswell. It was entirely beyond the capacity of Boswell to have invented this talk. His own free composition never approached the level of his Johnsonian records. By sheer retentiveness of memory, and by that alone, could the extraordinary quality of this conversation have been preserved.

Johnson made a point of always talking as well as he could, but he would only talk to a congenial audience. He was perfectly willing to sit talking to Boswell from eight or nine o'clock in the evening until one or two o'clock in the morning. It is difficult to see how those who imagine Boswell to have been a mere fool can explain this, unless they imagine that Johnson was a fool as well.

A very little reflection is enough to shatter the extremely crude hypothesis of Macaulay. Johnson talked freely and well to this young man, not only because he liked him, but because the young man had the liveliest appreciation of conversational episode and the happiest way of playing suggestively or provokingly with a new theme. These are not the gifts of a great man or an eloquent man, but they are not those of a fool. To suppose that we owe the most astonishing literary portrait in the world to the random jottings of an irresponsible ass is clearly absurd.

The meetings with Johnson, at first separated by long periods of dissipation, became more frequent in July. On the 1st of July there was a meeting of Johnson, Boswell and Goldsmith at the Mitre.

Goldsmith was then in his thirty-fifth year. He was beginning to emerge from a dreary career of hackwork. He had published the *Citizen of the World* in 1762, but the plays and poems and the novel by which he is known to us had not yet been written. His ambitions in the way of dress had probably got to the stage of crimson breeches, though not to the full-blown splendour of Tyrian blooms, queen's blue silk and gold sprig buttons. Boswell disliked him. He called him sententiously "one of the brightest ornaments of the Johnsonian school," and loved to expose his vanity. Goldsmith had been taken under the wing of Johnson for a little over a year, and their friendship was another proof of Johnson's benevolence and discernment.

On the day after this meeting, Boswell wrote to Dalrymple:

"I am now upon a very good footing with Mr. Johnson. His conversation is very instructive and entertaining. He has a most extensive fund of knowledge, a very clear expression, and much strong humour. I am often with him. Some nights ago we supt by ourselves at the Mitre Tavern, and sat over a sober bottle till between one and two in the morning."

A few days later he wrote to Temple, complaining of "a langour and absence of ideas." He had moved from his Downing Street lodgings because of the rudeness of his landlord (so he says) and was now in Temple's own chambers in Farrar's Buildings. Temple himself was at Trinity Hall, Cambridge. Boswell shared the rooms with Temple's young brother, Bob, who was a gay, noisy lad, with an unpleasant habit of asking for the loan of money, and a more unpleasant habit of treating the loan as a gift. He held a commission in a line regiment, but did not take his duties too seriously.

Johnson's household at this time included the blind lady, Mrs. Anna Williams, and the "obscure practiser in physick," Mr. Levett. Nothing displays better the domestic tenderness of Johnson than his concern for the affliction of the one and his touching admiration of the mediocre abilities of the other. The negro servant, Francis Barber—"his Ethiopian"—was generally in attendance.

On the 19th of July, Boswell ascended four flights of stairs with Mr. Levett to the dusty attic at the top of the house where Johnson kept his books and papers, and the chemical apparatus with which he used to amuse himself. From the windows they could see the dome of St. Paul's, "and many a brick roof." Everything was dirty and everything in confusion. Sheets of paper, covered with Johnson's handwriting, were scattered over the floor. It was here that he retired when he wanted to be alone, to work or to meditate, or to write those piteous and passionate prayers in which he begged so humbly for the mercy and the guidance of heaven. Boswell had penetrated to the secret apartments of the great man; he had won already the most intimate privileges of friendship. He looked at the tumbled papers with "a degree of veneration," and also with a degree of pride. Nor was pride out of place, although the supreme privilege of drinking tea with Mrs. Williams was not obtained until a fortnight later.

Next day there was a memorable evening at Farrar's Buildings, when Boswell entertained his uncle (Dr. Boswell), Johnson, and Mr. George Dempster—a gentle, speculative young man of thirty, who had recently been elected the member for Forfar. Mr. Dempster quietly defended the social teaching of Rousseau. On the following morning Johnson thus expressed his opinion of Mr. Dempster: "I have not met with any man for a long time who has given me such general displeasure. He is totally unfixed in his principles, and wants to puzzle other people." At night, Boswell and Johnson had supper together in a private room at the Turk's Head coffee-house, and Johnson admitted his fantastic inclination to visit the Hebrides. They talked of Boswell's approaching departure for the Continent. "My dear Boswell! it would give me great pain to part with you, if I thought that we were not to meet again."

By this time the influence of the Johnsonian philosophy was palpably changing the moral and social orbit of Boswell. Wilkes, a man so famous, was not lightly to be abandoned, but we hear nothing more of Churchill, Lloyd and the others, unless by way of literary criticism. You cannot worship a man unless you feel in harmony with his principles. The nicest regard for social convenience is unable to produce genuine alternations of infidelity and belief. So Boswell wrote to Dalrymple on the 23rd of July:

"I must own to you that I have for some time past been in a miserable unsettled way, and been connected with people of shallow parts, altho' agreeably vivacious. But I find a flash of merriment a poor equivalent for internal comfort. I thank God that I have got acquainted with Mr. Johnson. He has done me infinite service. He has assisted me to obtain peace of mind. He has assisted me to become a rational *Christian*. I hope I shall ever remain so. I shall leave England upon an infinitely happier footing now, than when I was tost by every wind, full of uneasy doubt. When I am abroad, I shall studiously preserve my good principles. . . . When I return from abroad I hope I may easily drop loose acquaintance. One mind can hardly support itself against many. But when we are with good men, whose opinions agree with ours, we are the more firmly fixed."

All his life, this poor man was trying to get himself firmly fixed, trying to preserve the comforting principles of a rational, sober Christian. If he could have lived for any length of time in close touch with Johnson it is possible that he might have done so. Whenever he came within the sphere of that benign influence he was immediately steadied; and as he receded again, he strayed in the fatally erratic ways of weakness and of dissipation.

In the month of July Boswell and Johnson met on twelve occasions, and spent a great deal of time together. The one listened while the other, with strange contortions of body, denounced or affirmed, and gave advice or judgment. Once more the future traveller was recommended to "perambulate Spain."

Boswell asked for advice as to the best method of studying at Utrecht. "Come," said Johnson, "let us make a day of it. Let us go down to Greenwich and dine, and talk of it there."

Two days later they took a sculler at the Temple stairs, landed at the Old Swan and walked to Billingsgate. They did this in order to avoid the dangerous rapids of London Bridge, where numbers of impatient or adventurous people were drowned every year. Here they took another boat and rowed quietly down the river. London Bridge was now behind them, and as they passed down the long reach towards the Pool they saw with delight the tall ships moored in the stream, the hoys and wherries, the barges full of gay folk who, like themselves, were pleased to be afloat on such prosperous waters and upon a day so calm and sunny. It was during this voyage that Boswell introduced the subject of Methodism, and Johnson admitted the success of Methodist preachers among the common people.

A letter to a friend shows that Boswell had carefully prepared a little scene at Greenwich. He had put Johnson's poem of *London* in his pocket, and from this poem, at the appropriate time and place, he recited with enthusiasm four of the worst lines that Johnson ever wrote:

"On Thames's banks in silent thought we stood,
    Where *Greenwich* smiles upon the silver flood:
    Pleas'd with the seat which gave Eliza birth,
    We kneel, and kiss the consecrated earth."

Perhaps Johnson did not like this; his *London* was written twenty-five years before, and few men like to be reminded of their early work. At any rate, he quickly remarked that "Greenwich hospital was too magnificent for a place of charity." Presently he burst into "an animating blaze of eloquence" on the unpromising theme of study at Utrecht; and Boswell, dazzled and gratified, could not remember a word of it. After dinner they walked in the park.

"Is not this very fine, Sir?" said Johnson, though he would have been quite unmoved by the finest view in the world. Boswell immediately realised the proper answer: "Yes, Sir; but not equal to Fleet Street." "You are right, Sir."

In the evening they came back to town, and the wonderful day was brought to an end with supper at the Turk's Head.

It was now that Johnson gave to the young man the most astonishing proof of his friendship. Boswell had arranged to leave England by the Harwich packet for Helvoetsluys on the 6th of August. Upon hearing of this, Johnson declared: "I will accompany you to Harwich."

To appreciate this gesture, it has to be remembered that Johnson was a lazy man, averse to any break in the comfortable disorder of his life. He was frequently in bed when people called to see him at twelve o'clock in the morning. When he got up to his penny loaf and his large pot of tea, he knew that he would soon be talking to a group of literary visitors. Early in the afternoon he sauntered out to dinner. After this he would go to some tavern, or to the house of a friend, or to a club or a beefsteak house. He would return late, often with a few squeezed-out oranges in his pocket, the peel of which he neatly cut into small pieces before retiring. He did not often travel, though he loved the motion of a good carriage on the highway, and he could ride a horse "as well as the most illiterate fellow in England." When he did travel, it was generally to Oxford or Lichfield or Ashbourne, where he could see old friends and places familiar to his eyes. But London was the true centre of his existence. That he should have willingly spent four days in a stage coach in order to see a raw Scotch boy embark for Holland is obviously very remarkable. He had only known this boy for a little over two months and a half, and already he was giving him the assurance of a most extraordinary

27

degree of affection. In studying the relations between Boswell and Johnson, the trip to Harwich is a point of the utmost importance: it proves, among other things, that Boswell had then the makings of a good companion, worthy of a privilege that would have honoured men of much greater ability or intelligence.

But this charming friendship had its ups and downs like any other. Only two days before the departure for Harwich there was a sharp explosion. Boswell and Johnson were spending a final evening together at the Turk's Head, and Boswell committed the first of his many indiscretions. He never knew that he was indiscreet, and it seemed to him the most natural thing in the world to tell Johnson what other people said about him. "Why, Sir, they ascribe to you the most peculiar sayings. As an instance very strange indeed— ha, ha, ha!—David Hume told me you said you would stand before a battery of cannon to restore the Convocation to its full powers." Johnson was marching heavily up and down the room. He now towered, thundering and shaking, above his young friend, who was sitting at the table. "And would I not, Sir? would I not? Shall the Presbyterian *Kirk* of Scotland have its Assembly, and the Church of England be denied its Convocation?" Such a thought was enough to bring rage into the heart of any true Englishman, and Johnson was never so fierce as when he was defending the Crown or the Establishment. These ranting Presbyterians! these vile Whigs! Certainly he would face a battery of guns for the honour of the Church or the Constitution. Boswell, after a momentary droop, quietly swung back to his balance: he led Johnson to expatiate "on the influence which religion derived from maintaining the church with great external respectability."

The two travellers set out early in the morning of the 5th of August, they spent the night at Colchester, and reached Harwich on the following day in time for dinner— that is, by about three o'clock in the afternoon. In the evening they walked together to the beach. After an affectionate embrace and a promise to correspond, the young man went on board the packet. "As the vessel put out to sea, I kept my eyes upon him for a considerable time, while he remained rolling his majestick frame in his usual manner; and at last I perceived him walk back into the town, and he disappeared."

Boswell did not see Johnson again for two and a half years. It is, indeed, necessary to remember that he did not see him often. Those who read the *Life* inattentively, and without observing dates, are apt to get the idea that Boswell and Johnson were almost continually together. This illusion is produced by the extraordinary mass of detail relating to Johnson and by a tendency to regard the two men as inseparable. The friendship lasted for a period of slightly over twenty years. During the whole of this period there were approximately 870 days on which Boswell could have met Johnson. In other words, Boswell and his eminent friend were only within reach of each other for about two years and five months distributed over a period of twenty years. As a matter of fact, they were frequently in the same place (London) without meeting each other at all for considerable periods, and a computation of the days and hours they actually spent in each other's company would give a very surprising result. At three separate times Boswell was absent from Johnson for more than two years together; at three other separate times he was absent for about a year and a half; and they were only together for any considerable time (ninety-seven days) during the excursion to the Hebrides in 1773.

Yet even when operating unseen from a distance the influence of Johnson was unquestionably the one influence which gave occasional sense or direction to the unsteady career of Boswell. After the visible friendship was broken by death in 1784, Boswell, though fitfully sustained for a few years by his devotion to the memory of the great man, or by his exploitation of that memory, felt himself lost and hopeless—as indeed he was. He owed the preservation of what was best in him, as surely as he now owes his imperishable literary fame, to the genius and character of Dictionary Johnson.

CHAPTER III

THE YOUTH ABROAD

AMONG the admirably vivacious pastels of La Tour there is none more enlivening than a head of Isabella van Tuyll (or de Zuylen), now in the Louvre. It is the gay head of a young woman prepared to enjoy her life fully though honestly, bright with candour and health and amusement.

Isabella van Tuyll was the daughter of a Dutch nobleman, Diederick-Jacob van Tuyll, who lived in Utrecht. Although she looked so gay when she sat for La Tour, she was not a fortunate girl. She was bored by the prim society of Utrecht, and she wanted to meet people who were more entertaining. In the winter of 1763 she met a sprightly fellow in a green and silver dress; he called himself Boswell d'Auchinleck, and he had come to the University to study law.

Boswell had found Utrecht dull enough at first, but he had good introductions, and before long he was enjoying himself prodigiously. His great-grandmother, the wife of the Earl of Kincardine, was a daughter of the noble Dutch house of van Sommelsdyck; and he had therefore made himself known to the Sommelsdycks at the Hague, who greeted him as a kinsman. The Countess of Nassau-Beverwerd ("she is the finest woman upon earth") made him acquainted with people of fashion. He went to assemblies twice a week, and to private parties nearly every evening. "There are so many beautiful and amiable ladies in our circle that a quire of paper could not contain their praises tho' written by a man of a much cooler fancy and a much smaller handwriting than myself."

Where is the Johnsonian example now? Have the amiable ladies prevailed? By no means. Boswell has drawn up an Inviolable Plan, to be read every morning. He is aware of the perils of mere frivolity and is determined to save himself. Above all things, let him be a respected gentleman.

There were trips to the Hague, and trips to Leyden, but the principal affair of Boswell's Dutch winter was the affair with Isabella van Tuyll, or, as he called her, *Zelide*.

In love young Boswell had a heavy and romantic style, and the influence of Johnson had added to this a new quality of solemn exhortation. We know now that Boswell fancied himself in love with Zelide, wished to marry her, and actually sent to her father a serious proposal. But Zelide was too frivolous, too flighty and fond of teasing. Poor Boswell, with his new Johnsonised ideas of courtship, was baffled—and what is more baffling to a serious lover than a woman who is always too gay?

All good European society affected to be French. Young Boswell (we know not how) soon acquired the use of this elegant language; he wrote and spoke in French with considerable ease and felicity, adapting it in the most comic way to his own requirements.

Although she did not accept him, Zelide remained for some years the mistress of his imagination, and to her he wrote many letters, some in French and some in English. The famous English letter, first published in full by Dr. Brown in 1921, was written at Berlin in the summer of 1764. It is apparently the longest private letter that Boswell ever wrote, and certainly the most astonishing. Boswell abroad, during the earlier stages of his tour, is more vividly illuminated by this document than he is by any of his other writings. Those who would understand him must read—and remember—the following passages:

"You know I am a man of form, a man who says to himself, Thus will I act, and acts accordingly. In short, a man subjected to discipline, who has his *orders* for his conduct during the day. . . . And who gives these orders? I give them. Boswell when cool and sedate fixes rules for Boswell to live by in the common course of life, when perhaps Boswell might be dissipated and forget the distinctions between right and wrong, between propriety and impropriety. . . . When such a man as I am employs his great judgment to regulate small matters, methinks he

31

resembles a giant washing teacups or threading a needle,
both of which operations would be much better performed
by a pretty little miss. . . . My dear Zelide! let me
prevail with you to give up your attachment to pleasure
and to court the mild happiness. Believe me, God does
not intend that we should have much pleasure in this
world. . . . My notions of God's benevolence are grand
and extensive. I puzzle not myself with texts here, and
texts there, with the interpretation of a gloomy priest, or
with the interpretation of a gay priest; I worship my
Creator and I fear no evil. . . . Pray make a firm resolution never to think of metaphysics. Speculations of that
kind are absurd in a man, but in a woman are more absurd
than I chuse to express. . . . My dear Zelide! You are
very good, you are very candid. Pray forgive me for
begging you to be less vain. You have fine talents of one
kind; but are you not deficient in others? Do you think
your *reason* is as distinguished as your imagination?
Believe me, Zelide, it is not. Believe me and endeavour
to improve. . . . Respect mankind. Respect the institu-
tions of society. If imagination presents gay caprice, be
amused with it. But let reason reign. Conceal such ideas.
Act with reason. I have had a most agreeable journey.
My Lord Marischal was most entertaining. . . . If you
love me own it. I can give you the best advice. If you
change tell me. If you love another tell me. . . . '*Je suis
glorieuse d'être votre amie*.' That is the stile. Is not this a
long letter? You must not expect me to write regularly.
Farewell, my dear Zelide. Heaven bless you and make
you rationally happy. Farewell."

Beware of metaphysics! Let reason reign; be rationally
happy! We are not very far from the Mitre tavern, we are
listening to the unmistakable echo of a great voice. And
what shall we say of this cool and sedate fellow, who gives
himself daily orders for the preservation of propriety? Is
he less absurd than the fellow who seriously advises his
mistress to improve her understanding? Perhaps the odd
creature is partly to be explained by a reference to a letter

which he had received in Holland from Samuel Johnson: "Let all such fancies, illusive and destructive, be banished henceforward from your thoughts for ever. Resolve, and keep your resolution; choose, and pursue your choice. Begin again where you left off, and endeavour to avoid the seducements that prevailed over you before."

About two years after her final break with Boswell, Zelide married a Swiss, de Charrières, her brother's tutor. She was never rationally happy after all. At forty-four she produced a little book called *Lettres Neuchâteloises*, which was praised by Saint-Beuve. This book was followed, two years later, by a novel, *Caliste*. She wrote many other little works, all of them simple and pleasing. Her name was not unknown to literary people; she was the friend of Benjamin Constant and of Madame de Staël, and she is warmly commemorated by Saint-Beuve. But her Swiss husband could never understand her; the dull people of Neuchâtel got on her nerves; she knew the quiet sorrows of unrequited vivacity.

Having done with Professor Trotz, Boswell put on his elegant suit of flowered silk and began what he called "A Tour through the Courts of Germany." But first he went to church (in the flowered silk), worshipped his God, and determined to be a worthy gentleman.

He travelled to Berlin with old Marischal Keith and that perplexing Turkish lady, Emet Ulla, who had been taken by General Keith at the siege of Oczakov, and was assumed to be the adopted daughter of the Marischal.

George, Earl Marischal Keith, was a Jacobite lord, the close friend and companion of Frederick the Great. He had received a pardon from George II in 1759, but he preferred to live in Germany, and he was now on his way back to Potsdam after a final visit to his Scotch estates. In 1752 he was the governor of Neuchâtel (then a Prussian principality) and here, ten years later, he entertained Jean-Jacques Rousseau at the summer residence of Columbier. He had been a member of that extraordinary group at Potsdam which gave a welcome to Voltaire in 1750.

The record of his German tour shows Boswell gradually drifting from the ideals of Johnsonian rectitude. He fell often into that dangerous melancholy from which he tried to escape by means neither wise nor effective. His pathetic notion of giving himself orders and of reading his Plan every morning shows that he was aware of his fatal weakness. His private journals refer ominously to gloom and indolence and a carking dread of melancholia. He felt that he was already old, tired and disillusioned. Too old at twenty-three; and there was Milord Marischal cracking his jokes at seventy-five.

Writing to Mitchell, the British envoy at Berlin, he said: "To escape from the gloom of dark speculation, I have made excursions into the fields of amusement, perhaps of folly. I have found that amusement and folly are beneath me. . . . In the mean time I can see little advantage to be had at Berlin." He wanted to travel south, to see Voltaire and Rousseau (to both of whom he had introductions) and to visit Rome: "I am no libertine, and have a moral certainty of suffering no harm in Italy." But Lord Auchinleck had written stiff, disapproving letters, and Boswell tried to obtain the sanction of Mitchell.

It is a pity that Boswell never met Frederick the Great. He saw him on parade, reviewing the grim lines of his tall grenadiers, but he never had a chance of speaking to him. The rigid confidence of that stern, neat little figure made its due impression upon his mind.

He met company of all sorts, including the numerous minor royalties of the German states. He visited Brunswick and Hanover, Mannheim and Baden, Dresden and Saxe-Gotha. He toyed foolishly with pretty girls, washerwomen or purveyors of chocolate. Temptation, in a form neither subtle nor gallant, assailed him, and he fell, after a whole year of chastity.

Not long after this fall, he was in Wittenberg, writing to Samuel Johnson with his paper resting on the tomb of Melancthon, and his mind full of religious thoughts. The letter was not handed to Johnson until thirteen years later, "lest he should have appeared too superstitious and too romantick."

By the beginning of December he was in Switzerland,

preparing himself to meet Rousseau. At that time Rousseau was living in sad retreat at Motiers in the Val de Travers, about sixteen miles from Neuchâtel.

Boswell had a letter from Keith introducing him to Rousseau, but he decided not to make use of it. He would write a letter of his own and send it to Motiers. His romantic genius, he said, induced him to rely upon his own merit. His letter pleased him immensely. He felt certain that no other man could have written such a letter and then lived up to its ample commendations. No other man would have said so, at any rate. The letter is fortunately preserved in the Public Library at Neuchâtel. It is written in Boswell's amusing though passable French. The most Boswellian portions are here translated:

"I am an ancient Scots gentleman. You know my rank. I am twenty-four years old. You know my age. . . . I present myself, Sir, as a man of singular merit, a man with a feeling heart, a spirit keen yet melancholy. Ah! if all that I have suffered gives me not a singular merit in the eyes of Monsieur Rousseau, why have I been created thus? and why has he thus written? . . . You know the pride of the Scots. Sir, I come to you that I may render myself worthier of belonging to that nation which has produced a Fletcher of Saltoun and a Lord Marischal. Forgive me, Sir; I feel myself deeply moved. I cannot restrain myself. Oh dear Saint-Preux! Enlightened Mentor! Eloquent and amiable Rousseau! My presentiment tells me that a friendship of the noblest kind will be born to-day. I find myself in serious and delicate circumstances, upon which I ardently desire the advice of the author of the *Nouvelle Héloïse*. . . . Open your door, then, Sir, to a man who dares assure you that he is worthy of entering. Have confidence in a singular visitor. You will not repent of it. But, I pray you, be alone. . . . I await your reply with impatience.   "BOSWELL."

Whatever may be said for the young man who wrote this, he was not wrong in talking about singularity. Rousseau had certainly never read anything of the kind before, and it may have been curiosity alone which induced him to receive the visitor: he sent a card, saying that he was not well, and begging that the interview might be a short one.

The man of merit accordingly made his preparations. He put on a scarlet coat and waistcoat trimmed with gold lace. He slipped his legs into buckskin breeches. He wrapped himself in a great coat of green camlet lined with fox-fur, and with a fur collar and cuffs. He then put on his head a fine hat decorated with what had every appearance of being solid gold lace, and strolled pensively by the banks of the Reuss. As he looked up at the Jura hills, the rocks, pines and glittering snow, he thought of Scotland, he thought of Killiecrankie. It was all very solemn and very thrilling. He was about to present himself before the Great Judge of Human Nature. He had sent before him a character that he was bound to sustain, at all hazards. Yet even singular merit needed singular fortitude on this occasion. . . . At last he knocked at the door of a decent house in the main street of Motiers, and the door was opened by Thérèse Levasseur, the mistress-housekeeper of the Great Judge.

The dialogues with Rousseau, set down both in French and English, are as vivid as anything Boswell ever wrote, and it is odd that he never thought of publishing them. They are now published by Colonel Isham in one of his magnificent volumes of the *Private Papers*, and we are thus informed of what took place when Rousseau and Boswell met each other, and also of the conversation with Voltaire at Ferney. Rousseau was in his Armenian dress: he gave the impression of a dark, genteel man, and he spoke rapidly and forcibly. Boswell had no reticence in the matter of questioning. There was a moment of high tension when he pressed Rousseau about his religious belief; he fixed the wild philosopher with a solemn and searching eye and forced him to admit that he prided himself on being a Christian.

The first meeting took place on the 3rd of December. Rousseau, although he was ill, allowed Boswell to see him again on the two following days, and again on the 14th and

15th. Here is another proof of the young man's peculiar charm—for it cannot have been anything else. Mere pertinacity would never have admitted and re-admitted him to the house of the most unapproachable man in Europe.

The Scots gentleman had now realised a state of supreme felicity; he felt the exultation of a heart swelling with joy. Rich, flattering ideas crowded into his mind, and assembled themselves in the most entrancing patterns. He, Boswell d'Auchinleck, was now the friend, the intimate confiding friend, of Jean-Jacques Rousseau! Could any living man hope for a nobler measure of rational happiness? a more splendid recognition of merit? He gave Rousseau a sketch of his life; he gave him, without shame, a packet of Zelide's letters, asking for his views on her character. In a letter of his own he begged ardently for a continuation of this inspiring friendship: "O deign to preserve a true Scot. Milord Marischal is old. This illustrious oak of Scotland must presently fall. You love this ancient country. Preserve at least one sapling."

Then came the turn of Monsieur de Voltaire.

It is probable that Boswell had with him two introductions to Voltaire, one from a friend at the Hague and one from Keith. At any rate, he was at Geneva by the end of December, and was presently on his way through the snow to Ferney.

Voltaire was now in his seventy-first year. He was living in his castle, the Patriarch, the *Seigneur du Village*. He called himself a sick man, a dying man, but he spoke and wrote and laughed and capered in a blaze of glorious and bewildering energy. He was flinging out those blasting satires which terrified or amused the whole of Europe. The great defence of Calas was not yet brought to a conclusion. The tragedy of La Barre was yet to be grimly played in the square of Abbeville. *Candide* had not long been written, and the *Dictionnaire Philosophique* had just made its appearance.

Those who visited Voltaire found a small, withered, grimacing creature, looking so dry, brittle and slender that he might have been a skeleton animated by a devil. He generally wore the dark, unpowdered wig of an earlier period, with a little black velvet cap on the top of it. His

D

dress, if he was not entertaining company, was plain, with a large dimity waistcoat reaching to the knees. His eyes were like two points of black fire; the corners of his long thin mouth were always twitching up maliciously; his gestures were rapid, with a cracking or snapping of joints; his voice continually rose to a pitch of unendurable shrillness.

Young James arrived at Ferney on the 28th of December, and presented his introduction. It was gratifying to be received by two or three footmen (and how different from the wild retreat of Motiers!), but the interview with the Patriarch was not successful. The instinct or the courage of Boswell appears to have failed him. Voltaire was bored: he sat bolt upright in his chair, and merely simpered. A second attempt was necessary.

Next day, Boswell sent a letter to Madame Denis, the mercenary and pretentious niece who kept house for the Patriarch. The letter, according to Boswell, was written in the finest humour and was full of wit: it produced not only another interview, but an invitation to spend the night at Ferney.

After dinner there was a truly astonishing dialogue between Voltaire and his guest. Boswell (in his flowered velvet) was not only confident but audacious, he was braced for the adventure, cheered by his entertainment; to him there was nothing absurd in the idea of a conversation upon equal terms between Boswell and Voltaire. (From his early youth he had adopted the grand Cæsarian method of speaking, thinking and writing of himself as *Boswell*, leaving that famous name to carry its own glory.) He asked Voltaire if he would speak in English. "No," said the old man. "To speak in English you have to put your tongue between your teeth; and I have lost my teeth." Then the young visitor got to work in earnest.

Before long they were raging furiously over the problems of religion. *Ecrasez l'infâme!* They got a great Bible and put it on the table between them. They argued with vehemence. For a time Boswell fancied that he held his ground. But soon the blaze of ridicule confounded his understanding. He was lost, though supremely exhilarated. The aged frame of the Patriarch shook with devilish excitement, until he reached a stage of real or assumed collapse: all at once he fell back in his chair; he was motionless, with closed eyes. Instead of pulling the bell-rope, or doing something to improve the condition of his host, the young visitor sat there and watched him with curiosity. Voltaire came back to life, and young James was ready for him: "Now, Sir;— the Master of the Universe—the soul—immortality— judgment——" Incredible youth! It was desirable to have peace at any price, and the old man tamely admitted his veneration of the Supreme Being, and even the possibility (though nothing more) of such a thing as a soul.

Boswell retired in triumph to his elegant bedroom and sent the valet for a book of his master's plays, which he read with inexpressible delight.

A short account of this visit was included in a letter from Boswell to Rousseau. The letter is in French, but there are no subtleties in the style of Boswell that need embarrass a translator:

"I have been with Monsieur de Voltaire. His conversation is the most brilliant that I have ever heard. . . . He spoke of his natural religion in a very striking manner. . . . In spite of all that has happened, you would have loved him that evening. I said to myself, *Aut Erasmus aut Diabolus.* . . .

"To-morrow I start for Italy. I beg you to advise me how I may receive the greatest benefit from that land of the arts. I love antiquities. I love painting. I shall have the finest opportunities for perfecting myself in both. I have a true taste for musick. I sing passably well. I play a little upon the flute. But I despise it. Two years ago I began to learn the violin, but I found it so difficult that I left it alone. I was wrong. Tell me, should I not do well if I applied myself seriously to musick, up to a certain point? Tell me what should be my instrument. 'Tis late, I confess. But should I not have the pleasure of making continual progress, and should I not be able to soothe my old age by the sounds of my lyre?

39

"You know me well, Sir, for you have read my life. But I forgot to relate one incident which disturbed me——"

There follows an account of a scene at one of the German courts, when his foolish tongue nearly forced him into a duel.

For more than nine months Boswell perambulated Italy. He visited, in the following order, Turin, Rome, Naples, Rome again, Terni, Venice, Mantua, Florence and Siena.

It goes without saying that the tour in Italy, in spite of the assurance to Mitchell, was too much for Boswell's good resolutions. The daily orders for good conduct, if they were given at all, were certainly not observed; the Plan was violated, the poor respected gentleman was driven away. Still, there were moments of agonising reproach. Attempts were still made to fix the wandering character. The great thing was to *be* something, to realise identity with some tremendous figure of solid virtue. Be father; be Johnson—or let us invoke a thing even more immovable: be the Rock of Gibraltar. It may be of some use, in times of temptation, to think oneself the Rock of Gibraltar; but such a useful thought, however much he might recommend it to himself, never saved James Boswell. The freedom of the Italian ladies led him astray in the most humiliating manner. How he was fooled or foiled, how his romantic overtures were treated with cynical disdain or with a cruel affectation of surrender, how he was only victorious with trulls or cast-off mistresses looking for subsistence, how he grovelled in the beastly despair of unsatisfied sensuality and ran the risk of what he most dreaded, all this makes a sorry story, and need not be told in detail. In his folly and fatuity there are already the signs of a disordered mind; and the signs occur again in complaints of drowsiness and melancholy.

Perhaps it was unlucky for Boswell that John Wilkes happened to be in Italy at the same time.

Wilkes had been expelled from the House of Commons on the 19th of May 1764, and outlawed on the 1st of November. After staying in Paris with his mistress Corradini, he had come to Italy at the heels of this beautiful though troublesome woman. When Boswell first heard of him, early in January, he was at Turin, though only for three or four days. Boswell himself reached Turin at the same moment, and at once wrote to Wilkes, inviting him to "a feast of most excellent wine and choice conversation." It seems evident that Wilkes declined the invitation, and sent Boswell a note in which he told him of the death of Churchill at Boulogne. Boswell replied by suggesting an appropriate talk on the immateriality of the soul. That he met Wilkes more than once at Turin seems improbable, but he spent a considerable time with him at Rome, and again at Naples.

"When Wilkes and I sat together, each glass of wine produced a flash of wit, like gunpowder thrown into the fire —Puff! puff!" And puff! puff! it probably was; little squibs of ribaldry or the sputtering nonsense that is happily forgotten by a sober mind.

In Boswell's own memoir of his life, he treats this friendship as one of the most important features of his tour: "Nor was it a circumstance of small moment that he met at Turin, Rome, and Naples, the celebrated John Wilkes, Esq., with whom he had always maintained an acquaintance upon the most liberal terms, and with whom he enjoyed many classical scenes with peculiar relish." Boswell, in speaking of him, nearly always contrived, however ostentatiously, to bring in the term classical. He did this, no doubt, in order to prove the essentially respectable nature of their friendship; if you knew nothing more of him, you might have imagined that he was talking of an English schoolmaster on a holiday. 'My classical companion, Mr. John Wilkes . . . a certain classical connection," and so on.

But the exiled hero of liberty could not have been a safe companion for a young man with a weak head. It is vastly important, in a biography, to remember ages; and we must not forget that Boswell, at this time, was only twenty-four, a very unsettled, impressible youth; Wilkes, on the other hand, was thirty-eight—a tough, disillusioned man of the world, not without generosity and courage, but entirely without those principles which are generally considered proper and are certainly convenient.

Boswell spent more than a month in Rome, where he met Lord Mountstuart, the eldest son of the third Earl of Bute. The young lord was just twenty-one, he took a liking to Boswell, and they travelled together for some time. To him, in 1766, Boswell dedicated his *Disputatio Juridica*.

Roman antiquities were viewed with due respect—indeed, with "venerable enthusiasm." A course, under the guidance of a hired antiquary, did much to inform the traveller's mind and to give him correct ideas about pictures, churches and palaces. But the traveller is ready to admit his limitations. His taste is only formed "up to a certain point." He is a little disappointed, although he can truthfully say *meminisse juvabit*. And still, there is always one advantage in true insensibility to the arts—you can make it appear like independence of judgment.

The earlier correspondents were neglected. As far as we know, Boswell never wrote to Temple during the whole of his tour. He says that he wrote to Johnson whenever he had anything "worthy of communicating," but that Johnson "did not favour him with a single letter for more than two years." There is nothing, in the published correspondence, to Sir David Dalrymple. The most vivacious letters written during the Italian tour are certainly those addressed to Wilkes—gay John Wilkes, classical Wilkes, *il Bruto Inglese*, the Whig, the libertine, the enemy of kings.

"Dare I affirm that I have found chearfulness, knowledge, wit and generosity even in Mr. Wilkes? I suppose few crucibles are so happily constructed as mine; and I imagine that I have a particular talent for finding the gold in your honour's composition. . . . At your hours of leisure I hope you think of your friends alive and dead. Of the first, it is difficult to know which are which. Of the last I know only two. Methinks I see Churchill bouncing into the regions below, making even Cerberus dread his brawny force, while poor Lloyd is lounging on the fatal shore, for want of a halfpenny to pay his freight.

. . . In the course of our correspondence, you shall have the various schemes which I form for getting tollerably through this strange existence. If you would think justly of me, you must ever remember that I have a melancholy mind. That is the great principle in my composition. . . . My liberal disposition will ever remain, should I even live in the very heart of a Court. . . . O John Wilkes, thou gay, learned, and ingenious private gentleman, thou thoughtless infidel, good without principle, and wicked without malevolence, let *Johnson* teach thee the road to rational virtue and noble felicity."

But while he could thus exhort to rational virtue, cleverly hinting that piety was the best policy, the poor youth was neither rational nor virtuous nor pious in demeanour. Writing in May to Rousseau, he told him that his Italian tour was nearly finished, and that he was thinking of his excursion to Corsica; and yet he wandered in Italy for more than five months after this, passing from town to town, and offering to each pretty lady who would speak to him the gift of his transitory and foolish love. Perhaps the company of young Mountstuart may have led him astray, and given him an excuse for seeing places that he would not otherwise have visited. Lord Auchinleck sent him letters denouncing this prolonged vagrancy, and still the youth wandered, feeling no doubt that he was forming himself into a devilish fine fellow.

But there were times when his melancholy thoughts presented him with another picture, less flattering; he thought at those times of Johnson's rolling majestic frame, or the enviable steadiness of the Rock of Gibraltar.

43

CHAPTER IV

CORSICA

THE Corsican tour was in many ways the happiest as well as the most creditable episode of Boswell's career. It gave him a taste of wholesome adventure, and supplied him with the materials for his first literary work of real merit—*The Journal of a Tour to Corsica; and Memoirs of Pascal Paoli*. He got upon a rock in Corsica, he said, and jumped into the middle of life. Some notion of personal publicity may have entered the scheme, but the main impulses were generous, adventurous and worthy of a man.

It is not easy to say when the idea of this excursion first came into his mind. He certainly mentioned it to Rousseau at Motiers, and he wrote to him from Rome, asking for a letter of introduction.

The Corsicans, under the noble leadership of Paoli, were fighting their masters, the Genoese: a fight for independence. Rousseau was keenly sympathetic. He had written in the *Contrat Social* (1762) a famous passage: "Il est encore en Europe un pays capable de législation; c'est l'isle de Corse. La valeur et la constance avec laquelle ce brave peuple a su recouvrer et défendre sa liberté mériteroit bien que quelque homme sage lui apprît à la conserver." Who should be "l'homme sage" if not Rousseau himself? Paoli would gladly have received him in the island, and he was actually invited, but the matter never got beyond the stage of graceful compliments and fruitless negotiations.

Boswell found waiting for him at Florence a letter from Rousseau, available as an introduction either to Buttafoco, a captain of the Royal Corsican Regiment, or to General Paoli.

Pasquale Paoli was a figure in the grand heroic tradition. He was the son of Giacinto Paoli, leader of the island rebels, and after training in the Neapolitan army he himself had become the leader of the Corsicans in 1755. Before long he had driven the Genoese to a precarious footing on his rocky shores. Genoa still professed to hold the island, and applied to France for assistance. Certain towns were therefore garrisoned, with a purely defensive intention, by French troops commanded by the Count de Marbœuf. Under the prevailing conditions of warfare the mountainous geography of the island was favourable to a strong resistance, as it still is to brigandage. But the French military occupation had brought about a period of relative calm, Paoli had come to an understanding with de Marbœuf, and there were no open hostilities.

Dalliance with the "angel of Siena" delayed young Boswell for so long that he does not appear to have reached Leghorn, whence he was to sail over to the island, until the beginning of October.

At Leghorn he was not to be delayed by people who told him that Corsica might be dangerous. He was only afraid of the Barbary corsairs, whose great lateen sails might swoop down upon him and bear him away to Africa. He was reassured by the Commodore of that famous old ship, the *Centurion*, then lying in the bay of Leghorn. "If the Turks did get you," said the Commodore, whose name was Harrison, "they wouldn't keep you long. But I will give you a very ample and particular passport—though I sincerely hope that you will have no occasion to make use of it."

He left Leghorn, accompanied by his Swiss valet, in a Tuscan vessel bound for Cape Corso. After a calm passage, during which he helped to pull an oar, they reached the harbour of Centuri on the evening of the second day. He had a recommendation from Count Rivarola, the Sardinian consul at Leghorn, to Signor Giaccomini, who would no doubt have received him courteously had it not been for the fact that he had just died. Boswell therefore went to Giaccomini's cousin, Antonetti, and presented the letter from the consul. He found in Antonetti's house a very kind reception, and a small copy of St. Michael and the Dragon by Raphael—not a good copy, but to see the thing at all was astonishing.

People were not in the habit of visiting Corsica, and there is no doubt that Boswell was looked upon, from the first, either as the representative of the British government, or a recruiting officer, or the agent of a trading concern. The flowered silk, the sea-green and silver were put aside: he wore scarlet and gold, more becoming to the friend of heroes, with a full suit of black in reserve. When it became known that he was on his way up to the mountains to see the General he was treated with uncommon respect.

Passed on from one friendly house to another, sometimes eating the simple fare of a convent and sometimes getting a dinner served on real Dresden, he presently arrived at Corte. Here he put on the full suit of black, and paid his respects to the Supreme Council. He was lodged at the Franciscan convent in Paoli's quarters, for the General was away at Solacaro, a mountain village.

It was here, in Corte, that Paoli had founded a university, but the term was over, and Boswell could only see the empty rooms. He saw other things of interest; most of all he delighted to see the tortured prisoners in the Castle and the poor Sicilian hangman. (His life-long interest in crime and death, we are told, was really due to extreme sensibility and a craving for strong emotions, especially those of a pitiful kind; it was, in fact, caused by an overflowing of pure good-nature.) And when he had seen everything, he remembered that he still needed a passport for the journey over the mountains. He went to the Chancellor's house; and when the passport was ready, a little boy who was playing in the room was told "to run to his mother, and bring the great seal of the kingdom."

Boswell's peculiar delight in his Corsican tour is not to be explained simply by his immediate response to environment. Even in 1765 people were beginning to look rather peevishly at their bric-à-brac civilisation, with all its ridiculous pagodas and frippery and fragile elegance. Some were more than peevish; they were rudely kicking to bits the pretty brittle trifles that once looked so admirable and so conclusively symbolic. Rousseau was being read everywhere. There was a stirring of new romantic and religious ideas (for the two revivals are always associated); and out of this came touching views of the child of nature and a surprising though illusory belief in the happiness of primitive man. Nothing can be done without exaggeration. The most over-dressed and over-fed people that ever lived were beginning to think with misguided envy of an imaginary though noble creature, who lapped the water of the fountain and ate herbs, berries or nuts. And now take this admirable passage from Boswell's own book of his tour:

"Next morning I set out in very good order, having excellent mules, and active clever Corsican guides. The worthy fathers of the convent who treated me in the kindest manner while I was their guest, would also give me some provisions for my journey; so they put up a gourd of their best wine, and some delicious pome-granates. My Corsican guides appeared so hearty, that I often got down and walked along with them, doing just what I saw them do. When we grew hungry, we threw stones among the thick branches of the chestnut trees which overshadowed us, and in that manner we brought down a shower of chestnuts with which we filled our pockets, and went on eating them with great relish; and when this made us thirsty, we lay down by the side of the first brook, put our mouths to the stream, and drank sufficiently. It was just being for a little while, one of the 'prisca gens mortalium, the primitive race of men,' who ran about in the woods eating acorns and drinking water."

He was among "brave rude men," and it pleased him to think that he was brave enough and rude enough to under-stand them.

At Bastelica he was lodged in a convent. A large company of the gallant islanders came into the room where he was sitting; they gathered round him, leaning on their muskets, and began to talk. Boswell had picked up enough Italian for the conveyance and the understanding of simple ideas Here was an opportunity not to be lost. He saw before him a group of heroes: those muskets were the arms of men fighting for liberty, those ragged coats were more glorious than uniforms of red and gold. He realised that a speech

47

would be appropriate, and he stood forth and made a speech to the men of Bastelica. Nor did he fail to raise a mood of superb enthusiasm. Loud voices, in more correct Italian, repeated the noble sentiments. Ah, Paoli!—they would fight with him and die with him for the honour of Corsica. The Englishman (for to these good fellows a Scotchman was English) knew very well what he was talking about.

At last he came within sight of Solacaro, where the General was attending to the duties of government.

For once, Boswell doubted whether he was equal to the occasion. From what the islanders had told him of Paoli, he expected to find some one almost "above humanity." Boswell had already hunted down the two most famous men in Europe—not a bad performance for a youth of twenty-four —but he had not yet acquired the brassy confidence of a veteran. Besides, he was really affected by greatness. A simple brave man, the leader of s.mple brave men, may very well have appeared to him as a singularly exalted character. And Paoli was more than this: he was a man of learning, a giver of laws and a patron of science. He was by accident a soldier; his mind was that of a scholar, well stored with history and literature and with a variety of knowledge. He had a little of the severity, and all the resolution, of an ascetic: virtue, he said, is the food of our hearts.

Young Boswell passed with some hesitation through the guards at Solacaro, passed the General's antichamber, and was shown into Paoli's room.

He found the General alone. He saw a tall, strong, handsome man of about forty, who received him courteously but with a definite reserve. "For ten minutes we walked together backwards and forwards through the room, hardly saying a word, while he looked at me with a steadfast, keen and penetrating eye, as if he searched my very soul."

The General's own impressions were conveyed, some years later, to Fanny Burney: "He (Boswell) came to my country, and he fetched me some letters recommending him; but I was of the belief he might be an impostor, and I supposed . . . he was an espy; for I look away from him, and in a moment I look to him again, and I behold his tablets. Oh!

he was to the work of writing down all I say! Indeed I was angry. But soon I discover he was no impostor and no espy; and I only find I was myself the monster he had come to discern. Oh—is a very good man; I love him indeed; so cheerful! so gay! so pleasant!"

It may be doubted if these were the actual words of Paoli. Fanny Burney disliked Boswell, and spread with malicious glee the fable that he always had a note-book in his hand for the purpose of taking down conversation.

Still, Paoli was cautious, until, like all the others, he was melted by the good humour, the obviously sincere admiration and the whimsical talk of the young man. Boswell had the satisfaction of being placed next to the General at dinner, and by the time they had gone into another room for coffee he felt himself rising to the level of his entertainment. He listened eagerly and joyously to "the illustrious commander of a nation."

There followed, for Boswell, several days of almost un-mitigated happiness. He was allotted quarters in the empty house of Signor Colonna, where his morning chocolate was presented to him on a silver salver bearing the Corsican arms. He dined and supped constantly with the General, he was visited by the nobility, and when he rode out to see the country he was given an escort of guards. Once he was actually mounted on Paoli's own horse, his buckskin breeches proudly associated with a rich furniture of crimson velvet, and his mind gloriously intoxicated with ideas of pomp and power.

His time was passed, he said happily, in "a luxury of noble sentiment." Even at dinner the General's talk was elevating: it seemed to him a suitable time for speaking of "the being and attributes of God." On another occasion he repeated with sonorous dignity a line from Virgil:

"*Vincit amor patriae laudumque immensa cupido.*"

He was no actor, no rhetorician: his gestures and words were those of one to whom dignity was natural. And although he afterwards appeared to the Streatham circle "soft and

mild in speech, as if he came from feeding sheep in Corsica,"
Boswell saw him speak to a traitor with the fierceness of a
lion and an awful darkening of brow: "One could see that
his thoughts of vengeance were terrible."

Boswell, admitted to the familiarity of this great and good
man, and seeing him among his "heroick nobles," was
realising what was best and nearest nobility in his own
nature. He was out of mischief. There was nothing to
interfere with his idealisation of Paoli. The bracing air of
the mountains was a tonic to his body, as the gallant company
was a tonic to his mind. There were no ladies to run after;
and if there had been it is doubtful if he would have pursued
them. There was no drinking, there was no buffoonery or
dirty talk at the headquarters of patriotism. It was a fine
adventure, and even the comical fancies of Boswell were
chastened, if they were not elevated, by the splendours of
manly romance.

"Corsica has fought a hard battle," said Paoli, "has been
beaten to the ground, and with difficulty can lift herself up.
The arts and sciences are like dress and ornament. You
cannot expect them from us for some time. But come back
twenty or thirty years hence, and we'll show you arts and
sciences, and concerts and assemblies, and fine ladies, and
we'll make you fall in love among us, Sir."

"He smiled a good deal," says Boswell, "when I told him
that I was much surprised to find him so amiable, accomplished, and polite; for although I knew I was to see a great
man, I expected to find a rude character, an Attila king of
the Goths, or a Luitprand king of the Lombards."

There might be a tendency to suppose that Boswell
exaggerated the attention paid to him by Paoli. But let it
be remembered that Boswell published his *Tour to Corsica* in
February 1768. In that year Genoa sold the island to
France, and in September 1769 Paoli fled to England. The
General soon found his way into the Johnsonian circle,
where his fine character and the vigour of his mind were duly
appreciated. The *Tour to Corsica* had been translated into
Dutch, German, Italian and French, and at least 10,000
copies of the original book had been sold in England. Paoli

had probably seen an early copy of the book, which was dedicated to him. He would certainly have resented anything untrue in the account of himself and his people. But he was not only pleased with the *Tour*; he treated Boswell with unaltered friendship and with splendid hospitality, and even visited Scotland in order to meet him. Nor should we forget the unfriendly though just observation of Gray: "Of Mr. Boswell's truth I have not the least suspicion, because I am sure he could invent nothing."

Paoli remained loyal to Boswell—even in circumstances which made loyalty extremely difficult—and Boswell preserved to the end of his life a warm sentiment for Corsica.

The soldiers and peasants of the island shared the General's liking for one whom they insisted on calling the English ambassador. They were delighted to see him strut, "with an air of true satisfaction," in the famous Corsican dress. Paoli gave him two of his own pistols, "made in the island, all of Corsican wood and iron, and of excellent workmanship." He obtained all the other accoutrements. The national dress and the national arms raised him to even higher flights of enthusiasm and gave him a greater sense of importance. He told his audiences to hope for an alliance with Britain—implying, of course, that he would be the irresistible negotiator. This went down well enough with the soldiers, but not with Paoli. "The less assistance we have," said the General, "the greater will be our glory." Still, Boswell could not be restrained. He "threw out many flattering ideas of future political events." Undeterred by the invariable nature of our foreign policy he saw beautiful images of "the British and the Corsicans strictly united both in commerce and in war." He quoted with fervour the eighth chapter of the first book of the Maccabees.

In his lighter moments he was remarkably diverting. One day he was asked to play a tune on his German flute. He did not play well, and he knew it; but he saw that he could not refuse to play without being churlish or affected. So he gave them one or two Italian airs, "and then some of our beautiful old Scots tunes, 'Gilderoy,' the 'Lass of Patie's Mill,' 'Corn Riggs are Bonny.'"

Very good, said the Corsicans; and now let us have an English song. Boswell, who never refused an invitation to sing, struck up cheerily "Hearts of Oak." Bravo! cried the heroic islanders; what does it mean? *Cuore di Quercia*, replied Boswell, and he gave them a translation. Whether he performed the feat of singing the translation is not recorded. Having got some idea of the words, the effect upon the audience was greater than ever—"Cuore di Quercia! Bravo Inglese!" "It was quite a joyous riot. I fancied myself to be a recruiting sea officer. I fancied all my chorus of Corsicans aboard the British fleet." And surely this amiable Scots gentleman of twenty-four, singing "Hearts of Oak" with a chorus of armed Corsicans, is a better man than the noisy casuist who blustered over the Bible with Monsieur de Voltaire.

If Boswell could invent nothing (and thank goodness for that) he had at least one quality of the artist—an abnormal degree of suggestibility. He could not readily discern the different values of ideas; he was indiscriminate, dazzled equally by Wilkes, Johnson, Rousseau, Lord Lonsdale and Mrs. Rudd. But he did receive, whether from persons or situations or ideas, an extraordinarily vivid impression of their meaning, and very often a true impression.

That is why he made himself so popular with the islanders. He threw himself into the proper attitudes instinctively; he breathed the authentic air of liberty; he said what was, or seemed to be, appropriate. Even the gravity of Paoli was relaxed by his flow of amusing talk.

"Every day I felt myself happier." He could not truthfully have written that line at any other period of his travels, and hardly at any other period of his life. He was treated with marks of outward respect that were never shown to him in any other place. The inconvenience of Colonna's ruined house was nothing when you thought of its great size and magnificence. The humble guard of musketeers was, after all, a real guard. Perhaps the nobility of Corsica, now his friends, could not always display the fitting splendour of rank, but they were a real nobility. And the heroism and greatness of Paoli were certainly real.

Any proper man would have been proud and excited in such company.

Paoli talked to him without reserve. Boswell is careful to convey the idea that they usually talked Italian, but he knew French better than Italian, and as the General knew French extremely well they probably used this language as much as any other. Paoli's English was never very good.

The General talked upon a great variety of subjects. He strode up and down as he talked, for he seldom sat on a chair except at meals. He was not married, but he often spoke about marriage, which he believed to be the proper state for ordinary men; Boswell, he said, would never be truly happy until he had found a suitable wife. He talked about the intelligence of beasts, the gift of clairvoyance, or the pleasures of speculation. But his chief delight was to explain the character and reveal the courage of his islanders. Noble islanders! Let them but hear a few words reminding them of honour, and there was not a man of them who would give way in battle. "I wish you could see one of them die," he said to Boswell, thinking, with pride greater than sorrow, of what he had seen himself among the mountains. Neither Rome, Thebes nor Sparta could show a loftier patriotism. Every single man was as good as a regiment. If they won they would be called the great defenders of liberty, if they lost they would be called unfortunate rebels. Boswell asked him how he could possibly have a soul superior to interest. "It is not superior," he replied. "My interest is to gain a name. I know well that he who does good to his country will gain that: and I expect it. Yet could I render this people happy, I would be content to be forgotten. I have unspeakable pride. The approbation of my own heart is enough."

Presumably Boswell did not see much of the General until the evening, but the "English ambassador" was well entertained. He had the society of those members of the General's staff who were free.

There was Signor Suzzoni, who had been in Germany, and who amused Boswell by talking German. There was also Signor Gian Quilico Casablanca, of a most ancient family, who gave him a long and exact account of the

E

Corsican government. There was the Abbé Rostini, "a man of literature, and distinguished no less for the excellency of his heart." And perhaps the most friendly of all was the secretary of the General, Father Guelfucci of the Servite order. Boswell rode and walked and went a-shooting with these gentlemen; they showed him all the beauties and curiosities of the neighbourhood, the village fairs, the sports of the common people.

The common people were hardy enough. They were fond of baiting cattle with large mountain dogs, and thus promoting a useful degree of bravery among dogs, cattle and Corsicans alike. It is only on mountainous islands that you will find people with so much spirit. A Neapolitan, for example, would have run away at the mere sight of one of these dogs. Paoli himself, not relying upon guards and sentries alone, always had five or six of these brutes, either in his room or just outside the door: not only a practical device, but another point of resemblance with the heroes of antiquity. The dogs, we are told, would have torn to pieces anyone who tried to approach the General after he had retired, but they were fortunately "extremely sagacious," and knew all the members of the staff.

When they were not engaged in the manly exercises of warfare or hunting, the islanders lay about in the open, talking of their brave deeds or singing offensive songs about the enemy. Brave simple men of all periods are very much alike.

Before he left Solacaro, Boswell had taken Paoli into his confidence. He made the sad confession that already, at twenty-four, his mind was a camera-obscura, and he felt the *non est tanti* and the *omnia vanitas* of a man who has tasted all the sweets of life. He had reasoned beyond his depth (and he need not have gone far); he had "intensely applied himself to metaphysical researches; he had grown weary with dull repetition." It was useless for him to think of any sort of activity. In saying this, he had two motives: that of relieving his mind, and that of appearing singular. "All this," said the General, "is very melancholy. I know the arguments about fate and free will and so forth. But let us leave these disputes to the idle. I hold firmly at all times one sublime thought." Johnson would not have dealt with him so gently or brought the argument to a nobler or more sensible conclusion.

At last Boswell produced the character of his illustrious friend, the *Rambler*. "I repeated to Paoli several of Mr. Johnson's sayings, so remarkable for strong sense and original humour. . . . I felt an elation of mind to see Paoli delighted with the sayings of Mr. Johnson, and to hear him translate them with Italian energy to the Corsican heroes." Here we may well say, as he said after meeting Rousseau—What a rich assemblage of ideas!

Boswell parted from Paoli with agitation, but also with a sense of gratified pride. He was conscious of a new resolve. His *omnia vanitas* gloom had lifted. He, too, would be a useful man, he would distinguish himself, if he was capable of doing so. Best of all, he need not fear future timidity in the presence of great men; for where could he find a man greater than Paoli?

He was indisposed when he left Solacaro. The wind and rain got into the old house of Colonna and gave him an ague.

"I was accompanied a part of the road by a great swarthy priest. . . . He was a very Hercules for strength and resolution. He and two other Corsicans took a castle, garrisoned by no less than fifteen Genoese. . . . This priest was a bluff, hearty, roaring fellow, troubled neither with knowledge nor care. He was ever and anon shewing me how stoutly his nag could caper. He always rode some paces before me, and sat in an attitude half turned round, with his hand clapped upon the crupper. Then he would burst out with comical songs about the devil and the Genoese, and I don't know what all. In short, notwithstanding my feverishness, he kept me laughing whether I would or no."

At Bogognano, near the residence of the Chancellor, he was again received by the Franciscan fathers. His ague became more troublesome and he was kept within doors for several days. When he was a little better he walked to Corte, simply in order that he might write a letter to Mr. Samuel Johnson from another *locum solennium*—the palace of Pascal Paoli.

He remained some days at Vescovato, and eventually reached Bastia about the middle of November, accompanied by Signor Buttafoco.

Here he was introduced to de Marbœuf, the commandant of the French troops in the island. De Marbœuf was living in elegance and comfort, in a state very different from that of Paoli up in the mountains. He received Boswell with charming hospitality, took him into his own house and nursed him through another attack of the ague (probably malaria). Boswell stayed for some time in Bastia, equally well entertained by French and Corsicans. He was certainly ill, but he did not leave until he had seen all that was remarkable in the town. The commandant looked after him like a father; he saw that he only ate and drank what the doctors allowed him, and lent him books when he was kept in bed.

At the beginning of December, Boswell arrived in Genoa. Later in the same month he reached Marseilles.

On the 4th of January 1766 he wrote to Rousseau from Lyon, but Rousseau, on that very day, had left Paris with Hume and de Luze on his flight to England. The letter was never delivered. It is a richly Boswellian letter, written in French, and shows that Boswell had heard the news of Rousseau's flight: he promises himself the felicity of introducing the wild philosopher to Johnson. It is inconceivable that Johnson, who wanted to send Rousseau to the plantations, would ever have agreed to this; in any case, Boswell took the side of Hume in the crazy quarrel with Rousseau, and his friendship with the wild philosopher came to an end.

In Paris, where he stayed for a few days, Boswell found a letter from Johnson and the society of Wilkes. And here he found Thérèse Levasseur, and agreed to escort her to England.

The character of Thérèse Levasseur, more often attacked than defended, is naturally of some interest. Rousseau had met her in 1744 when she was a sewing-maid at the hostel of Saint Quentin in Paris, and he had taken her as a mistress, a cook, laundress, housekeeper and companion, and to some extent as a nurse. Except for one or two necessary desertions on his part, when he was actually in flight or preparing for flight, he lived with her to the end of his life, and she has at least the merit of having endured for thirty-four years the intimacy of a man with whom scarcely anyone could live for a week on terms of ordinary friendship. But then, she was not handicapped by intelligence or delicacy. She could never read, write or count with anything like correctness. The names and the sequence of the months of the year were for ever a mystery beyond her grasp. After twenty years of instruction she was only just able to tell the time by the clock. Her manners were coarse and homely. It is impossible to avoid the conclusion that she was a mental defective. When Boswell took charge of her in Paris she was about forty-one years old.

Among the private papers of Boswell in the Malahide collection there was an account of the journey to England with Thérèse Levasseur. Before those papers were handed over to Colonel Isham, that account had been destroyed; but Colonel Isham had seen it and remembered it.

The account was destroyed, whether rightly or wrongly, because it was not fit to be published, even in the pages of a very expensive and limited private edition. It showed that Boswell and Mademoiselle Levasseur behaved with comic though repellent indecency. Our knowledge of this episode, though it does not affect any previous ideas of Boswell, certainly does affect our view of Thérèse Levasseur, who, in spite of contemporary gossip, has generally been given the credit of sexual fidelity. Every future biographer of Rousseau, if he knows of this, will have to reckon with its implications: he will perhaps find it necessary to review his opinion of Grimm, Diderot, and the Holbach circle, and to look with a little more indulgence at Voltaire's ugly picture of the sorceress *Vachine*.

CHAPTER V

LAUGH AS YOU PLEASE

IF every man who was capable of doing so wrote down the full circumstances of his life, and then printed them, our whole conception of life and society would be changed, and probably not improved. This is no cynical reflection, but a matter of plain common sense. Nothing could be more catastrophic than a revelation of the entire truth in regard to personality.

Boswell, who was a journalist or daily scribbler in the true sense of the word, set down the facts of his life with a frankness that most people would consider insane. He enjoyed the luxury of confession. Not only in his more or less private records (and there was never a man with less regard for privacy), but in his letters to Temple, he babbled about things one might have supposed him anxious to conceal—things not merely discreditable, but vapid, silly or trifling. He has prepared, for the peering psychologist, a garbage-pie of the most extraordinary dimensions.

Had this exposure of himself been the instrument of a personal reformation, or even made with a sincere moral purpose, it would have been less objectionable. True, there are crises of remorse and vows of repentance; and then the story goes on again, with crackles of stupid laughter and all the sorry antics of a disordered vanity. For the history of the four years that follow (1766–1769) it is necessary to draw more largely upon the Temple correspondence than upon any other source, and these letters disclose, with astounding clarity, the particulars of what good-humoured people would call an eccentric life.

Towards the middle of February 1766 Boswell arrived in London after an absence of about two and a half years. He found that Rousseau was lodging at Chiswick, and he met him at least once and gave him a report of the Corsican tour. In March, Rousseau had retired to Davenport's house at Wootton, and before long he was accusing Hume and all his other friends of black perfidy.

Johnson had moved to Johnson's Court, Fleet Street, where he had put Mr. Levett in the garret and Mrs. Williams on the ground floor. He received Boswell with kindness, but it must be observed that he could never be worked up to any pitch of enthusiasm about Corsica. Indeed, he wrote a letter to Boswell some time afterwards in which he spoke of the island with considerable petulance.

To Boswell the affairs of Corsica were supremely important. He spoke of himself as the friend of Paoli. On several occasions he appeared in the Corsican dress. He composed for the *London Chronicle* a whole series of paragraphs, many of them pure inventions, in which he tried to surround himself with mystery: for example "he had a good many papers about which he seemed very anxious, and he avoided talking freely of what he had seen in his singular tours." Not content with nonsense of this kind, he invented Signor Romanzo (whose name was enough to excite suspicion) the island courier. He invented also the most fantastic stories about Paoli: Prince Heraclius of Georgia had sent the General six beautiful camels—and so on.

By such means, and by the free employment of a babbling tongue, he endeavoured to excite popular sympathies; and he also endeavoured to show James Boswell, Esq., as a fascinating fellow, unique in style and adventure, the man who could say so much more than he chose to say, the subtle diplomat, the dashing hero, and the favoured representative of an oppressed nation.

He was not entirely unsuccessful. He did obtain an interview with Pitt, and he certainly roused interest in the character of Paoli. Nor should we suppose him to have been moved only by the paltry designs of a publicist or mountebank. Publicity he certainly desired, but we cannot doubt the sincerity of his romantic zeal for the Corsicans.

Although he had received the news of his mother's death while he was in Paris he showed no great haste to return to Scotland. He did not reach Auchinleck much before the end of April. On the 29th of July he was admitted a Scotch advocate at Edinburgh, and before the year was out he had begun to practise.

He had not been long in Edinburgh before he picked up a "dear infidel"—Mrs. Dodds or "the Moffat woman." Mrs. Dodds was a free though unfortunate lady, deserted by a wicked husband. She had three children. Boswell at first carried on his intrigue with the connivance of "a sober widow," but in the spring of 1767 he determined to rent a house for his mistress and to establish what he was pleased to call a "family." "In this manner," he wrote to Temple, "I am safe and happy and in no danger either of the perils of Venus or of desperate matrimony."

He was anything but safe or happy. Unpleasant stories about the dear infidel found their way to his ears. He was tortured by ignoble jealousies and sickened by ignoble craving. The lady was loud, boisterous and rude. And yet she had advantages. There seemed to be no end to the crazy alternations of lust and loathing, of sentimental folly and maudlin fears, of rapture and abasement. The state of his mind is best illustrated by quotations from a long letter to Temple:

"In a former part of this letter I have talked a great deal of my sweet little mistress. . . . But I have had more intelligence of her former intrigues. I am hurt to think of them. I say 'Damn her lewd minx.' I am jealous. What shall I do? . . . Friend of my youth, explain to me how we suffer so severely for what no longer exists. How am I tormented because my charmer has formerly had others! I am disgusted to think of it. . . . Besides, she is ill-bred, quite a rompish girl. She debases my dignity. She has no refinement. But she is very handsome, very lively and admirably formed for amourous dalliance. What is it to me that she has formerly loved? So have I. . . . What shall I do? I wish I could get off; and yet how aukward would it be! and after all, can I do better than keep a dear infidel for my hours of Paphian bliss? But, alas, since yesterday I am cooled. . . . This is a curious epistle to a clergyman. . . . To return to where it winces, might I not tell my charmer that really I am an inconstant being; but I cannot help it? Or may I let my love gradually decay? Had she never loved before, I would have lost every drop of blood rather than give her up. There's madness! There's delicacy! I have not had such a relief as this for I don't know how long. I have broken the trammels of business and am roving unconfined with my worthy Temple."

There's madness! The delicacy is not so apparent. Before the end of the letter he told him how, in payment of a bet "that he would not catch the venereal disorder for three years," he gave a supper to two or three friends. After the supper he was outrageously drunk, and spent the night with a prostitute. "Next morning I was like a man ordered for ignominious execution. But by noon I was worse; for I discovered that some infection had reached me. Was not this dreadfull? I had an assignation in the evening with my charmer. How lucky was it that I knew my misfortune in time . . . Bless me! what a risque!" To the charmer he confessed the whole situation as, in later years, he made similar confessions to his wife. He kissed her feet, he spoke with "the eloquence of a young barrister," and he was forgiven.

So the squalid, crazy account goes on from letter to letter. "What is the meaning of this, Temple? You may depend upon it that very soon my follies will be at an end, and I shall turn out an admirable member of society." But the follies never came to an end. There was a gardener's daughter at Auchinleck, with whom he was briefly though madly in love, and whom he seriously thought of marrying; though he was soon able to look at her with perfect unconcern while she laid the fire or tidied his room "like any other wench." The series of mawkish loves and of shoddy adventures ran almost without a break through all the remaining years of his life. He was incurably amorous and brutishly indiscriminate. And the situation is not much improved by the fact that he was invariably absurd.

With Mrs. Dodds for a while in the background, he began

to think of respectable marriage. He thought of his kins-woman, Miss Bosville in Yorkshire, and then of Miss Blair who lived at Adamtown near Auchinleck: "Her picture would be an ornament to the gallery." And then we learn from his chatter that "my late Circe . . . is with child." "What a fellow am I!" he exclaims.

By June 1767 Miss Blair or "the Princess" was in the ascendant. He adored her in the groves of Auchinleck, where she came with her mother on a visit. He drank her health so many times in such brimming bumpers that he staggered out into the streets of Edinburgh and spent the night in a brothel.

He gave Temple a paper of instructions which he was to observe when he visited Miss Blair as the ambassador of Boswell: "Give Miss Blair my letter. Salute her and her mother; ask to walk. . . . Talk of my mare, the purse, the chocolate. . . . Praise me for my good qualities—but talk also how odd, how inconstant, how impetuous, how much accustomed to women of intrigue. Ask gravely, Pray don't you imagine there is something of madness in that family? . . . Think of me as the great man at Adamtown—quite classical too! Study the mother. . . . Stay tea." The question about insanity is not unreasonable, though curiously introduced. Perhaps it is better to be insane than to be uninteresting.

Temple visited Adamtown, but there was an ominous silence on the part of Miss Blair. What was the matter? Was she really unmoved by the mare, the purse, the chocolate? Did she not perceive the advantages of a man who was accustomed to women of intrigue? Another suitor, Mr. Fullarton, had put in his appearance, he was "a formal nabob," "an East Indian"—possibly he was going to outweigh the good qualities and the singularity of young Boswell.

Shameful maladies were followed by shameful apprehensions, and then by a more determined pursuit of Miss Blair. "Miss Blair is my great object at present," he wrote to Temple, "I enclose the latest papers upon the subject. . . . Read these papers in their order. . . . What condescension, what a desire to please! . . . Adorable woman. Don't you think I had better not write again till I see her?" Next day he enquired nervously, "Tell me, can I honestly ask so fine a woman to risque her happiness with a man of my character?" In the meantime the dear infidel drank tea with him once or twice a week.

Presently there is such a confusion of amorous hopes, of raillery, despair, foppish vanity, ranting, canting and sheer nonsense that we do not know, any more than Boswell himself did, where he actually stood. Zelide and the angel of Siena again floated in his fancy; again he thought of his Yorkshire cousin. He wrote "a strange Sultanick letter" to Miss Blair, and left her alone for three weeks.

At the end of that time he came to Adamtown in a chaise. He was dressed in green and gold, and was accompanied by a mounted servant who wore a claret-coloured suit and a silver laced hat. This magnificence was the sign of honourable and serious intentions. Unfortunately, Boswell, "the proud Boswell," found himself out of countenance, and could only speak "in a very aukward manner." She was cunning, he thought, and saw his weakness. Then he heard of three people in Ayr who "abused her as a d—d jilt." What a lucky escape! And yet—perhaps it was not true.

But that was enough of Scotch lasses for a time. "I am a soul of a more southern frame. I may perhaps be fortunate enough to find an Englishwoman who will be sensible of my merit, and will study to please my singular humour."

All very well; but the next day the singular and Sultanic young man is pursuing Miss Blair again. Oh yes!—he loves her with his whole heart. He is entirely in her power. He is ready to consecrate his life to her for ever, if only she will learn to play the harpsichord and to speak French. Is it possible that she can think of marrying any other man?

In the midst of these uncertain pleasures, these alarms, these febrile vacillations, Boswell engaged himself warmly on the side of Douglas in the famous legitimacy case, and accomplished the infinitely more important task of writing the *Account of Corsica*. His contributions to the publicity of the Douglas case were *Dorando*, a version of the case in a fictitious form, various poems and newspaper paragraphs, and the *Essence of the Douglas Cause*. He also edited, or helped to edit, the *Letters of Lady Jane Douglas*. These efforts were by no means contemptible. *Dorando* is a rather careless *pièce d'occasion*, but the *Essence* was the result of much labour and gives in a very succinct form the legal outline of the dispute—its effect, we are told, "was said to be considerable in a certain important quarter."

But these essays were of little moment in comparison with *Corsica*, "my Corsican monument." The book, almost immediately after its appearance in February 1768, established Boswell as an author of repute, and it is undoubtedly true that it was more widely read on the Continent than any work by Samuel Johnson.

This effect was anticipated by Boswell. The publication was to mark a definite phase in his career. "Temple, I wish to be at last an uniform pretty man. . . . I am always for fixing some period for my perfection as far as possible. Let it be when my *Account of Corsica* is published. I shall then have a character which I must support."

And then Princess Blair came to Edinburgh and there were fresh transports and perplexities and hesitations. A fatuous, meandering conversation was recorded for the benefit of Temple. All the old questions were revived: What does the girl mean? Where am I now? How long must I suffer? How must I do? Shall I shake her off? Is it not below me to be made uneasy by her? Am I living up to my character as the friend of Paoli?

Before Christmas (1767) the Moffat woman gave birth to "the finest little girl I ever saw." This did not fulfil the expectation of "Edward the Black Prince," but it seems to have pleased Boswell, who named the child Sally. He resolved to look after the mother, but not to live with her again.

At last the pursuit of Miss Blair seemed hopeless. After all, she was not worth it. She had not fire enough. She did not know the value of her lover. It was time to break the enchanting fetters.

In February 1768 Boswell wrote, "All is over between Miss Blair and me." And it certainly looked like it. He met Mr. Fullarton, the "formal nabob," and together they joked about the Princess. They paid her a visit in company; and when they left, both exclaimed together, "Upon my soul, a fine woman!" Then they visited a lady cousin of Boswell's, and afterwards went to a tavern and became fast friends over "the good old claret." Boswell then wrote a crambo song on Miss Blair, and felt his mind "twice as enlarged as it had been for some months." Once more the gay, emancipated fellow is full of hope: "You cannot say how fine a woman I may marry, perhaps a Howard or some other of the noblest in the kingdom." Perhaps.

The *London Chronicle* for the 27th of February 1768 announced: "James Boswell, Esq., is expected in town." On the 22nd of March there was a further announcement: "Yesterday James Boswell, Esq., arrived from Scotland at his apartments in Half-Moon-street, Piccadilly." Both announcements, like innumerable others, were forwarded to the paper by James Boswell himself.

Corsica had been published, the period of perfection had come, it was time for the reformation, time to support the character of Paoli's friend and the author of a great book. Mrs. Barbauld, in a poem of extraordinary magnificence, told the world how Boswell had turned from polished Gallia's soft delicious vales and the grey relics of imperial Rome to animated forms of patriot zeal. With a little steadiness, all might be well. There was Johnson with his thundering morality, and a most encouraging chorus of applause rising from all parts of the kingdom.

Johnson had gone to Oxford, and after a few days in town Boswell followed him. The Doctor's cool treatment of Corsica must have been a disappointment to the young man. "I wish you would empty your head of Corsica," he had written in March; and he was annoyed with Boswell for having ostentatiously thrust into the *Tour* a passage from one of his own letters. He was also annoyed, we may suppose, by what he considered the foolish praises bestowed upon a mediocre performance. He wanted to preserve Boswell in a position of decent inferiority. Young James putting on the airs of an author was like a woman preaching or a dog standing on his hind legs; it was neither becoming nor desirable. You cannot be on good terms with a man who threatens to become eminent in your own profession. To Johnson, the value of this young man was that he gave him companionship without the possibility of rivalry.

Boswell returned to London, leaving Johnson at Oxford. It is not unreasonable to suppose that the Oxford conversations had never reached a high level of cordiality; and that supposition is confirmed by an attentive reading of the *Life*.

Boswell had renewed his correspondence with Zelide, and his volatile ardours were now concentrated upon the idea of possessing her. He wrote to his father for permission to start for Utrecht at once. Ah! she was so sensible and so accomplished, and knew him so well and liked him so much! The charming Dutchwoman for Boswell! Sir John Pringle gave him a ready backing, and Zelide, of course, would never hesitate.

"What think you of this, Temple?" Temple thought it a crazy notion; and Lord Auchinleck thought it a great deal worse, and put down his foot with emphasis. And that was the last phase of the Zelide infatuation.

In the meantime, let us remember that Corsica Boswell, Paoli Boswell, had reached the critical turning, the new resplendent phase of his career. The applauded book was briskly circulating; and now he was to prove himself a solid, sagacious and respectable man. It was only a matter of simple resolution. Remember the Plan. Remember that you are the friend of Johnson, of Paoli, of Sir John Pringle and Sir Alexander Dick.

On the 16th of April he wrote to Temple:

"To confess to you at once, Temple, I have, since my last coming to town, been as wild as ever, and for these ten days I have been suffering justly for my conduct. I have upon honour been tormented this time; and I am positive I shall never go astray, were it for nothing else but the absolute dread of pain. I shall be confined a week yet."

Even to Dick he says frankly: "Since I last came to London I have been if possible more extravagantly fond of the ladies than ever." Sad indeed; but merely a postponement. "I shall never again behave in a manner so unworthy the friend of Paoli. My warm imagination looks forward with great complacency on the sobriety, the healthfulness, and the worth of my future life."

By the middle of April there was a partial recovery, in every sense of the word. The treatment by Mr. Forbes of the Horse Guards (doubtless a very experienced man) had been successful. Johnson had returned to town. Boswell gave literary dinners in Half-Moon Street; he was visited by Hume and Johnson in the forenoon of the same day; he entertained Benjamin Franklin, General Oglethorpe, Sir John Pringle and Garrick. At the Crown and Anchor he gave a supper to Johnson, Dr. Percy and Dr. Douglas (both on the way to episcopal rank), Bennet Langton, Dr. Hugh Blair and Mr. Tom Davies: Johnson "tossed and gored several persons," and everything was really splendid. On the 20th of May he had a notable conversation with Lord Mansfield. Anything was possible: he thought of writing a comedy. "I am the *Great Man* now. . . . I shall be moral for the future." Before he left London he made in St. Paul's a solemn vow to abstain from licentious adventures for a period of six months.

Not long after his return to Scotland there was a new infatuation. At Lainshaw, the home of David Montgomerie who had married Boswell's aunt Veronica, he met the finest creature he ever beheld, a perfect Arcadian shepherdess, not seventeen, a most angelic miss, all youth and softness and coy sensibility, *La Belle Irlandoise*, with the crowning advantages of a Dublin education and the prospect of a very pretty estate. She was related to the Montgomeries of Lainshaw and her name was Mary Anne. As soon as Boswell saw her, he realised that he had never been so much in love before. Here every flower was united, with no thorns or prickles. "What a fortunate fellow am I! what a variety of adventures in all countries!" He received no small encouragement from the father, mother and aunt of this lovely girl; he was allowed to walk with her; he "repeated his fervent passion again and again"; he carved the first letter of her name on a tree; he tasted the exquisite pleasure of snipping off a lock of her hair. The aunt went so far as to say, "Indeed, Mr. Boswell, I tell you seriously there will be no fear of this succeeding, but from your own inconstancy." He was invited to Ireland. He felt that he was fixed at last. This glowing, delicious virgin was not like the cautious, prevaricating Miss Blair, and even less like the Moffat woman. It was lucky, too, that *Corsica* had run to a third edition in Ireland—with a third edition he might suppose himself irresistible. And the solemn vow of St. Paul's was not forgotten: "I have given up my criminal intercourse with Mrs. —— . . . *Maria* has me without a rival." Fortunate Maria!

His amorous fancies never distracted Boswell from the sterner and more heroic devotion to Corsica. At this time he raised by private subscription more than £700, and purchased from the Carron company various pieces of ordnance. In August he sent to the island two 32-pounders, four 24-pounders, four 18-pounders, and twenty 9-pounders, with 150 balls for each gun. This was a feat more extraordinary than may appear at first sight. The money was entirely raised in Scotland, and it was raised for a purpose in which no Scotchman had any obvious interest. Although the facts are openly recorded in the Temple correspondence, no one seems to have paid much attention to them or to have realised their implication of zeal, energy and pertinacity. Corsica had been sold to France in May 1768, and Boswell's artillery must have put heart into Paoli's gallant though now hopeless defence.

Boswell also continued a vigorous Corsican propaganda by means of newspaper items and by the collection of *British Essays in Favour of the Brave Corsicans*. This collection, though dated 1769, actually appeared in December 1768.

His fame as the defender of Corsica and his literary fame grew together. He concluded the Preface of the third edition of *Corsica* with a most delightful and characteristic passage:

"May I be permitted to say that the success of this book has exceeded my warmest hopes. When I first ventured to send it into the world, I fairly owned an ardent desire for literary fame. I have obtained my desire: and whatever clouds may overcast my days, I can now walk here [at Auchinleck] among the rocks and woods of my ancestors, with an agreeable consciousness that I have done something worthy."

In the winter of 1768 Miss Blair suddenly regained her empire. Boswell incautiously wandered to Adamtown, and found that she was not to marry Sir Alexander Gilmour as had been supposed. There was a rapid kindling of the old flame. Young Boswell knelt. He became "truly amorous." But—can you believe it?—Miss Blair would not go beyond the stage of chilly friendship and soothing assurances of regard. She liked him well enough, but she would not marry him. For three weeks he fervently wrote letters full of passion to the frigid, unalterable Miss Blair: she did not answer them.

This might have gone on for more than three weeks, had it not been for the arrival of a letter from Ireland. The aunt of the Arcadian shepherdess wrote with kindness and encouragement. Miss Blair was forgotten. Insensible creature—let her go!

Before the winter was over there was another sad relapse.

Among the amiable habits of the Scotch, one of the most prevalent was that of long drinking in company. The morning drams of whisky were followed after dinner by bottles of claret, hock and port. A willingness to be helplessly drunk was a sign of good fellowship and manly complaisance. In this peculiarly northern form of sociability Boswell never refused to play his part. But unluckily he was not the sort

F

of drinker who falls in sodden oblivion beneath the table and may be quietly transported to bed. After drinking he was fiery and foolish, with a tendency to stagger out into the street and to fall into the most deplorable kind of mischief. Although he regarded this as a dangerous weakness, he was never able to prevent its recurrence and never able to escape the resulting moral and physical degradation. In spite of repeated vows, occasional abstention, and frequent moods of terrifying remorse, he was, by the age of thirty, an incurable drunkard—perhaps the penalty of being too friendly in a northern climate.

In the latter part of 1768 he was drinking hard. He committed his usual indiscretions, and was again violently enamoured of the dear infidel. On this subject he wrote to that exemplary clergyman, Temple:

"Tell me sincerely, Do I right to insist that my dear little woman shall stay? She was married very young. But she has three children. I hate to think of it. No matter. She is like a girl of eighteen. She has the finest black hair. She is paradisial in bed. Is it not right that I should have a favourite to keep me happy? But, alas, I love her so much that I am in a kind of fever. This is unworthy of Paoli's friend. . . . By the by, she is now more affected by my bad conduct than she was at first."

From his earliest years Boswell had known his cousin Margaret Montgomerie, the daughter of David Montgomerie of Lainshaw. She was a gentle, homely, dutiful young woman, and she seemed to Boswell's relations to be a very proper person to become his wife. He himself did not at first share this opinion. But he liked her, and she was the only young woman of his acquaintance whom he treated always with respect. And that proves that she was neither dashing nor artful nor conspicuously handsome.

The first mention of Margaret Montgomerie in Boswell's correspondence is in a letter to Sir Alexander Dick from Lainshaw, in which he says: "Miss Montgomerie, who is sitting by me, joins in best compliments to all." In April

1769 she accompanied him to Ireland. On the very eve of their departure he had offended her by getting drunk.

The purpose of this trip to Ireland was to visit, and if possible to capture, the Arcadian beauty. The result was by no means what Boswell anticipated. He was received in a very gratifying manner by the Irish; he met Lord Charlemont, Dr. Leland, Mr. Flood, the Lord Lieutenant Townshend, and "the celebrated George Falkner, the social though laughable friend of Swift and Lord Chesterfield." He dined with the Duke of Leinster at Carton. In county Down he was introduced to much good society by Mr. Sibthorpe, his relation by marriage. He found in most places a natural sympathy with Corsica, and everywhere the most delightful praises of his book. His propaganda, zealously urged, was evidently successful. This was very pleasing; but what about *La Belle Irlandoise*? She is mentioned casually in a letter to Sir Alexander Dick; she was amiable; she danced a jig with Boswell to the tune of Carrickfergus; and that was all.

The truth is that Boswell's affections were veering again, and this time in the direction of his cousin Peggie. Perhaps he turned to Miss Montgomerie for consolation after his failure with the Arcadian nymph. Be that as it may, his growing love for his cousin—no sudden, flaring folly—was more estimable and certainly more rational than any he had known before. She had been, so he said, "the constant yet prudent and delicate *confidante* of all his *égarements du cœur et de l'esprit*." She knew something about him: that she knew everything is inconceivable. Her kindness and good sense had calmed him in the midst of his futile distractions, and had kept alive in his own mind the sentiment of honour and esteem. Of all the innumerable women with whom he philandered or flirted, she alone really cared for him. The result of the Irish tour was a formal engagement between James Boswell and Margaret Montgomerie. In his own words: "This jaunt was the occasion of Mr. Boswell's resolving at last to engage himself in that connection to which he had always declared himself averse. In short, he determined to become a married man."

This projected marriage was cordially sanctioned by

71

David Montgomerie and by Lord Auchinleck. It may seem necessary to find excuses for them. The wildness and folly of Boswell must have been known to both families. But David may have thought of the noble Auchinleck estate, and old Alexander may have believed in the sobering effect of marriage with a wise and virtuous woman. At any rate it is clear that the match was not only approved of, but was actually plotted, by these careful and affectionate fathers and by the cleverly associated effort of uncles, aunts and cousins.

The proximity of any woman not wholly unpleasing was enough to kindle the desires of Boswell and to fill his mind with a turmoil of gusty sentiment. To this propensity marriage made little difference. Nearly ten years after his marriage Boswell wrote in the series of *Hypochondriack* essays for the *London Magazine*, the following piece of auto-biography:

"A man who is actuated only by sensual desire will indulge it with any female he may meet, and like a glutton, who ravenously devours many dishes, will indiscriminately embrace a plurality of wenches. . . . I know that there are numerous gradations of the passion, and that the heart may sometimes be divided into many sections, though no doubt there is always a pre-eminent object, as in every seraglio there is a favourite sultana. . . . It is the violent passion of Love which is the subject of these lucubrations. For the truth is, that an *Hypochondriack* rarely knows a milder species."

The heart of Boswell was perpetually divided in many sections, and a new section was ready at a moment's notice. But still, it is true that poor Mrs. Boswell did become the "pre-eminent object." There was never a definite evil intention in the mind of Boswell; he was a rake and a drunkard through sheer weakness or insanity; contemptible, perhaps, but not substantially wicked; deserving pity rather than a heavy burst of moral indignation.

Before his marriage took place (on the 25th of November 1769) there was a journey south.

72

Boswell arrived in London early in the autumn and found that Johnson was away at Brighton with Mr. and Mrs. Thrale. He now made up his mind to attend the Shakespeare Jubilee at Stratford-on-Avon. As he never travelled without the Corsican dress, this appeared to be a first-rate opportunity for display. He therefore went to a tailor and had a cap made in the appropriate style, with the stirring device of *Viva la Libertà* embroidered in letters of gold.

CHAPTER VI

STRATFORD JUBILEE

THE ordinary people of Stratford were very much surprised, and they had some reason to be surprised, by the Shakespeare Jubilee designed by Mr. Garrick.

Mr. Angelo, Mr. Garrick and other London gentlemen, had turned the whole place upside down. They set up a great booth which they called Shakespeare's Hall or the Amphitheatre, on the lines of the elegant Rotunda at Ranelagh, though not so large, supported by a colonnade of the Corinthian order and illuminated by a chandelier of eight hundred lights. This Amphitheatre was made beautiful and interesting by means of painted curtains and other pretty devices. In front of the orchestra there was a magnificent statue of Shakespeare, presented to the town by Mr. Garrick. The town hall was also prepared for the occasion: at one end of it there was a fine picture of Shakespeare meditating (as well he might, in view of what was going on), and at the other was Gainsborough's portrait of Mr. Garrick. There were transparencies in the windows, which had an agreeable effect when they were lighted up at night. There were other transparencies on the bank of the Avon, opposite the Amphitheatre, which were also very pleasing. But the most noble transparency of all was undoubtedly that which covered the house in which Shakespeare was born, and which represented in a superb manner a rising sun breaking through the clouds. And this was all due to the ingenuity and the unselfish enthusiasm of Mr. Garrick.

The Jubilee was to begin on Wednesday the 6th of September. By Tuesday afternoon most of the available rooms in the town were occupied. Handsome coaches, with bright escutcheons on their panels, brought visitors of nobility and elegance. People of a more dashing sort flew along the road in chaises at a speed of nearly ten miles an hour. The humbler folk took places in the expensive though perilous "machine," and were most damnably jostled and shaken together. Sporting gentlemen rode their own nags, accompanied by servants with pack-horses. Most of them brought large trunks decorated with brass nails and full of laces, brocades, caps, ruffles, curlie-wurlies, bag wigs, bob wigs, grizzle bobs, hats, buckles, and resplendent clothes for the morning, the assembly and the masquerade.

It was a fashionable crowd that came to Stratford. The Shakespeare Jubilee of Mr. Garrick was not patronised by serious men, by men of letters or learning. And yet the entertainment was varied enough. There was to be an oratorio, a horse-race, an ode by Mr. Garrick with music by Dr. Arne, a dinner with a real turtle, a fancy dress ball and a prodigious number of fireworks. How could Shakespeare (and Mr. Garrick) be more suitably honoured? How was it that men like Johnson and Steevens turned up their nose at the whole performance?

Stratford policy was divided by the apprehension of divine wrath (for this Jubilee was a very profane business) and the desire to fleece the visitors. Half-a-guinea a night was charged for the standing of a single horse, without oats or hay; and the worst beds in the town went for not less than a guinea. Mr. Foote merrily declared that he paid nine guineas for six hours' sleep. When it came to meals, you were lucky if you got the desiccated remains of a cold chicken. You had to pay double and treble the London prices for everything, and you got miserable substitutions, dirt and impertinence, ragged quilts and filthy pewter.

Before dawn on Wednesday morning the Jubilee began with a serenading of the ladies. This was done by a party of Mr. Garrick's people from Drury Lane, and it may have been tolerable: the words they had to sing were bad; so bad that it may be doubted if any pageant poetry was ever worse.

> "Let beauty with the sun arise,
>   To Shakespeare tribute pay,
> With heavenly smiles and speaking eyes,
>   Give grace and lustre to the day.

75

> Each smile she gives protects his name,
>   What face shall dare to frown?
> Not envy's self can blast the fame,
>   Which beauty deigns to crown."

Then came a song by Mr. Garrick, in a style of rollicking familiarity:

> "Ye Warwickshire lads and ye lasses,
>   See what at our Jubilee passes,
> Come revel away, rejoice and be glad,
> For the lad of all lads was a Warwickshire lad,
>   Warwickshire lad,
>   All be glad,
> For the lad of all lads was a Warwickshire lad."

Before the Drury Lane singers had finished their delightful performance, a fine burst of artillery greeted the rising sun. Boys ran from house to house distributing programmes. There was a rumbling of drums, a squeaking of fifes and braying of trumpets: the military music of the Warwickshire militia. The gay Jubilee people tumbled out of bed and prepared themselves for the public breakfast in the town hall; they put on their rainbow ribbons, their Shakespeare medals and Shakespeare favours.

Mr. Garrick came to the breakfast-room soon after eight. He was received by the mayor and corporation and was presented with a medallion of Shakespeare carved on a piece of the famous mulberry-tree and richly set in gold. Mr. Garrick made a suitable reply, and hung the medallion round his neck. The company began to arrive: a very noble company, including the Duke of Dorset, the Duke of Manchester, Lord Beauchamp, Lord Grosvenor, Sir Watkin Williams Wynne, Lord Spencer, Lord Denbigh, Lord Pigot, and James Boswell, Esq.

Boswell knew Garrick, but he was anxious not to be recognised until the masquerade, when he could make a surprising appearance as the armed Corsican chief. So when the people said, "Pray, Mr. Garrick, who was that odd, serious-looking fellow who spoke to you just now?" Garrick answered, "Mum's the word!—he's a clergyman in disguise."

Leaving the town hall after breakfast, the company went to the church, to hear Dr. Arne conduct his own oratorio of *Judith*. This, although it had little to do with Shakespeare, was a very fine work. The chorus and the orchestra were admirable. The solo parts were taken by Mr. Vernon, Mr. Champness, Master Brown, Mrs. Barthelemon, and the truly divine Mrs. Baddeley of Drury Lane. Boswell listened with rapture to the music, and he looked with rapture at Mrs. Baddeley. Still, he disapproved of the oratorio: "I could have wished that prayers had been read, and a short sermon preached; it would have consecrated our jubilee to begin it with devotion—with gratefully adoring the Supreme Father of all spirits, from whom cometh every good and perfect gift."

After the oratorio there was a procession to the Amphitheatre, led by Mr. Garrick and his players, and accompanied by a band and chorus under Mr. Vernon. At three there was a public ordinary in the Amphitheatre, with occasional songs and catches by picked singers. The ordinary, provided by the manager of the White Lion, was a miserable affair. Eighteen-and-sixpence was charged for a dinner which consisted mainly of neck of beef washed down by a cheap and sour Southampton port.

No sooner had the ordinary come to an end than people were hurrying off to get ready for the assembly. Dancing began at ten o'clock; the minuets (some of them written for the Jubilee) continued until midnight, and were followed by country dances which lasted until three in the morning.

But the second day was to be the great day for Boswell and for all the jubilee-makers.

Boswell had certainly come to Stratford with the idea of exhibiting himself. The precise nature of his exhibition is generally misrepresented. Carlyle and Macaulay both repeat the fable that he walked about wearing on his hat a placard which bore the words *Corsica Boswell*. It is also supposed that he stood in a conspicuous place and offered to any who would take them free copies of a poem on Corsica. There is nothing improbable in these particulars; but they are not true.

The idea of attending the Jubilee masquerade in the character of an armed Corsican chief had come into Boswell's head before he left London. However absurd he may have looked in his Corsican dress, he was not without some excuse for choosing it. His book had made him well known, both as a writer and as the friend of Paoli. For the purpose of a masquerade the Corsican dress was therefore as appropriate as any other; the absurdity was not in the choice of the occasion, but in the appearance of such a person in such a dress. The cap specially made to go with the dress carried the device of *Viva la Libertà*, not *Corsica Boswell*; it was made of black cloth, and on one side of it there was a great bunch of blue feathers with a cockade. The fable of *Corsica Boswell* is probably due to the impersonation of Boswell by an actor in Garrick's dramatised version of the Jubilee at Drury Lane.

The distribution of the poem on Corsica was not part of the original plan; it was a happy thought on the first or second day of the Jubilee. A desperate effort was made to get it printed off locally in time for distribution at the masquerade. A printer was found, who sent a breathless boy to the masquerade at two o'clock in the morning with a proof. But the gallant endeavour was made too late, and the distribution never took place.

Whether any copies of the *Verses in the Character of a Corsican* were given away at Stratford is uncertain. The poem consists of a folio leaf, printed on one side only, unpaged and unpriced, and is now exceedingly rare. It was published in several newspapers, and, although an extremely bad poem, it is well above the level of the other Jubilee productions.

On the second day of the festival, divine wrath showed itself (according to the religious) by letting fall upon Stratford a desolating downpour of rain. There was to have been a procession of Shakespeare characters after breakfast, but the rain put a stop to that. The company, in sodden cloaks and overcoats, made their way to the Amphitheatre to hear Mr. Garrick's Ode.

Inside the Amphitheatre there was a noble sight: Mr. Garrick in a suit of brown with rich gold lace, his wooden medal on his breast, and a chorus of blooming ladies on each side of him. And there were the fiddles and flutes, the bass viols, the trumpets and the harpsichord, to be conducted by Dr. Arne. Mr. Garrick rose and bowed to the assembly, gracefully holding in one hand the steward's rod; there was a great noise of applause; and then, as Dr. Arne raised his wand, a silence in which you could hear the rain drumming on the roof. One, two, three! Down came the wand and away went the band and the chorus:

> "To what blest genius of the isle,
>   Shall Gratitude her tribute pay,
>   Decree the festive day,
>   Erect the statue, and devote the pile?"

A noble chorus, a rousing band; and yet the splendour of their harmony was nothing to the declamations by Mr. Garrick. At the proper place, Mr. Garrick rose and spoke his lines. In none of his various performances, we are assured, did he appear to greater advantage. He distinguished himself (in the words of Mr. Victor) as a Poet, an Actor, and a Gentleman. His dress, to be sure, was that of a gentleman; his gestures and speech were those of a supremely great actor; but it may be questioned if the verses he uttered were those of a poet. Mr. Garrick had written those verses, and Mr. Garrick alone could make them worth hearing. The Jubilee audience of elegant lords and beautiful ladies had never heard anything so fine; the noble voice of declamation, the sweeping chords of Dr. Arne's music, the trilling and booming of the chorus were positively superb.

> "From the dark cloud the hidden light
>   Bursts tenfold bright!
>   Prepare! prepare! prepare!
>   Now swell the choral song,
>   Roll the full tide of harmony along;

Let Rapture sweep the trembling strings,
And Fame expanding all her wings,
With all her trumpet tongues proclaim
The lov'd, rever'd, immortal name!
Shakespeare! Shakespeare! Shakespeare!"

To Boswell, stirred as he was by the spirit of occasions, all this must have been really magnificent. Such rank and beauty! Such an assemblage of poetical fancies! Were they not gloriously and elegantly united in honouring the memory of the immortal bard, the Swan of Avon, the Will of Wills? But there were other thoughts in his mind, as well. If the Corsican verses were not actually written, they were contemplated with anxious concern; and if they were already finished, there was the question of a printer.

And of course there were inevitable distractions. Boswell guarded, as best he could, his pure affection for Miss Montgomerie. He was trying to be steady and sober, and trying to preserve inviolate the holy devotion of a reforming philanderer pledged to an honourable marriage. It was to be another period of perfection; he made up his mind to be respectable, to be worthy and sedate, to be a solid, uniform, exemplary character. That was not easy for a man who was capable of falling in love every five minutes.

He had been introduced at Stratford to Mrs. Sheldon, the pretty wife of Captain Sheldon of the 38th Foot. Mrs. Sheldon was a gay Irish lady, and she immediately fascinated Boswell. Something had to be done. He looked at Mrs. Sheldon listening to the Ode. Yes; he was falling in love, and there was only one way out of it. He gazed earnestly at Mrs. Baddeley of Drury Lane, and the image of Mrs. Sheldon faded out of his mind. In such homœopathic remedies there may be a risk, it may be only a fatal hop out of the frying-pan. But Mrs. Baddeley was inaccessible; she was a distant though living image of beauty, and might safely be used for the purpose of effacement.

When the Ode was over, Mr. Garrick delivered a prose encomium on Shakespeare, which was quite as fine as anything else he had done; it finished with a challenge to the enemies of the poet.

Upon this, Mr. King, that famous comedian, rose up and came into the orchestra. He took off his greatcoat, and was seen to be dressed in a suit of blue with silver frogs—clearly he was in the fashionable character of a Macaroni. Those who knew Mr. King "expected something extremely whimsical," and those who did not know him were not a little astonished. He denounced Shakespeare with considerable ingenuity; and then Mr. Garrick got up and addressed the ladies in a poetical speech.

During this part of the performance there was an unrehearsed diversion. The benches in various parts of the Amphitheatre suddenly gave way, and many illustrious people were bumped on the floor, and a door fell on Lord Carlisle.

But nothing can disturb for long the dogged good-humour of an English assembly when it has made up its mind to enjoy itself. In given circumstances, whatever happens is amusing. Inanities that even the mind of a fool could scarcely tolerate in solitude become in the highest degree pleasurable when they are shared by many. That is why the success of an English party depends only upon getting together a sufficient number of people and providing them with a simple method of destroying thought.

The Jubilee crowd had made up its mind to enjoy itself. With the exception of Lord Carlisle, no one cared much if the doors and benches of the crazy Amphitheatre did give way. The people listened cheerfully to Mr. Garrick's verses, and cheerfully ate something called turtle, but which, according to Musidorus of the *Chronicle*, was really beef. As for the rain, falling so dismally and so steadily, damping the ingenious fireworks of Mr. Angelo and splashing upon the gay panels of the coaches, it was nothing more than a slight inconvenience.

To Boswell, the masquerade was the crowning event. Not many people watched the curtailed display of the fireworks, most of them only sputtering with a deal of smoke and smell; but the entire company (except Lord Carlisle) attended the masquerade.

It was a brave show. Those who could not afford dresses of their own hired them at extravagant prices. The stewards were lenient, and some were admitted whose only disguise was a mask. Lady Pembroke, Mrs. Bouverie and Mrs. Crewe appeared as the witches of *Macbeth*, and Miss Nancy Ladbrooke was Dame Quickly. Lord Grosvenor was dressed in a rich oriental habit. Mr. Yates as a waggoner was excellent; on the other hand, some unlucky man who represented the Devil "gave inexpressible offence." Nobility had to keep its proper distance—for this was only a provincial affair after all—and for the most part wore plain dominoes; the rest could do as they pleased, they could be nuns or Turks, pedlars, Jews, shepherds, Punches, harlequins or Patagonians. Such dresses, though amusing and pretty, had been seen before. The celebrated friend of Paoli, James Boswell, Esq., had determined to produce an effect peculiarly his own. Dancing began at eleven, but the armed Corsican chief did not arrive until midnight.

The Corsican dress was undoubtedly a good one, although a musket slung over the back may be a little awkward in dancing. But there was a curious addition which had nothing to do with Corsica: Boswell carried a long staff "with a bird finely carved upon it, emblematical of the sweet Bard of Avon." It may have been finely carved, though it looked more like a snake than a bird—or, to be exact, like a serpent with the head of a duck. The friend of Paoli could not wear a mask; and it was never Boswell's policy to hide his face.

"So soon as he entered the room," wrote Boswell himself, "he drew universal attention. The novelty of the Corsican dress, its becoming appearance, and the character of that brave nation concurred to distinguish the armed Corsican chief. He was first accosted by Mrs. Garrick, with whom he had a good deal of conversation. Mr. Boswell danced both a minuet and a country dance with a very pretty Irish lady, Mrs. Sheldon . . . who was dressed in a genteel domino, and before she danced threw off her mask."

It had evidently been his intention to recite his verses to the company, even if he could not get the copies in time for distribution. Victor makes the suggestion that he endeavoured to do this, "but was prevented by the crowd." However that may be, the verses belong properly to the history of the Stratford Jubilee. They are addressed to the Jubilee crowd, and they are now, perhaps, the best known expression of Boswell's ardent Corsican propaganda. In sentiment they are generous, in diction at least equal to the better sort of newspaper poetry:

> "From the rude banks of Golo's rapid flood,
> Alas! too deeply ting'd with patriot blood;
> O'er which, dejected, injured freedom bends,
> And sighs indignant o'er all Europe sends:
> Behold a *Corsican*. . . .
> I come not hither sadly to complain,
> Or damp your mirth with melancholy strain:
> In man's firm breast conceal'd the grief should lye,
> Which melts with grace in woman's gentle eye;
> But let me plead for Liberty distrest,
> And warm for her each sympathetic breast. . . .
> With generous ardour make *us* also *free*;
> And give to *Corsica* a *noble Jubilee*!"

There are forty-six lines in the poem, none of them better, or worse, then the lines quoted above. They illustrate very well that odd compound of generosity and vanity, of solemn fervour and puffing ostentation, which makes up so much of Boswell's external character. Yet we should note that a sense of congruity prevents him from speaking of himself in the poem. He is one of Paoli's musketeers. He is playing a part, and he is guided by his appreciation of the part. And so the verses illustrate something else in Boswell—his obvious though fumbling perception of the essentials of drama.

Boswell did not stay to see the last of the Jubilee. Having shown himself at the masquerade, there was nothing to keep him in Stratford. The great event was over. He was not interested in the horse-race for a cup of £50 value, won in nearly a foot of water by Mr. Pratt the groom on his own colt Whirligig. Nor did he care to attend the dinner in the Amphitheatre (which was now being gradually flooded and was falling to bits) with its music of clarinets and French horns. He was not present when the rain ceased, and at last the Grand Firework was played off.

The Stratford Jubilee may seem to us, as it did to many of its contemporaries, a piece of ridiculous mummery, designed as much to advertise Garrick as to celebrate Shakespeare. It did not appear in that light to Boswell. He did not agree with Dempster, who said it belonged to "the chapter of whims." He was vexed by the ribaldry of Mr. Foote, who spoke of "an ode without poetry, music without melody, dinners without victuals and lodgings without beds, and a gingerbread amphitheatre which, like a house of cards, tumbled to pieces as soon as it was finished." To him, the Jubilee had been a really tremendous occasion. In his account written for the *Scots Magazine* he declared enthusiastically: "I am now returned to London; and I flatter myself that, after being agitated as much as any body, I have recovered my tranquillity, and am in a condition to give a few remarks on this celebrated jubilee of genius, which I am persuaded will engage the attention, not only of all ranks of this island, but of the learned and ingenious in every part of Europe." And he wrote in the *Life of Johnson*: "When almost every man of eminence in the literary world was happy to partake in this festival of genius, the absence of Johnson could not but be wondered at and regretted." Here is an exaggeration as foolish as it is unnecessary. Not a single man of literary eminence had anything to do with the festival; nor could the absence of Johnson have been surprising to anyone who knew him. Boswell tried to persuade himself, and did persuade himself, that Garrick's entertainment was really a matter of importance for the entire civilised world. He reflected with intense delight that his figure in the Corsican dress was being engraved on a most genteel plate for ten thousand copies of the *London Magazine*.

Soon after Boswell's return to London, Johnson came back from Brighton. On the 6th of October, Boswell visited Thrale's house at Streatham for the first time. He had met Mrs. Thrale at Johnson's in the spring of 1768.

But Johnson was not at this time his principal concern.

Paoli had come to England. The French had beaten down
the last resistance of the islanders, and the General had only
escaped with difficulty and some peril: on the 21st of
September he had landed at Portsmouth.

The arrival of Paoli was naturally an event of the highest
importance for Boswell. He had a European reputation as
the friend of this illustrious man, and his book had introduced the noble character of the General to thousands of
English readers. He could now associate openly with the
hero, and be of real service to him in ways both friendly and
practical. In such display and in such devotion Boswell
could find his best employment.

Johnson, in spite of his petulant sallies against Corsica,
or against Boswell's heady enthusiasm for Corsica, met Paoli
with true satisfaction. Their talk, though fluency was hardly
possible, was congenial from the very start. The Doctor
afterwards told Boswell that Paoli had "the loftiest port of
any man he had ever seen." From this time until the end of
Johnson's life the Doctor and the General met often, and
never without a manly regard for each other.

On the 16th of October Boswell gave a dinner at his rooms
in Old Bond Street. His guests were Johnson, Reynolds,
Garrick, Murphy, Goldsmith, Bickerstaff and Tom Davies.
It was on this occasion that Goldsmith boasted about his
new bloom-coloured suit, and Johnson made his brutal
remark about the pride of the tailor in being able to make a
good coat even with a colour so ridiculous.

Let it be observed that Boswell's company included four
of the most famous men of the period. Reynolds was then in
his forty-seventh year, he was the President of the recently
founded Royal Academy, and was at the height of his fame.
Goldsmith was forty-one; he had written all his best works,
except *She Stoops to Conquer*. Garrick was fifty-two, and had
been the most famous English actor for nearly thirty years.
The Great Cham of literature was in his sixty-first year, and
Boswell had not yet celebrated his twenty-ninth birthday.
It seems worth while to note the ages and the attainments of
these men, to consider their eminence, and then to remember
the comparative youth of Boswell, asking ourselves whether

such company would have accepted the invitation of one who was in truth the exasperating fool described by Macaulay in the *Edinburgh Review*.

Before the middle of November, Boswell had left for Scotland, and he did not see Johnson again for nearly two and a half years.

Boswell and his father were both married on the 25th of November: young James to Peggie Montgomerie, and old Alexander to his cousin Elizabeth, the daughter of Claude James Boswell, afterwards Lord Balmuto. The most extraordinary account of his own marriage was afterwards written by Boswell in one of the *Hypochondriack* essays (April, 1781):

"After having for many years cherished a system of marrying for money, I at last totally departed from it, and marryed for love. But the truth was, that I had not been careful enough to weed my mind; for while I cultivated the plant of interest, love all the time grew up along with it and fairly got the better. Naturally somewhat singular, independent of any addition which affection and vanity might perhaps have made, I resolved to have a more pleasing species of Marriage than common, and bargained with my bride, that I should not be bound to live with her longer than I really inclined; and that whenever I tired of her domestick society, I should be at liberty to give it up."

Such were the admirable sentiments of a man whose marriage contract had been witnessed by Samuel Johnson and Pasquale Paoli.

CHAPTER VII

GOOD SOCIETY

VAGRANCY of character is usually checked by marriage, even if there is no permanent reform. Boswell's marriage certainly had the effect of reducing his moral oscillations and of giving him the illusion of balance for two or three years. To some extent he was again playing up to his idea of being "a uniform pretty fellow," a model of distinguished respectability. But he was also aware of the true affection, the care and the plain good sense of his wife. His affection for her was of a more settled kind than his previous affections and was based upon worthier sentiments of gratitude and esteem.

The love letters of Boswell are simple and manly. His courtship was frank and honourable. He spoke freely of his failings; he made no foolish promises. The odd "Sultanick" agreement that he mentions in his essay is to be taken as a mere flourish of originality; at no time did he contemplate such a thing as desertion.

For at least two years after his marriage there is a marked sobriety in the life and correspondence of Boswell. Indeed, there is very little correspondence. He left Johnson without a letter for nearly a year and a half, and when at last he did write he gave him a staid account of his "comfortable life as a married man, and a lawyer in practice at the Scotch Bar."

This break in the correspondence with Johnson is extremely significant. It implies a break with London associations and the acceptance of a new domesticated scheme of life. Even the project of Johnson's tour to the Hebrides, once the subject of lively discussion, was left alone. Boswell had come under an influence that seemed likely to change him for the better; the influence, not of the philosophic Johnson or the heroic Paoli, but of Peggie his wife.

Periods of personal improvement are biographically barren. The edifying year of 1770, in which Boswell tried to be diligent, sober, and completely rational, is entirely without episodes or excitement. He disappears, for a time, in the decent obscurity of a good citizen. He lived blamelessly in his Edinburgh house (Chessel's Buildings, Canongate), anxious to build up a sound legal practice and to be the respectable head of a respectable family. *Quid mea?* he might say, looking back on his variegated career, *ego in portu navigo.* He observed with satisfaction that his father's wife showed "no appearance of multiplying."

At the end of August his first legitimate child was born, and died soon after birth. In spite of sober philosophic reasonings, this was a real sorrow. "I have experienced this," he wrote to Temple, "and there is no arguing against it."

In September he received a most welcome visit from Temple. This was delightful to both of them, and Boswell felt that he would be perfectly happy if he could find a northern living for his friend.

So he lived, uprightly and worthily. It was truly a period of reform and settlement. From a strictly moral point of view, it is to be regretted that Boswell ever broke away from his moorings, and that his life eventually became a dreadful warning and not a profitable example. But from other points of view we might have regretted even more his continued application to business and his acquiescence in a rigid household discipline: there might have been no *Tour to the Hebrides* and no *Life of Johnson.*

In the early autumn of 1771, General Paoli, accompanied by Count Burzynski, the Polish ambassador in London, paid a visit to Scotland. These illustrious men reached Edinburgh *incogniti* on the 3rd of September. They were received by James Boswell with the utmost enthusiasm. Two days later, Boswell conducted them on a little tour. They saw the iron works of the Carron company, where Boswell had placed his order for the Corsican guns. Afterwards they travelled to Glasgow, and visited the elegant press of the Foulis brothers and the University. But the chief purpose of the tour was a visit to Auchinleck. Paoli and the Count were the guests of Lord Auchinleck for two nights. "You may figure the joy of my worthy father," said Boswell, "at seeing the Corsican hero in our romantick groves." Somehow, it is not so easy to figure this joy: old Alexander had called Paoli "a land-louping scoundrel," and we cannot imagine him responding emotionally to the spectacle of a hero in romantic groves. On Sunday, the 7th, they set out with an escort of the Auchinleck tenants, and breakfasted with Campbell of Treesbank. After a short excursion in the Glasgow district they returned to Edinburgh and spent a whole day with Boswell. On the 12th of September the visitors left for London, and Boswell hastened to write his account for the *Scots Magazine*.

In February 1772, Boswell wrote to Johnson and told him that he was coming to London in order to appear in a case which had been sent from the Court of Session to the House of Lords. It was the case of a schoolmaster who had been deprived of his post because he was "somewhat severe in the chastisement of his scholars." The Court of Session had reinstated him, but his enemies had lodged an appeal. Johnson replied with one of the kindest of his letters, assuring Boswell of a welcome: "Whether to love you be right or wrong, I have many on my side: Mrs. Thrale loves you, and Mrs. Williams loves you, and what would have inclined me to love you if I had been neutral before, you are a great favourite of Dr. Beattie."

This visit to London (March 1772) may be taken as the end of Boswell's reformation period. There is no immediate visible collapse, but the old ruinous tendencies reappear, and London life goes to his head again.

On the 21st of March, after long absence, he found himself in Johnson's apartments. The Doctor was extremely cordial.

Like all friends meeting after absence, they wanted to talk about a number of things. The conversation flowed easily and delightfully from one subject to another.

First they discussed the prospects of the schoolmaster and his appeal. Johnson was heavy on the side of discipline. "Severity must be continued until obstinacy be subdued, and negligence be cured." Then they talked of Johnson's political pamphlets, *The False Alarm* and *Thoughts Concerning Falkland's Islands*.

"*Johnson*: 'Well, Sir, which of them did you think the best?' *Boswell*: 'I liked the second best.' *Johnson*: 'Why, Sir, I liked the first best; and Beattie liked the first best. Sir, there is a subtlety of disquisition in the first, that is worth all the fire of the second.' *Boswell*: 'Pray, Sir, is it true that Lord North paid you a visit, and that you got two hundred a year in addition to your pension?' *Johnson*: 'No, Sir. Except what I had from the bookseller, I did not get a farthing by them. And, between you and me, I believe Lord North is no friend to me.' *Boswell*: 'How so, Sir?' *Johnson*: 'Why, Sir, you cannot account for the fancies of men.—Well, how does Lord Elibank? and how does Lord Monboddo?' *Boswell*: 'Very well, Sir. Lord Monboddo still maintains the superiority of the savage life.' *Johnson*: 'What strange narrowness of mind now is that, to think the things we have not known are better than the things we have known.' *Boswell*: 'Why, Sir, that is a common prejudice.' *Johnson*: 'Yes, Sir, but a common prejudice should not be found in one whose trade it is to rectify errour.'"

A gentleman came in, who was going as mate with Mr. Banks and Dr. Solander. Then came a debate between Mrs. Desmoulins and the Reverend Mr. Stockdale; and then came the praises of Dr. Beattie. Johnson then spoke of St. Kilda, the most remote of the Hebrides, and Boswell said he had thought of buying it.

"Pray do, Sir!" cried the Doctor merrily. "We will go and pass a winter amid the blasts there. We shall have fine fish, and we will take some dried tongues with us, and some books. We will have a strong built vessel, and some Orkney men to navigate her. We must build a tolerable house: but we may carry with us a wooden house ready made——"

So he roared and rambled, and Boswell said, "Are you serious, Sir?" and Johnson replied, "Why, yes, Sir, I am serious."

Here was life again!—London, Johnson, literature, politics, glorious conversation, good society! It seemed a long way to the house in the Canongate. He went out into the Strand, and there were the pretty purchasable girls. He only looked at the girls, but that was enough to make him realise that it would be unsafe to come to London without his dear Peggie.

He talked with Lord Mansfield, who said that he was glad to see him at any time; he breakfasted with the Earl of Eglinton, and saw with delight a proper Scots table with marmalade, honey, currant jelly, and muffins both buttered and toasted. Another noble countryman, Sir Alexander Macdonald, received him with genial hospitality.

Paoli was in London, and Boswell might go to his house whenever he pleased. He was equally sure of a welcome at the house of that boisterous, benevolent old man, General Oglethorpe. (After fighting with distinction under Prince Eugene, Oglethorpe had interested himself in prison reform and had founded the colony of Georgia in 1732.) At his own rooms in Conduit Street he could entertain his friends and pour out innumerable cups of tea for Doctor Johnson.

Johnson had given up wine. He looked with a rational man's contempt upon those who believed that sociability depended, in a large measure, on a readiness to get fuddled and the toleration of drunkards. Indeed, the worst instances of his rudeness occurred when he fancied that the person addressing him was not perfectly sober. Boswell, on the other hand, took delight in what he called "convivial indulgence." Again and again he argued with Johnson in a futile effort to soften the hard countenance which frowned upon the tippler. He was always trying to win from Johnson a few pieces of moral sophistry in justification of his own failings; he could win a qualified apology for licentiousness, a quibbling extenuation of adultery on the part of a man, but never an excuse for the poor inebriate. "No, Sir!—it is all very well to talk about truth in wine. That may be an argument for drinking, if you suppose men in general to be lyars. But, Sir, I would not keep company with a fellow who lyes as long as he is sober."

A day or two after this defeat Boswell tried again. Wearisome pertinacity was one of his worst faults. He said bumptiously: "You know, Sir, drinking drives away care, and makes us forget whatever is disagreeable. Would not you allow a man to drink for *that* reason?" Johnson replied: "Yes, Sir; if he sat next *you*." This was one of those "grand explosions" which filled Boswell (if we are to believe him) with perverted joy. Yet he takes care, in the *Life*, to conceal his own identity, and to name the speaker only as "a gentleman." An attentive perusal of the *Life*, and a comparison with his private journals, makes it clear that the nameless "gentleman" is very often Boswell himself.

Now, the attitude of Boswell towards Johnson is not so easy to understand as might be imagined. During the visit of 1772 he undoubtedly became more closely intimate with the great man than he had been before; and it has to be remembered that Boswell only met Johnson during a series of visits or excursions. He was therefore anxious to make the most of his time. Before the end of this book we shall have to study in some detail the relations between the two men, which were certainly relations that were neither constant nor obvious; but here it is only necessary to observe that Boswell looked upon Johnson with as much curiosity as reverence. He treated the Doctor as a kind of entertainment which he imagined himself perfectly well qualified to control or exhibit; he loved to display his capacity for drawing him out and making him exert his powers in conversation. Actually, there is no doubt that Mrs. Thrale could draw him out quite as well, and Burke a hundred times better. Fanny Burney, again, could show a delightful aspect of Johnson which Boswell could not even perceive. But it was Boswell whose varying and irresponsible fancies, plausible solemnity and absence of restraint, led the Doctor from one theme to another until he had covered the whole range of the topics which are interesting to ordinary men. He was then able to record, in a style of dialogue which is absolutely unrivalled, the results of his exploitation. What we have to remember is that he was playing a part not unlike that of a showman, whether he had in his mind persons immediately present or the vaster audience of posterity. The *Life of Johnson* is not a complete portrait; it is very far from being such a thing: to realise that, you have only to read Madame d'Arblay's *Memoirs*, the *Anecdotes* of Mrs. Piozzi (a little book which is too much neglected), and the writings—particularly the letters—of Johnson himself. Boswell has preserved, in a form bright, imperishable and perpetually astonishing, the appearance, the manners and the talk of Johnson, thus making him a vividly comprehensible figure; Macaulay is right in saying that "his book resembles nothing so much as the conversation of the inmates of the Palace of Truth."

It is therefore important to bear in mind that Boswell's performance is really a superlatively fine piece of journalism, and not the work of a man distinguished by great intellectual acuteness. Unless this is remembered, it is impossible to understand Boswell's attitude, or to see the definite purpose in many of his absurd actions or absurd questions.

By virtue of his fidelity in recording, Boswell has given us a volume of truth richer and more illuminating than he himself was able to comprehend. Indeed, it is highly improbable that he ever saw his own character as clearly as we are now able to view it through his writings. What distinguished him was the kind of sensitivity which invites comparison with a chemical or mechanical process, though admitting a certain power of æsthetic rejection. And it is also important to remember that it was only towards the end of his life that he began to renounce the idea that he was himself a man of real eminence.

Johnson was therefore an entertainment, an example, and a centre of illumination. He was also an intrument for testing the value of ideas, and a measure for checking the moral edifice. He was the guide, the arbiter. "Pray, Sir, how do I speak now? Is there not some improvement?" "Sir, your pronunciation is not offensive."—"But, Sir, is there any harm in forming to ourselves conjectures as to the particulars of our future happiness?" "Sir, there is no harm."—"Suppose, Sir, that a bookseller should bring you a manuscript to look at." "Why, Sir, I should desire the bookseller to take it away."—"But, Sir, would it not be better to follow Nature, and go to bed and rise just as Nature gives us light or withholds it?" "No, Sir!"—It does not matter if the question is absurd or serious; the answer comes with a smack and a rap and the heavy assumption of absolute finality. It is not often a vague answer, as in the case of Cave's ghost: "Pray, Sir, what did he say of the appearance?" "Why, Sir, something of a shadowy being."

The idea of writing Johnson's life had occurred to Boswell almost as soon as he made his acquaintance. It was frankly admitted to Johnson himself on the 31st of March 1772, after they had dined at Paoli's and had gone to Boswell's rooms for tea before visiting the new Pantheon in the Oxford Road. "I said, that if it was not troublesome and presuming too much, I would request him to tell me all the little circumstances of his life; what schools he attended, when he came to Oxford, when he came to London, etc. He did not disapprove of my curiosity."

The visit of 1772 was probably one of Boswell's happiest periods in London. Although the weakness of his moral fabric is perceptible, there are no disastrous lapses. He was floating decently upon a high social level. He was on excellent terms with Paoli and Oglethorpe, with Goldsmith, Garrick and Reynolds, and certainly on friendly terms with Sir Adam Ferguson, Sir Alexander Macdonald, Lord Elibank, Lord Mansfield, Langton, Beauclerk, and scores of others. He had the delight of supping with Johnson at the Mitre and of drinking tea with Mrs. Williams. He had now a reasonable hope of enticing Johnson to the Highlands. His note-book and journal were filled with Johnsonian dialogue.

He returned to Edinburgh hoping that Johnson would actually come to Scotland in the autumn. But the Doctor was too unwell or too indolent. He assured Boswell that he was "very sincere in his design to pay the visit and take the ramble." Boswell therefore spent the autumn in collecting "the antiquities of the feudal establishment." In this year he published *Reflections on the Bankruptcies in Scotland*.

Boswell's eldest daughter, Veronica, was born on the 15th of March 1773. On the same night, *She Stoops to Conquer* was produced at Covent Garden. A fortnight later Boswell wrote to Goldsmith congratulating him on the success of his comedy, and telling him that he would shortly be in London. The purpose of this letter was the same as that of many other letters written by Boswell. He collected documents from famous people and stored them in his "archives." He says to Goldsmith, "While you are in the full glow of theatrical splendour . . . let me see that you can *stoop to write* to me." And he adds an urgent postscript: "My address is James's Court, Edinburgh. Write as if in repartee." It was the same thing when he wrote to Wilkes: "I beg that your letters may be signed John Wilkes. . . . I beg that you may put John Wilkes at the end of your letters, that they may not look like unsigned title-deeds."

It is to be observed that Boswell, as long as he was trying to maintain the equilibrium of a reformed character, avoided Wilkes. He evidently avoided him after the Stratford Jubilee, and he avoided him in 1772. The bloody riots of the Middlesex election were over, and Wilkes, in 1771, was a Sheriff of London and one of the most popular heroes. But a man whose mind is full of good resolutions and feudal antiquities naturally avoids a gay, profligate Whig, no matter how classic or how entertaining he may be. The famous dinner at Dilly's did not take place until 1776, and by that time there were no further serious attempts at reform.

There must have been misgivings in the mind of poor Mrs. Boswell as her husband set out for London at the end of March (1773). She regarded Johnson first as an inconvenience and then as a positive danger; and she was right. James loved London above all other places, and he thought more of Johnson than of anyone else; but James could never keep his head or his resolutions in a place where he was so continually excited and flattered. London would be his ruin —and that was equal to saying that Johnson would be his ruin.

To Boswell himself, a return to London was a return to all the best things in life. On the evening of the 3rd of April he was again drinking tea with Mrs. Williams and waiting for the Doctor to come home.

The 9th of April was Good Friday. Johnson, Levett and Boswell had a breakfast of tea and hot-cross buns. Then

Johnson took Boswell to the church of St. Clement Danes, where he had a seat in the north gallery. This day was always observed by the Doctor in a mood of dark religious abstraction. He went to church in the morning and evening, and in the interval between the two services he did not dine or talk, but read his Greek Testament. The attendance at the church and the quiet interval of reading formed a ceremony deeply impressive, and one in which Boswell often took a part. He sat in the Doctor's room, looking at books, while the Doctor, with low muttering and whistling and singular contortions of muscle, turned over the pages of his Testament. So they sat together, not speaking, and Boswell fancied himself truly pious. Perhaps he was. In a character where everything is mutable and flowing it is not easy to discern the more stationary elements or to identify those which are most likely to predominate.

Johnson invited him to dinner on Easter Day. "I have generally a meat pye on Sunday," he said: "it is baked at a publick oven, which is very properly allowed."

Boswell thought, or pretended to think, that his dinner would be a very crude affair. "I supposed we should scarcely have knives and forks, and only some strange, uncouth, ill-drest fish: but I found everything in very good order." They had soup, a boiled leg of lamb and spinach, a veal pie, and a rice pudding. There was no other company except Mrs. Williams and a young lady whose name is not recorded. After a light conversation on many subjects, Boswell again pressed the Doctor for the particulars of his early career. "You shall have them all for twopence," cried Johnson. "I hope you shall know a great deal more of me before you write my Life."

During the weeks that followed there was a noble series of dinners and conversations. They dined at General Oglethorpe's and heard Goldsmith sing Tony Lumpkin's song while the ladies drank tea. They dined at General Paoli's and met Signor Martinelli, the ingenious author of an Italian history of England. They dined with Mr. Elphinston of the Kensington Academy, and they dined with Mr. and Mrs. Thrale at Southwark.

At this time Boswell had a fondness for the twittering vivacity of Mrs. Thrale. He never admired a woman for her understanding, or believed that she could have any worth speaking of, but Mrs. Thrale was undeniably pretty, even at the age of thirty-three and after ten years of marriage. She was a real literary lady, too. Her first essays had appeared in the *St. James's Chronicle* before she was fifteen. Her knowledge of the English and Latin classics was remarkably good, though she could not approach Mrs. Carter in the matter of Greek, and she excelled in the little parlour-firework displays of quotation. Boswell had not yet made a fool of himself in Thrale's house, he had not yet preposterously claimed an exclusive right to Johnson, and Mrs. Thrale liked him. Of Thrale himself, a man only distinguished by a capacity for making money out of beer, there is little to be said. He was a heavy, deliberate man, who never said anything that anyone remembered, and who was inordinately fond of eating and not averse to a ponderous kind of flirtation. He died of an apoplexy in 1781.

The most memorable of the dinners was that of the 30th of April at Beauclerk's. There was a meeting on the same evening of the Literary Club, and Boswell, proposed by Johnson, and warmly supported by Beauclerk, was a candidate for membership.

To be received into this club was to be admitted to the most brilliant intellectual society of London. During the lifetime of Boswell the membership did not exceed thirty-five, and included Johnson, Reynolds, Burke, Goldsmith, Gibbon, Thomas and Joseph Warton, Fox, Banks, Dr. Burney, Sheridan, Malone, Dr. Percy, Chamier, Steevens, Lord Ossory, Lord Spencer, Lord Palmerston, Colman, Courtenay and Garrick. A single black-ball excluded a man. Garrick was nearly excluded by his own confidence of election: "*He'll be of us?*" said Johnson, angrily quoting the words of his friend, "how does he know we will *permit* him? the first Duke in England has no right to hold such language."

That Johnson should have proposed Boswell to the Club is obviously a point of considerable importance. There have always been plenty of clubs for fools, but you cannot admit the idea of a fool being invited to join such a club as this. Johnson regarded Boswell as a proper candidate; Reynolds, Beauclerk and Lord Charlemont were of the same opinion. On the other hand, several members of the Club wished to keep him out of it, and Burke said that he doubted if he was good enough. Judging from a conversation which took place on the Scotch tour in 1773 it seems likely that Johnson bullied the opposers and insisted on having his way: if Boswell did not get elected, the Doctor would see to it that no one else was elected as long as he was there to drop a black-ball into the box. Whether that was the case or not, the actual facts justify us in assuming that the reasons for excluding Boswell were quite as good as the reasons for admitting him.

His *Corsica* had given him a literary reputation, but not the solid reputation of a first-class writer, and his other performances were negligible. On his own showing, his conversation was never brilliant. Everyone who knew him was aware of his weakness and absurdity.

But there was something about him—something valuable —which had won the friendship and the esteem of Johnson; mere good-humour was not enough. One is led to the belief that Boswell's chief social recommendation lay in his responsiveness, his readiness to be assimilated, and his engaging quality of enthusiasm or complaisance. Johnson knew this, and Johnson did not hesitate in proposing him to the Club.

After Beauclerk's dinner, the gentlemen went off to the Club, and Boswell had to wait for the result of the ballot. He sat in a state of anxiety. He was a little cheered by Lady Di Beauclerk, but even her loveliness and her amusing chatter could not wholly divert him. Presently he was informed of his election. He ran to the place of meeting, and there he saw for the first time Mr. Edmund Burke and such a group of eminent men as could not have been found anywhere else.

Three days before Boswell's return to Scotland there was another dinner with much good society. The dinner was given by Charles and Edward Dilly, the booksellers, and the company included Johnson, Boswell, Langton, Goldsmith,

Dr. Mayo, the faithful Temple, and the Reverend Augustus Montagu Toplady.

Toplady (though Boswell ignores him) was a very singular young man. At that time he was thirty-three years old, and he died five years later. He was a Calvinistic clergyman of the Church of England, and one of the most violent enemies of John Wesley. As long as he was writing on the solar system, on birds or meteors, or the sagacity of brutes, he could be amusing and graceful; but when he attacked Wesley he put aside the first principles of decency and moderation. Depressed by the bleakness of a Somerset landscape he composed "Rock of Ages," one of the best known English hymns.

The conversation which took place at the Dilly's is the first to be recorded at great length in the *Life of Johnson*. They talked about the South Sea voyages, the nidification of birds, religious toleration, the Roman Catholics, and (very properly) the sale of books. Toplady concluded the religious argument by saying to Johnson, "Sir, you have untwisted this difficult subject with great dexterity."

And it was Toplady who inadvertently caused an outbreak of petulance on the part of Goldsmith. While Johnson was booming out his views on toleration, Goldsmith made vain efforts to speak: at last he flung his hat on the table, with a bitter though senseless exclamation of "Take it!" There was a pause, in which clouds were gathering in silence, and then it seemed to Goldsmith that Toplady was going to speak and that Johnson prevented him by showing signs of beginning again. At this he lost control of himself. "Sir," he cried to Johnson, "the gentleman has heard you patiently for an hour: pray allow us now to hear *him*." The Doctor looked at him sternly: "Sir, I was not interrupting the gentleman. I was only giving him a signal of my attention. Sir, you are impertinent."

The last dinner of this notable series was at General Paoli's on the 9th of May, the day before Boswell started on his northern journey. Johnson was unwell, and left the company early, asking Boswell to meet him later at Mr. Robert Chambers's in the Temple. The Doctor was "very ill" when Boswell came to Chambers's rooms, but he presently gave way to an astounding burst of hilarity.

Mr. Chambers (afterwards Sir Robert) was a lawyer, and he had on that very day been employed by Langton to make a draft of his will. There must have been something funny in the idea of Langton making a will, though we do not know what it was. Johnson began to laugh boisterously, making great sport of his friend and calling him *the testator*. "Ha, ha! I dare say he thinks he has done a mighty thing. He won't stay till he gets home to produce this wonderful deed: he'll call up the landlord of the first inn on the road, and, after a suitable preface upon mortality and the uncertainty of life—ha, ha!—will tell him that he should not delay making his will; and here, Sir, will he say, is *my* will, which I have just made with the assistance of one of the ablest lawyers in the kingdom; and he will read it to him—oh, ha, ha, ha!" So he went on, joking and bellowing, and hoping that Chambers had not certified the understanding of the testator, and vowing that he would turn the will into a ballad, until Mr. Chambers was very much annoyed and plainly showed that he was anxious to be rid of his visitors.

But this was not the end of it. Johnson rolled out of the Temple in spasms of huge jocularity, gusts of humorous invention, and finally reached a climax of stupefying merriment. "He burst into such a fit of laughter that he appeared to be almost in a convulsion; and, in order to support himself, laid hold of one of the posts at the side of the foot pavement, and sent forth peals so loud, that in the silence of the night his voice seemed to resound from Temple-bar to Fleet-ditch."

This gargantuan mirth was not by any means usual. Johnson's ordinary laughter is described elsewhere in the *Life* as "a kind of good humoured growl"—which is a very different thing. Such an exhibition of "the awful, melancholy and venerable Johnson" moderated the sadness of Boswell at the moment of parting. He must also have reflected with triumphant joy on the prospect of Johnson coming to Scotland in the autumn, rambling across the Highlands and going over the sea to Skye.

However much Boswell is to be pitied as a weak man, he

was at least happy in realising the most fantastic of his ambitions. There could have been nothing more fantastic than the idea of seeing Johnson with a blue bonnet and a broad-sword at a gathering of Highlanders; yet even this came to pass.

CHAPTER VIII

URSA MAJOR IN SCOTLAND

THE fine daring of Johnson's trip to the north in 1773 is not always properly understood.

The Doctor was in his sixty-fifth year. Although he was able to ride a horse and was not unduly fatigued by carriages, his life was one of sedentary ease or gentle perambulations: he was more often an idler than a rambler. He liked to be in motion, but he preferred stationary comfort. He was fond of meeting people, though he met them less gladly if they were Scotch. In London his felicity was almost complete. Any idea of travelling for health would have sent him in the opposite direction.

At the present day we may travel, if we can afford to do so, in a state of comfort unimaginable in the eighteenth century. But even now the route of the Johnsonian tour, if it was proposed for a holiday, would make some of us pause. At the actual time of this tour it was little short of adventurous. If you went to Scotland you might be expected to make a book, and a fairly exciting book, of what you had seen and heard. The Highland Scotch were a barbarous folk, certain to make you uncomfortable, and amongst whom you were sure to find a number of bitterly reproachful Jacobites. By extending your trip to the Hebrides, especially in the autumn, you delivered yourself to the perils of rude navigation along shores ragged with jutting rocks and washed by foaming races.

In the case of Johnson there was another matter to be considered. If he carried out the tour designed by Boswell, he might not be able to travel south before the cold weather had set in.

Travelling for long distances by coach was never pleasant; in winter it was frequently agonising. This refers merely to the unavoidable physical discomfort of riding in a coach, but you may include the risk of highway robbery, and the more ordinary risk of broken springs or loose wheels or the stranding of the vehicle in a muddy track. In the most favourable circumstances a fast "machine" could not do more than a hundred miles in sixteen hours, and it took two days to get from London to Shrewsbury. A speed of six miles an hour was a remarkably high average for a coach, and very few of them were able to keep it up. Actually, Johnson got from London to Edinburgh in eight days, which works out at an average of less than fifty miles a day; but then, he was taking his time. He was lucky enough to do the return journey, travelling in the "fly," in five days.

Johnson's desire to visit the Hebrides was not kindled, in the first place, by Boswell. In his youth he had read Martin's *Description*, and he had always wanted to see those wild islands. Boswell had merely provided the opportunity. He found in Boswell "a companion whose acuteness would help his enquiry, and whose gaiety of conversation and civility of manners were sufficient to counteract the inconveniences of travel."

Late in the evening of the 14th of August, Boswell received a note from Johnson saying that he had arrived at Boyd's Inn by the Canongate. Memorable and happy moment! At once Mrs. Boswell, gently apprehensive, was instructed to prepare a large pot of tea, and Boswell joyously ran off to the inn. The Boswells had moved from Chessel's Buildings, and were now in a flat in James's Court—their door was at the top of the house and was approached by a common staircase. David Hume, at one time, had occupied the same quarters.

Presently Mrs. Boswell—even more apprehensive, poor lady!—saw the immense figure of her guest in his wide overcoat, his black worsted stockings and his bushy wig. She disliked him at sight. She listened for a while to his great rumbling, growling voice; and she disliked him still more. "I have often seen a bear led by a man," she thought, "but never before have I seen a man led by a bear, as poor James is led by this crazy old philosophical Doctor of his; and indeed I don't understand what the man is talking about." And she had given up the best room—her own room—to this huge, uncouth and not very clean visitor.

Boswell never understood his wife's deep distrust of Johnson; but the Doctor felt it, and he tried by little courtesies to soften her heart. She was always polite, stiffly polite, and she once gave Johnson a pot of marmalade, but the aversion remained. Towards the end of his life she invited him to Auchinleck, touched at last, perhaps, by the knowledge of his melancholy state.

Johnson's opinion of Mrs. Boswell is to be found in a letter to Mrs. Thrale: "Mrs. Boswell has the mien and manners of a gentlewoman; and such a person and mind as would not be in any place either admired or contemned. She is in a proper degree inferior to her husband: she cannot rival him; nor can he ever be ashamed of her."

Dr. Johnson stayed with Boswell in Edinburgh from the 14th to the 18th of August. He viewed the city with only moderate interest: a man who knows London is not greatly excited by other towns. He did not like the smell of the open sewers, he made sly jokes at the expense of Scotchmen, but it pleased Boswell vastly to see him in the Advocate's Library, "rolling about in this old magazine of antiquities." Mrs. Boswell had to make special efforts for the entertainment of this great man and of the company invited to meet him. She got veal and grouse, she made puddings and sauces, she was assiduous in maintaining supplies of boiling water for perpetual tea, and she put out her best table-linen to be splashed or spotted by the uncouth visitor. And she could not, like Mrs. Thrale, consider herself amply repaid by listening to extremely fine conversation.

The conversation was indeed admirable. Johnson was braced by the notion of the tour, stimulated by the applause of a new and submissive audience, and he never talked more vigorously or delightfully. He met Robertson the historian, Sir William Forbes, Sir Adam Ferguson, Sir Alexander Dick, Lord Hailes, the learned Dr. Maclaurin, and scores of others. People who seldom visited Boswell's house came there willingly enough to meet Dr. Johnson. So many people came that Johnson was nearly overpowered by noise, warmth and cordiality. "At supper," he confided to Mrs. Thrale, "there was such a conflux of company that I could scarcely support the tumult. I have never been well in the whole journey, and am very easily disordered." He admired the rooms, which, he said, were "very handsome and spacious."

On the morning of Wednesday, the 18th of August, the tour began. Johnson, thinking that he was about to travel among savages, had brought with him two pistols and a supply of powder and bullets. He was persuaded to leave these behind, and he also left behind "a pretty full and curious Diary of his Life." These things were deposited in an open drawer, and Boswell regretted that his wife did not take the opportunity of having the whole Diary transcribed. This only shows what may happen to a gentleman if he takes to journalising. Such a disgraceful breach of confidence, he thought, would have been excusable on the ground that it was all *pro bono publico*. Mrs. Boswell, who had not the slightest curiosity in the matter, did not even look at the Diary. "She did not seem quite easy when we left her: but away we went!"

There was doubtless a reason for the uneasiness of Mrs. Boswell. If she had seen her husband going off with another woman, she would have been more acutely miserable; but she dreaded the infatuation of James for this lumbering old pedant, and she foresaw the probable results of this infatuation. Johnson, the austere model of rectitude and virtue, was literally seducing Boswell, and making him dissatisfied with wife and home and country.

No intelligent man is more to be envied than one who reads for the first time Boswell's *Tour to the Hebrides*. As a book of travel and topography it has little value; as a study of character and situation it is perhaps the finest entertainment in English literature. There may be some excuse for stressing that particular quality in Boswell's writing which is more frequently employed in the *Tour* than it is in the *Life*: the quality that enables him to represent in simple and happy words the amusing or dramatic or suggestive relation between a character and its environment. He found æsthetic delight in treating Johnson as a spectacle; a figure to be looked at as part of a composition, whether in a social group or in a landscape. No matter if the effect is ludicrous or majestic:

the great thing is that it shall be duly observed. You are not surprised by the idea of Johnson rambling in Fleet Street, his appropriated scene, but here you have Johnson riding over the mountain, or stalking like a giant among the nettles and thistles of Inchkeith, Johnson floating in a gloomy cave, Johnson with a burgess-ticket in his hat, or a chieftain's buckler on his arm, or a Highland lady on his knee, Johnson arguing about nightcaps and bed-curtains, or being a fine gentleman to the Duchess of Argyll. Here is the wonderful presentation of a living man in scenes of living colour; not the result of casual scribbling, but of instinctively sound arrangement of words or details. Nor does it lessen the unique skill of Boswell if we remind ourselves that our picture of Johnson could never be so vivid without the portraits of Reynolds. Between them, Reynolds and Boswell have preserved in a manner without example the figure, the sound and movement of a man who is more real to many of us than men we have actually seen with our own eyes.

The travellers were accompanied by Joseph Ritter, Boswell's Bohemian servant, "a fine stately fellow above six feet high." Boswell had a map of Scotland given to him in Italy by Lord Mountstuart (a happy circumstance!), a Bible, and a copy of *Ogden on Prayer*. Ogden was carried in his pocket, and was often produced for reading aloud.

Johnson had the singular perversity of believing that no such thing as a tree could be found in Scotland. It is improbable that he could have seen a tree unless he was nearly touching it with his nose, but whenever he did see one, or was told of one, there was a lively debate. "A tree," he wrote, "might be a show in Scotland, as a horse in Venice. At St. Andrews Mr. Boswell found only one, and recommended it to my notice; I told him that it was rough and low. . . . This, said he, is nothing to another a few miles off." Colonel Nairne, at St. Andrews, showed him a plane tree in his garden and most unluckily said there was only one other large tree in the county. This, of course, provoked a peal of Johnson's enormous laughter. "But let it be considered," says Boswell gravely, "that, when Dr. Johnson talks of trees, he means trees of good size. . . . There are certainly not a great many; but I could have shown him more than two at Balmuto, from whence my ancestors came, and which now belongs to a branch of my family." So the jokes went on; and Johnson, when he lost his oaken staff, expatiated jocosely on the value of "such a piece of timber" to a poor Scotchman.

There was often in Johnson's attitude to the people he met a kind of stiffness which tended to become patronising. He showed this to the doctors at St. Andrews, and he showed it to that eccentric little Scotch nobleman, Lord Monboddo, and again to the university men of Aberdeen. His manners appear to have varied a good deal. Dr. Watson of St. Andrews was astonished by his "total inattention to established manners," while in Monboddo's house he politely rose when the ladies left the table after dinner. At times he was depressed, and grumbled about wasting his life in a country without saddles and bridles; at other times he was prodigiously merry; and most of the time he was obviously enjoying himself. His behaviour to his companion varied from the most gratifying tokens of regard, the most solemn exhortations, to "such keen sarcastick wit and such a variety of degrading images" that Boswell could not bear to think of them.

One of the oddest features of this excursion was the way in which Boswell wrote his account of it from day to day and gave it to Johnson to read, up to the 26th of October. It is true that Johnson had no idea of Boswell's intention to publish this account, or any form of it, and Boswell did not print his *Journal* until after Johnson's death. Nor can it be supposed that all the passages relating to Johnson were read by him.

It is often believed that Johnson's own account of the *Journey to the Western Islands* is greatly inferior to Boswell's *Tour*. To make such a comparison is ridiculous in any case. There is a vulgar traditional idea, propagated by the illiterate, that we should think nothing of Johnson to-day if it had not been for Boswell. There is always an obscure gratification in supposing that a great man may owe his fame to a lesser man.

Nothing could be more false. In the matter of writing

prose, as in the matter of thinking and reasoning, the superiority of Johnson is incontestable. Nor is it correct to say that Johnson's conversation was of more value than his literary work. Boswell regarded Johnson as an entertainment; but to imagine that Boswell could think or write better than Johnson is the purest absurdity, and invites a comparison that would never be suggested by any person with a real knowledge of literature. Boswell described himself well as "one who has the power of exhibiting an exact transcript of conversations." Therein lies the province of his peculiar genius, and it would be foolish to look beyond.

Johnson's unpretentious book is actually on a level of scholarship and of literature beyond the reach of Boswell. It is a philosopher's book of travel, in which the traveller is looking less for particular views than for general ideas. But in several matters it throws light on Boswell himself and on the circumstances of the tour.

From Johnson we learn that Boswell's inquisitiveness was "seconded by great activity," and we see him scrambling up the ruined abbey of Arbroath. We learn also that Boswell's name was a name of power, capable of bearing down objections and of opening doors that would otherwise have been shut. We discover how much was due to Boswell's enthusiasm or diligence. Mr. Boswell, said Johnson, "bent a keener eye on vacancy." And there are little pictures of Mr. Boswell catching a cuddy-fish with a borrowed rod or growing sentimental among the ruins of Iona.

It is Johnson, naturally, who talks with less restraint about the occasional roughness or discomfort of the journey. A house with slates and glass was "an image of magnificence." He wrote a most characteristic paragraph on the subject of Scotch windows:

"The art of joining squares of glass with lead is little used in Scotland, and in some places is totally forgotten. . . . Their windows do not move upon hinges, but are pushed up and down in grooves, yet they are seldom accomodated with weights and pulleys. He that would have his window open must hold it with his hand, unless, what may be sometimes found among good contrivers, there be a nail which he may stick into a hole, to keep it from falling."

But if there were hardships to be endured, there were occasional centres of elegance and learning to be enjoyed, there were books and pictures, fine ladies and courteous gentlemen, or the solid comfort of regimental quarters, isolated among the rocks and hills of a wild country.

The travellers crossed the north-east corner of Aberdeenshire, skirted the Moray Firth, and passed by way of Fort Augustus to the Atlantic shore. On the evening of the 1st of September they reached the inn at Glenelg, opposite the coast of Skye, and in full view of Ben na Cullick and Ben Aslak—rugged hills with barbarous names.

They were now approaching the Hebrides, the Western Islands, they were entering upon the picturesque and adventurous phase of their excursion. But the prelude was not happy. The inn could provide them with nothing fit to eat or drink, and had it not been for the kindness of Mr. Murchison, who sent them a bottle of rum and some sugar, they would have fared very badly. Johnson, according to Boswell, showed the calm philosophy of the Rambler; though in his own account he describes himself as "weary and peevish." The beds were not good enough to lie upon. They ordered hay: "I directed them," wrote Johnson, "to bring a bundle into the room, and slept upon it in my riding coat. Mr. Boswell being more delicate, laid himself sheets with hay over and under him, and lay in linen like a gentleman." On the following morning they crossed over to Skye.

Before long Johnson saw the hearty savages of his fancy. At Corrichatachin, under the Red Hills, he saw and heard Boswell joining the company in a Gaelic chorus; he saw them, invigorated by drams, jumping and stamping to the fierce rhythm of a Highland reel; he listened, without dismay, to the buzzing and squealing of the pipes and the howling of the dancers; and he then retired, to compose, no doubt by way of a balancing exercise, a Latin ode to Mrs. Thrale.

Other wild scenes were to follow. An open boat manned by a crew of half-naked islanders, took them to Raasay.

"Dr. Johnson sat high in the stern, like a magnificent Triton." The oarsmen shouted a chorus which it pleased the Doctor to call a "proceleusmatick song." Naval music, he observed thoughtfully, is very ancient. Boswell cried out, "We are contending with seas!" and the Doctor replied, "Not much," although a good scudding breeze was driving the spray in his face. "This now," he said, not quite truthfully, "is the Atlantick."

Johnson wrote, for Mrs. Thrale, a lively account of their entertainment by the Macleods of Raasay (he calls it Raarsa):

"At night, unexpectedly to us who were strangers, the carpet was taken up, the fiddler of the family came in, and a very vigorous and general dance was begun. We were two-and-thirty at supper; there were full as many dancers; for though all who supped did not dance, some danced of the young people who did not sup. Raarsa himself danced with his children, and old Malcolm, in his filibeg, was as nimble as when he led the Prince over the mountains. When they had danced themselves weary, two tables were spread, and I suppose at least twenty dishes were upon them. . . . The table was not coarsely heaped, but was at once plentiful and elegant. They do not pretend to make a loaf; there are only cakes, commonly of oats or barley, but they made me very nice cakes of wheat flour. I always sat at the left hand of Lady Raarsa, and young Macleod of Skie, the chieftain of the clan, sat on the right."

At Kingsburgh the Doctor met a little woman of genteel appearance who was known in her youth as Miss Flora Macdonald. At Dunvegan he was so much delighted by the hospitality of the Macleods that he cried joyously, "Boswell, we came in at the wrong end of this island." He shocked Lady Macleod by saying that no woman was naturally good.

On their return from the north of the island they spent three days with the homely and boisterous people (M'Kinnons and others) at Corrichatachin.

110

To these good people, "social honour" involved the drinking of many bowls of punch. On the first evening Johnson retired early. This was unfortunate for Boswell. Young Coll or Maclean had joined the travellers with the amiable intention of conducting them to the islands of Coll and Mull. It was an occasion for "social honour." Coll was paying his first visit to Corrichatachin. They had an enormous bowl of punch, and then a third and a fourth bowl of punch. After the third bowl they were "cordial and merry to a high degree." Their faces glowed cheerfully in the hot vapours of the steaming brew, though no one had a very clear notion of what was going on or what was being said. No doubt it was all very honourable, very pleasing and familiar. Boswell could recollect very little after the third round, except that he called the host "worthy Corri" or something of the sort. After the fourth bowl he was in a state of befuddled confusion, though still able to lift his glass like a man, and it was nearly five o'clock in the morning before he got to bed.

He woke next day at noon with a terrible headache. At one o'clock Johnson came into his room, luckily in a good humour. M'Kinnon came in, with some other friends, and forced him to swallow a dram of brandy. After that he got up, went to Johnson's room, and opened Mrs. M'Kinnon's Prayer Book. He opened the book at the twentieth Sunday after Trinity. He looked at the Epistle: "And be not drunk with wine, wherein is excess."

When the gentlemen sat down to another punch party, two evenings later, Boswell had sufficient resolution to retire. The merry fellows drank punch and sang Gaelic songs until morning. At five o'clock they all trooped up to Boswell's room, where some of them had beds. Here they found a bottle of cold punch in a corner; and having drunk this, "honest Corrichatachin" went for another. Such were the cheerful, social and manly habits of these gallant islanders.

The travellers were held back in Skye by foul weather, and it was not until the 3rd of October that they were able to set sail for Mull.

They were now to get a real taste of the Atlantic. The

wind appears to have blown from the north-east when they left Skye, but soon after they had sighted the point of Ardnamurchan it veered to the south-east and began to blow more stiffly. The crew consisted of the skipper Macdonald, two sailors, Mr. Simpson the owner of the boat, young Coll and his manservant. With Johnson, Boswell and Joseph Ritter, that made a total of nine persons.

In view of the difficulty of reaching Mull, with a gale blowing dead ahead, young Coll began to talk of running back to Eigg or Canna, or making for his own island. The skipper insisted on rounding Ardnamurchan and beating up against the wind in the hope of getting as far as Tobermory in Mull. Finding that he could make no headway, he then decided to lie off the northern shore of Mull until the morning. It was now night, very dark and blowing hard. Various plans were considered in turn. Simpson was willing to run for Coll if young Coll and his man could pilot them to a harbour, and this course was eventually chosen.

Macdonald, therefore, put up the helm and let his boat drive before the gale. But Coll is a low island not visible from a distance, and the task of making a harbour on a dark night with a high sea running was not an easy one. Boswell admits that he was terribly frightened. The boat was being driven hard under a sprit-sail of some kind, and as they were anxious to reach the island quickly they kept her under as much cloth as she would bear: she lay over at a most alarming slope while the sea roared and raced along her lee gunwale. In the stern of the boat stood a man with a blazing peat, to guide a wherry behind them, and as the sparks were blown inboard by the following wind Boswell thought of the dreadful results of a fire or explosion—for Coll was taking with him a parcel of gunpowder. As he listened to the shrill Gaelic voices of the crew, shouting to each other in the storm, his fears rose to a higher and higher pitch. He begged Coll earnestly to give him something to do. Coll put into his hand a rope, and told him to hold it until he got the order to haul away. The rope was merely fastened to the top of the mast, and served no purpose of navigation. But this device kept Boswell quiet: "Thus did I stand firm to my post, while the wind and rain beat upon me, always expecting a call to pull my rope."

At last they got safely into the harbour of Lochiern, piloted by Coll and the islander in the bow, and were presently riding at anchor. Johnson had all the time been lying "in philosophick tranquillity," with a greyhound at his back to keep him warm. Boswell says that he knew nothing of the danger. But Johnson, in any circumstances, was ten times more of a man than Boswell.

A normal person would not have recorded his fears and foolishness as Boswell recorded them, for the scorn or delight of the public. In describing his drunkenness at Corrichatachin, Boswell is careful to explain that he does so in order to introduce a new aspect of Johnson, although the aspect is contained only in a few trivial bantering remarks. But his behaviour in the storm serves no such purpose of introduction; it is a gratuitous display of mere cowardice. The episode of the rope was used by a contemporary carica-turist, and was chosen by Macaulay in his own devastating caricature of Boswell. These pointless exhibitions of folly and weakness—there are many of them in the published work of Boswell—are to be explained, if they must be explained, as the symptoms of inverted egoism and the indications of a state of mind not compatible with ordinary standards of sanity.

Johnson himself described the storm in one sentence: "After having been detained by storms many days at Skie, we left it, as we thought, with a fair wind; but a violent gust, which Bos had a great mind to call a tempest, forced us into Coll, an obscure island."

Sir Walter Scott, in a note written many years later, took a serious view of the position. He said: "Their risque, in a sea full of islands, was very considerable. Indeed, the whole expedition was highly perilous, considering the season of the year, the precarious chance of getting sea-worthy boats, and the ignorance of the Hebrideans."

Storms again detained them in Coll. They were there for ten days, and it was fortunate that Johnson found some books to entertain him. They got across to Tobermory on the 14th of October. Geographical knowledge, even of small areas, was then imperfect, and perhaps Lord Mountstuart's map was a very bad one; for nothing could be more inaccurate than Johnson's description of Mull as an island "not broken by waters, nor shot into promontories, but a solid and compact mass, of breadth nearly equal to its length."

In Mull they were handsomely entertained by the Macleans, and Johnson found that Miss Maclean was not only able to talk French, to sew and draw, to play on the spinet, to make boxes of shell-work and to milk the cows, but she was "the only interpreter of Erse poetry that he could ever find." They crossed the island, visited Ulva and Inchkenneth, and presently reached the holy island of Ilcolmkill or Iona, where they found lodging in a barn. On the 22nd of October, after riding and sailing along the southern coast of Mull, they returned to the mainland, and put up for the night in Oban.

At Inveraray, on the road to Glasgow, there was another episode that no one except Boswell could have recorded with complacency. The Duke and Duchess of Argyll were in residence at the castle. Boswell knew that the Duchess detested him, and he accounts for this by supposing her offended by his activities in the Douglas case. But the Duke, on the other hand, always treated him well.

The idea of passing a ducal residence without entering it and dragging Johnson with him could not be entertained by Boswell, a man who felt such holy raptures in the presence of high rank. For the sake of this rapture he was prepared even to defy the Duchess. He walked to the castle after dinner and was courteously received by Argyll, who said, "I hope you and Dr. Johnson will dine with us to-morrow."

Having attained his object, Boswell got up to go. But the Duke detained him by saying, "Mr. Boswell, won't you have some tea?" and they went to the drawing-room. The Duchess, who was sitting with her daughter, Lady Betty Hamilton, and several other ladies, took not the least notice of Boswell; his impertinence was hardly more deplorable than her rudeness. But that was nothing to the scene at dinner on the following day:

"I was in fine spirits; and though sensible that I had the misfortune of not being in favour with the Duchess, I was not in the least disconcerted, and offered her Grace some of the dish that was before me. . . . I knew it was the rule of modern high life not to drink to any body; but, that I might have the satisfaction for once to look the Duchess in the face, with a glass in my hand, I with a respectful air addressed her—'My Lady Duchess, I have the honour to drink your Grace's good health.' I repeated the words audibly, and with a steady countenance. This was, perhaps, rather too much; but some allowance must be made for human feelings."

After this, we are not surprised to find the Duchess remarking stiffly to Johnson, "I know *nothing* about Mr. Boswell." What is surprising is that Boswell could have related a humiliating circumstance which has nothing to do with the narrative of the tour and nothing to do with Johnson. It only ceases to be surprising if we adopt the same theory of reversed egoism that we used in order to explain the account of the storm. Nor must we shirk the conclusion that our best defence, in both cases, is very like the plea of insanity.

Irrelevance, however, is not to be alleged in the case of the family scenes at Auchinleck, in which Johnson was a principal actor.

Lord Auchinleck, we are told, invited Johnson out of pure kindliness. Exhilarated by the idea of placing Johnson among the groves of his ancestral domain, of seeing him by the castle ruins or in the handsome library of the new house, Boswell still feared a collision with his father. He carefully impressed on the visitor the necessity for avoiding like the pestilence all mention of Whigs or Presbyterians, of Tories or Jacobites, and especially of Sir John Pringle.

Dr. Johnson and Boswell arrived at Auchinleck in time for dinner on the 2nd of November, and stayed there for seven days. Of Lady Auchinleck we hear nothing at all. Old Alexander (he was then in his sixty-seventh year) could get on very well with his guest as long as they were discussing the beauties of Anacreon or the different editions of Tacitus. He had probably never read a line of Johnson's, and he called him "a dominie," "a Jacobite fellow," and "Ursa Major." In 1775, with more bitter recollections in his mind, he was still harping on James having wasted his time by "going over Scotland with a *brute*." But he preserved a grim tradition of ancient hospitality, he knew the merits of lordly condescension and of sternly correct behaviour.

Things might have gone on smoothly, even with a definite knowledge of compromise, if they had not taken it into their heads to look at a collection of medals. Among these medals there happened to be one of Oliver Cromwell, and that led to a rapid exchange of warm words. Neither Johnson nor Auchinleck, both of them magisterial men, and both of them judges in their own departments, could defend principles and control temper at the same time. Boswell had the mortification of seeing those two revered faces grow dark with anger, and of hearing warm words followed by the extreme violence of a noisy dispute. Whatever could be said for and against bishops, kings, presbyters, churchmen, Tories and Whigs, they said with rude vigour. Traditions of hospitality were rapidly melted by the hot blast of argument. The hard, yelping dialect of the old judge held its own for some time against the rising thunders of Johnson. Then the Doctor fiercely attacked the Presbyterian ministry, declaring that it had not produced a single writer of any merit; and Lord Auchinleck, luckily remembering a title in a catalogue, cried out, "Pray, Sir, have you read Mr. Durham's excellent commentary on the Galatians?" "No, Sir!" roared Johnson, perceptibly checked: but he called up the brutal resources of his rhetoric, and presently smashed his opponent by a retort "which," says Boswell, "I forbear to mention."

Happily for Boswell he was able to contrast this scene of horrid violence with a placid view of the Doctor in the romantic groves. The "illustrious Mentor," standing near the castle ruins, listened to Boswell expatiating on the antiquity and the grand alliances of his family, but he was a little startled when James pointed to a shadowy recess and told him it was the place where he intended to set up a classic memorial to Dr. Samuel Johnson. To Johnson, who could not bear to think of dying, nothing could have been more grievously inappropriate. He turned away brusquely: "Sir, I hope to see your grandchildren."

They reached Edinburgh on the 9th of November, after a tour which had lasted for nearly three months. Johnson stayed in Edinburgh, as the guest of Boswell, for nine days, but of this period Boswell gives no considerable account.

Mrs. Boswell disliked the Doctor more than ever when she found that she had to keep kettles boiling all day to supply him and his visitors with cups of tea. She must have been immensely pleased when he dined out with Lady Colvill, Sir Alexander Dick, Lord Hailes, or Professor Robertson. Boswell himself had returned to his work, or attendance, at the Court of Session, and his wife was therefore obliged to preside over Johnson's levees. One day the Doctor visited the Court of Session. He was not impressed by the mode of pleading: "This," he said, "is not the Areopagus."

Johnson took a place in the coach which was to set out for London on Monday the 22nd of November. He was invited by Sir John Dalrymple to come to Cranston on Saturday, and thus to pick up the coach at a later hour and a more convenient place. Boswell pretends that Dalrymple had spoken against Johnson, and had said that he wondered how any Scotch gentleman could allow himself to be seen in his company. He thinks this (whether true or not) a sufficient reason for treating Dalrymple with appalling rudeness. The invitation was accepted, but Boswell, who accompanied the Doctor, insisted on turning aside to see Roslin Castle and Hawthornden, and thus made it impossible to arrive at Cranston in time for dinner, although he knew that Dalrymple was expecting them. They saw Roslin Castle, dined at the inn, and then coolly proceeded to view the caves at Hawthornden. If Boswell is to be trusted, Johnson became facetious at the expense of his insulted host, and wantonly aggravated the insult by giving in Sir John's own historical style a ludicrous account of his imagined suicide through mortification. It is difficult to believe that Johnson could

I

have tolerated gross behaviour towards a man whose hospitality he had accepted, and still more difficult to believe that he made this behaviour the subject of a heavy joke in execrable taste. However that may be, there is no doubt of Boswell's deplorable taste in publishing this episode at the end of his *Tour*, to be read by Dalrymple himself, and to suggest to many readers that Johnson was actually the "brute" described by Lord Auchinleck.

The *Tour* marks the mid-way period of Boswell's acquaintance with Johnson. It kept them more or less continuously together, in many varieties of place and company, for nearly a hundred consecutive days. In the space of ten and a half years between May 1763 and November 1773, Boswell had been within reach of Johnson for about 460 days; in the remaining space (1774–1784) during which it was possible for them to meet each other, including a long stretch of eleven weeks in 1781, there were about 400 days on which they either were or might have been together. The time occupied by the *Tour* is therefore not only by far the longest period during which Boswell and Johnson were continuously in each other's company, but also a very considerable fraction of the time they actually spent together in the whole period (nearly twenty-one years) of their friendship.

CHAPTER IX

THE HYPOCHONDRIACK

ANY advance in social philosophy, accompanied by a wider diffusion of common sense and a more scientific denial of compromise, tends to make the drunkard less amusing. A defence of drunkenness, quite possible and acceptable in the time of Queen Elizabeth, could now only be imagined by some irresponsibly sentimental person trying to palliate his own weakness by a spurious anacreontic exuberance. On the other hand, to crush the poor tippler with pious invective or to shrink from his bloated monstrosity with anger or scorn would be equally unphilosophic and unscientific. We have to regard him as a particularly awkward case, a somewhat elaborate and lamentable piece of wreckage; we are not to meet him with foolish laughter or with indignation.

From 1774 the private history of Boswell becomes a drunkard's progress, with a tragically ample representation of all its deplorable stages. His descent had begun during his early youth in Edinburgh; an impulse towards reform at the time of his meeting with Johnson, and again in 1769–1771 in connection with his marriage, had kept him precariously balanced for a while upon a narrow ledge of respectability; in 1772 his foothold was clearly insecure; in 1773 there were ominous lapses, and in 1774 he was again proceeding with some rapidity and with a more pronounced loss of control, down the slope. Dissatisfaction with his dull work as a Scotch advocate, resentfully compared with Johnsonian rambles or the splendours of London society, led him the more readily to seek the common comforts of a weak man. He says that he had "a great aversion to the law," and had only taken it up in order to please his father. After the end of the tour he did not see Johnson again for a year and four months, and it is observable that, in 1774, he fell before long into a state of melancholy and of nervous collapse. The "black dog" drove him to the bottle, and the bottle drove him to the shabby creatures who prowled in the Edinburgh streets.

Unpleasant moral and physical sensations on the morning after a debauch, and a real grief at causing alarm to his wife, brought on fits of dismal repentance or periods of agitated sobriety. But soon the black dog was yelping, and then came the bottle again, and all the rest of it. The lowest point of Boswell's degradation was reached when he allowed himself to be drunk in the presence of Johnson and roared foolishly and rudely at the old man who still represented, for him, all that was most venerable and tremendous in the human character. That occurred more than once; it occurred for the first time in 1775.

Boswell's journal for 1774 shows him to have been often outrageously drunk. It might be after eating nine kinds of fish with Bob Chalmers at Musselburgh, or it might be after an expensive carouse at Fortune's Tavern, but the pain, remorse and futile vows of reform were always the same.

Poor Mrs. Boswell had to learn, from a succession of ghastly experiences, the misery and horror of being a drunkard's wife. While Boswell drank in the town, she sent him pathetic messages by his clerk; she watched him all night as he lay groaning on his bed, pale, sick and lamentably frightened. Once he threw a candlestick at her: on another occasion he flung an egg into the fire, and some beer after it. She had to apprehend things even worse than drunken violence, for she knew what happened after so many of the drinking bouts; indeed, Boswell frequently informed her, and with tears running down his piteous, owlish face implored forgiveness. At other times he would upbraid her for not studying his moods, or not appreciating his manly qualities.

Distortion of judgment, fixed ideas and obsessions are greatly encouraged by alcohol. In August 1774, Boswell became obsessed by the case of John Reid, a sheep-stealer.

John Reid was a very unfortunate man. He had stolen some sheep, unquestionably, in 1766: Boswell, only just admitted to the Bar, had been one of the defending counsel, and the jury brought in that excellent Scotch verdict of "not proven." Mr. Reid, if he had any sense, must have known that he would be closely watched after this episode; and now he was in trouble again. He was charged with stealing some more sheep. Boswell defended him. It seems probable that John Reid was innocent, but the court made up its mind that he ought to swing, if not for his present alleged offence, at any rate for his undoubted offence in 1766. He was found guilty and received the ordinary sentence of death.

From Colonel Isham's magnificent publication of the private papers we see how frantically Boswell worked to get a reprieve. He took to visiting John Reid in prison nearly every day. He cheered Mr. Reid with whisky (though he was a little embarrassed in drinking his health) and by telling him all about the differences in the Scotch and English methods of hanging people. Then he got the idea that he would have Mr. Reid cut down from the gallows, and brought back to life by a little party of medical advisers. The only difficulty was to get a room, because no one seemed anxious to lend one for this humane experiment, or indeed to receive the corpse on any terms. But the life-savers were not to be defeated, and at last they persuaded two half-witted persons to let them use a stable. While this was going on, Boswell thought of nothing, spoke and wrote of nothing, but John Reid. He ran to the bottle for courage or hope or mere oblivion, and then he ran to John Reid in the cell.

On the day of the execution John Reid's wife dressed him in a white grave-suit, with a high nightcap and black ribbons. The poor man shivered a little, and Mrs. Reid took off her green cloak and put it round him. Boswell stood there, trying as best he might to comfort these unhappy people; and presently the gaoler came in and asked them to follow him. They walked out of the cell, and as they went down the stairway the prisoners crowded to the rails above and peered down at them. In the hall there was a pause and a colloquy, and there was an awkward meeting. A man came up to John Reid and bowed respectfully. It was the hangman. Mr. Reid, looking grotesque and terrible in his white clothes, mournfully stared at the hangman; the hangman stared at John with decent embarrassment, but neither of them said a word—and indeed, what could they say? Of all imaginable meetings, none could be more dreadful. Boswell told poor John that he must not feel any resentment against a man who was only doing his duty, and John replied bravely that he felt no resentment and desired to forgive all mankind. At Boswell's request a glass of wine was given to Reid, and he drank to the health of the company. The prison door was then opened and the procession stepped out into the bright sunlight of the morning; in the midst of them, and walking with them, the tall, white, tragically absurd figure of the victim. Mrs. Reid was persuaded to stay behind: the others walked past the silent crowd, which presently followed them, and up the hill to the gallows. Any idea of rescue or resuscitation had to be abandoned. The body was left hanging for three quarters of an hour; the medical advisers gave it up as a hopeless case.

An imprudent newspaper comment on the Reid affair nearly involved Boswell in a duel with a boy of nineteen, Mr. Miller, the son of the Justice's Clerk. Boswell had to write an apology, the relatives arranged a friendly meeting with the young man, and the matter was brought to an honourable conclusion.

The case of John Reid certainly had a damaging effect on the mind of Boswell. It led him to wild extravagance, to crazy indiscretion, to something near madness. In the recoil of disappointment and of indignation he drank frantically. Again he tried to give interest or distinction to his miserable street amours by talking of "Asiatick" notions or the "manners" of the Old Testament.

In March 1775 he came south, reaching London on the 21st of the month. His fondness for wine was now beginning to overpower him. He disgraced himself by appearing at the Club when drunk, and asking Johnson why, if he could neither see nor hear, he had gone to Mrs. Abington's benefit. Had it not been for "worthy Langton," who kept the bottle out of his way, things might have gone from bad to worse: as it was, he got into the street and wandered among the women of the town. Next morning he sat in Old Slaughter's

Coffee-house, a melancholy fellow, sipping a little brandy and water. But a walk restored him to gaiety. It was on this day—the 1st of April—that he won a bet from Lady Di Beauclerk by asking Johnson the famous question about the orange-peel.

There is little to Boswell's credit at this time, and little to prove either sense or virtue, except his disapproval of Johnson's *Taxation no Tyranny*—one of the most unworthy and ridiculous of die-hard manifestos. On the question of American liberty Boswell decided to oppose Johnson. But any moral advantage that he might justly have claimed in this matter was neutralised by his views upon negro slavery, and here Johnson scored again. Negro slavery, according to Boswell, was part of the grand scheme of subordination designed by heaven for the benefit of superior whites: according to Johnson, and to John Wesley, it was a horror that no civilised man could think of without reproach.

John Wilkes, classical Wilkes, that jolly yet dangerous friend, was now Lord Mayor of London, and Boswell had a place at the Guildhall dinner on Easter Monday, the 17th of April. On the following day he set out to visit the Earl of Pembroke at Wilton, and his old friend Temple at Mamhead. At Mamhead he vowed "under a solemn yew" that he would abstain from the use of strong liquors.

He returned to London on the 1st of May, and attended commons at the Inner Temple. Discouraged by a sense of failure in Scotland, and feeling, no doubt, that he had lost ground by his own folly, he determined to qualify for practice at the English Bar. It is a recurring delusion of weak people that they are sure to do better in a new place. At the same time, he wrote to Temple complaining of a "dissipated state of mind." He was unable to fix his thoughts or to settle down to work. His record of Johnson's conversation breaks down miserably; he was listless and could remember nothing. Even the roaring virtue of Johnson had failed to raise him; even the noble mien of Paoli had left him unresponsive. He found a little consolation in flirting sentimentally with Mrs. Stuart, the daughter-in-law of the Earl of Bute, or in riding in General Paoli's coach.

This is obviously a period of mental decay, aggravated by the habit of excessive drinking, and by the deplorable *sequelæ* of drinking. Professor Pottle has very rightly observed that already, in his thirty-sixth year, Boswell showed slight but ominous indications of premature age. Had he continued to go down hill at the same rate, there would have been no *Life of Johnson*; in a few years there would have been no Boswell. Fortunately the velocity of descent was checked, although the movement of descent was continuous, and Boswell could prove that he had by no means lost his glorious faculty of "exhibiting an exact transcript of conversations." The most superb passages in the *Life* are undoubtedly those which belong to a later period (1778–1781), with a notable climax of brilliance in 1778.

When he returned to Edinburgh in 1775 he was badly "hypped," he was restless and gloomy. He could not bear "the unpleasing tone, the rude familiarity and the barren conversation" of the Edinburgh people. He despised his clients. He dreaded "the dull labours of the Court of Session." In the dark hours of the night he woke up "dreading annihilation or being thrown into some horrible state of being." He feared, so we believe, that he might become insane. The promise made under the solemn yew at Mamhead was no longer binding. His father was dissatisfied with him and treated his wife with a shameful lack of courtesy. It was only possible to endure his stepmother after the dulling of his faculties with immense quantities of strong beer.

The birth of another son on the 9th of October helped to lift him from a dangerous mood of dejection. His feudal sentiments were gratified, and he found a new outlet for gushing sensibility. Nor can it be denied that Boswell had at least the intentions of a good father. Had it not been for his mental instability and his fatal weakness he might have been a very good father indeed. The son was named Alexander after Lord Auchinleck.

But there were bad lapses in the winter. He ran after the drabs of Edinburgh, and then recorded his ignominy in a private journal, feebly substituting Greek for English characters when he came to incriminating words. He gave the journal to Mrs. Boswell to read, and was very much pained when she deciphered, or guessed, the meaning of the awkward passages. Parts of this loathsome record were heavily scored out in recent ink before the papers came into the hands of their present owner, Colonel Isham.

At the beginning of 1776 Boswell had a squabble with his father on the entail of the Auchinleck estate. He wrote to Johnson, who sent him a cloudy answer, and consulted Lord Hailes, who told him that his father was in the right. He came to London in no happy mood, on the 15th of March 1776.

But Johnson, magnificently diffusing common sense, benevolence and wit, saved him again. No sooner did he see that massive countenance, beaming over Mrs. Thrale's breakfast-table in Southwark, than he felt himself "elevated as if brought into another state of being." He was actually brought into another state of being; there was every prospect, if not of moral restoration, at least of some days of untroubled happiness. And his joy was increased when Johnson, after referring to his projected Italian tour with the Thrales, said, "But before leaving England I am to make a jaunt to Oxford, Birmingham, my native city Lichfield, and my old friend Dr. Taylor's at Ashbourne, and you, Boswell, shall go with me."

This little English tour lasted from the 19th to the 29th of March. At Oxford Boswell heard Johnson soliloquise in the common room of Pembroke: "Ay! Here I used to play at draughts with Phil Jones and Fludyer. Jones loved beer, and did not get very forward in the church. Fludyer turned out a scoundrel, a Whig, and said he was ashamed of having been at Oxford . . . but he had been a scoundrel all along to be sure."

On the 21st they visited Blenheim and rode through the park. Boswell, cheered by the bright morning, the fine view and the noble society of his friend, produced a unique specimen of original wit:

"When I looked at the magnificent bridge built by John Duke of Marlborough, over a small rivulet, and

125

recollected the epigram made upon it—'The lofty arch his high ambition shows, The stream, an emblem of his bounty flows:'—and saw that now, by the genius of Brown, a magnificent body of water was collected, I said, 'They have *drowned* the epigram.'"

As they drove rapidly in a post-chaise to Stratford, probably touching the remarkable speed of twelve miles an hour, Johnson said, "Life has not many things better than this." At Birmingham they met Johnson's old friend, Mr. Hector. Mr. Hector kindly took Boswell to see Mr. Bolton's great ironworks, where at least seven hundred people were employed, and Boswell had a new thrill at meeting a captain of industry, or, as he called him, "an iron chieftain." Boswell liked Mr. Hector and would have enjoyed more of his conversation, but Johnson decided to press on through the darkness to Lichfield. "Forty years ago, Sir, I was in love with an actress here, Mrs. Emmet, who acted Flora in *Hob in the Well*." On the morning of the 25th, still at Lichfield, Johnson received the news of the death of Thrale's only son. In the evening they saw *Theodosius* and the *Stratford Jubilee*: Johnson had recovered from the shock of the bad news and was "quite gay and merry." But the visit to Dr. Taylor at Ashbourne was curtailed, in order that he might quickly return to London, and offer to Mr. and Mrs. Thrale the solid comforts of piety and reason.

During this tour Boswell had been steadied by the moral weight of his companion and by his own desire to behave with such gravity as became a philosopher's friend; but he had no sooner got back to town than he broke away again in the most shocking manner. He indulged freely and brutishly his ordinary vice and his ordinary weakness. Then, with a typical impulse of remorse and alarm, he pledged his word of honour to Paoli that he would taste no "fermented liquor" for a year. He afterwards wrote to Temple: "I have kept this promise now about three weeks. I was really growing a drunkard." On Easter Day he received the Communion at St. Paul's and felt himself a real Christian.

Three days later he began to drink water only. He was so accustomed to being unsteady when he rose from table, that he was dizzy by habit, and found himself still tottering when he had drunk nothing stronger than water or tea.

Johnson went to Bath with Mr. and Mrs. Thrale towards the middle of April, and Boswell followed them on the 26th. Before leaving town he had made the acquaintance of a new celebrity, Margaret Caroline Rudd.

Mrs. Rudd was a singularly emancipated and charming woman, a good deal in advance of her time, though perhaps not quite up to the level of our own. She had been the mistress of one, or both, of the ingenious brothers Perreau who were executed for forgery, and in order to save her own life she had turned informer. Mrs. Rudd was also tried; she conducted her own defence, neatly dressed in "second mourning." She looked so pathetic and so beautiful that she was not only acquitted, but quickly became one of the most admired women in London. Everyone repeated with approval the opening words of her address to the jury: "You are honest men, and I am safe in your hands."

Boswell had a long and serious talk with Mrs. Rudd, and kissed her several times. An account of this interview was written for his wife, and sent to his clergyman friend, William Temple. Johnson, who was not always narrow-minded, said, "I envy him his acquaintance with Mrs. Rudd."

Shortly before his return to Scotland, Boswell arranged the famous meeting between Wilkes and Johnson at Mr. Dilly's table in the Poultry. The account of this episode forms one of the best passages in the *Life*, and one of the most superb conversation-pieces in English literature.

On the day after the dinner at Mr. Dilly's, Johnson wrote a letter to Mrs. Boswell in which he said:

"You will now have Mr. Boswell home; it is well that you have him; he has led a wild life. I have taken him to Lichfield, and he has followed Mr. Thrale to Bath. Pray take care of him and tame him. The only thing in which I have the honour to agree with you is, in loving him; and while we are so much of a mind in a matter of so much importance, our other quarrels will, I hope, produce no great bitterness."

In the autumn of 1776 and the winter of 1776–1777 the condition of Boswell was such as might have suggested a loss of sanity. There is a most ominous break in his correspondence between the 31st of August 1776 and the 8th of February 1777. His private journal shows that he sank to a lower level of mental decay and of moral deterioration than he had previously touched, even during a Scotch winter. His behaviour became openly scandalous; he was drunk in the churchyard at a funeral; he showed a tendency to insult, in his own house, young unprotected women of his wife's family. And yet, such were the odd mutations of this variable creature that he could look with glowing and worthy sentiments upon scenes of domestic felicity, upon the cheering fireside group of wife and happy children.

But his family life had actually become tragic. While he was drinking and whoring in the dark, foul streets of the old town, his wife was ill, miserable and humiliated. The very continuance of the household in a state of decency depended upon an allowance from Lord Auchinleck, and Auchinleck was more and more vexed by his son's wanton habits and by his inattention to business. There was little hope, now, of promotion; and younger men, like Henry Dundas, had been promoted already. Clients were not anxious to hand their cases to Boswell; and who could blame them? His Edinburgh reputation had become that of a worthless drunkard, a man notoriously immoral, indiscreet, without stability.

Now, of all the terms that a man is unwilling to apply to himself, drunkard is perhaps the most uncongenial. It is one of those terms that you cannot pass off as a joke, nor can you endow it with any sense of pathos. There is no dodging or softening the meaning of the word; it crashes down through all ambiguity and marks its man as a thing unspeakably contemptible.

Observe the totally different effect of the term hypochondriac, which can be made to cover drunkenness and a whole multitude of other failings or misfortunes. It was a term which, in Boswell's time, did not so much indicate a man tormented by imaginary ailments or morbidly pre-occupied with concern for health, as a man pursued by melancholy. The hypochondriac was not by any means despicable; he was interesting or pathetic; he suffered with many of his countrymen, and his ailment was known as the English Malady. When, in 1777, Boswell called himself a Hypochondriack and began to write a long series of essays under that name, he chose a technique and a designation extremely well calculated to afford him relief. He wrote those essays for the *London Magazine*, in which he had acquired an interest. The first essay was published in October 1777, and the last in August 1783. He thus provided himself with periodical literary work and with an excellent vehicle for the unloading of his mind.

The Hypochondriack could speak freely about love, marriage, drinking, letters, morals and religion, or anything that came into his head. He could extenuate his own lapses by referring to his peculiar malady. Anyone who suffered from hypochondria was at a terrible disadvantage, he felt everything more intensely than other people, and so he was less able to withstand the assaults of the devil. The following passages are chosen from a series of papers on drinking, in which Boswell exhibits very pathetically a fatal disorder and a fatal weakness:

"I do fairly acknowledge that I love Drinking; that I have a constitutional inclination to indulge in fermented liquors, and that if it were not for the restraints of reason and religion I am afraid I should be as constant a votary of Bacchus as any man. To be sensible of this is a con-tinual cause of fear, the uneasiness of which greatly counterbalances both the pleasure of occasional gratifica-tion and the pride of frequent successful resistance, and therefore it is certainly a misfortune to have such a con-stitution. My thoughts upon Drinking cannot be sup-posed to be quite uniform and fixed. Yet I flatter myself that as I have revolved the subject very often in my mind, and that too in very different states, I may bring together some particulars which will furnish a periodical essay sufficiently well. . . . An Hypochondriack is under peculiar temptations to participate freely of wine. For the impatience of his temper under his sufferings which are sometimes almost intolerable, urges him to fly to what will give him immediate relief. It has often occurred to me, that one must be obstinate to an extraordinary degree, who feeling himself in torment can resist taking what he is certain will procure him ease, or at least insensibility. . . . But we know from humiliating experience that men cannot be kept long in a state of elevated intoxication, and that drunkenness will be followed either by immediate frenzy or by such wretched ruin both of mind and body as must render its victims despicably miserable. . . . Writing upon Drinking is in one respect, I think, like Drinking itself: one goes on imperceptibly, without knowing where to stop; and as one calls for the other bottle to his friends, I press the other paper upon my readers."

The conclusion of the whole matter, according to the Hypochondriack, is that drinking should be the pleasure of old age. A greater confusion of muddled thought never resulted in a more luminous revelation of personality. In one line we are shown reason and religion as checks to intemperance; in another we find that the only hope lies in an extraordinary degree of obstinacy. We do not know whether "the pride of frequent successful resistance" is supposed to justify "the pleasure of occasional gratification." The one clear issue is that a hypochondriac is under peculiar temptation. This quotation is enough to show the mental haze in which Boswell's ideas presented themselves, and the desire for relief which actually made another point of resemblance between drinking and writing.

Johnson's affection for Boswell was not altered by the perception of his weakness. The Doctor despised insobriety, he warned Boswell, and he tried to keep him in order; but he was nearly always delighted to see him.

Again we have to remember the important fact, very seldom realised, that Boswell and Johnson rarely met each other. In the last seven and a half years of Johnson's life, the total of the various periods when they could have been together is only a little over ten months. Between 1779 and 1781 they did not see each other at all for a period of one year and five months; and between 1781 and 1783 they were separated for one year and nine months. The popular idea of Boswell as the attendant or parasite of Johnson is therefore crudely erroneous.

In September 1777 Boswell came down to Ashbourne, and spent ten days with Johnson at Dr. Taylor's. He did not see him again until the 19th of March 1778, the day after his arrival in London.

The year 1778 is known to students of the *Life of Johnson* as the year of the great dialogues. Boswell remained in London from the 18th of March to the 19th of May, and during that period he set down a series of conversations more brilliant than any other series in his book. Even if the dinner with Wilkes is to be regarded as the supreme achievement of Boswell in the historical and literary sense, it is run hard by the dialogue of the 3rd of April, when a company whose names are not given met at a place which is not revealed; by the account of the dinner at Reynolds's on the 9th of April; and by the superb record of the evening at Dilly's on the 15th of April, when Johnson met Mrs. Knowles, Miss Seward, Dr. Mayo and the Reverend Mr. Beresford. On Good Friday, the 17th of April, occurred the famous meeting between Johnson and his old school-fellow, the pleasing Mr. Edwards, the man who tried to be a philosopher but was defeated by cheerfulness. These are the outstanding conversations of the period, but there are more first-rate pages under this year than in any other equally long section of the book. To read only the Johnsonian dialogues of 1778, even with no other knowledge of Boswell and Johnson, would be a literary experience of the most delightful kind.

That noble Corsican, Paoli, shared with Johnson the task of keeping Boswell straight, and lodged him in his own house in South Audley Street (and later in Upper Seymour Street, Portman Square) during his visits to London.

Boswell probably owed as much to the friendship of this loyal and grateful man as he did to that of Johnson.

Burke was a tepid friend, if indeed he ever treated Boswell with more than mere urbanity; John Wilkes kept on the verge of cordiality with his "old classical travelling companion," but went no further; Reynolds, for the sake of Johnson, showed him a ceremonious benevolence; Mrs. Thrale began to dislike him. With the other members of the Johnsonian circle Boswell never lived on really intimate terms: the petulance and the occasional malice which he shows in writing of Goldsmith and of David Garrick is a proof of their own attitude. Goldsmith died in 1774, and Garrick in 1779. Temple, Boswell's lifelong and most devoted friend, could only exert his influence and offer his advice by means of letters. It is an undoubted fact that Boswell could never have swum on a high level of cultured society if it had not been for the prestige of his association with Johnson and Paoli, and the resulting social complaisance. He was not only becoming disreputable; he was known to have all the acid resentments of a weak or feminine character and all the dangerous drawbacks of a babbling tongue.

Boswell's son James was born in 1778.

There were two visits to London in 1779: one from the 16th of March to the 3rd of May, and the other from the 4th to the 18th of October. During the earlier visit Boswell suffered greatly from melancholia; his records of Johnson are poor and thin, he is fretful, distracted, a wretched being. In the interval between the two visits he refrained cantankerously from writing to Johnson in order that he might be reassured by a signal of anxious concern. Johnson wrote, displaying the desired anxiety, and the Hypochondriack placidly replied:

"What may be justly termed a supine indolence of mind has been my state of existence since I last returned to Scotland. . . . I was willing to take advantage of my insensibility, and while I could bear the experiment, to try whether your affection for me would, after an unusual

silence on my part, make you write first. . . . I am doubtful
if it was right to make the experiment, though I have
gained by it."

This neurasthenic dalliance with emotion, in which the
real motive is the recovery of self-esteem, was very properly
denounced by the Doctor as a foolish trick, not to be played
more than once.

The second visit of 1779 was occasioned by the recruiting
campaign of Colonel James Stuart, who invited Boswell to
accompany him to Leeds, and thence to London and other
places. England was trying to fight or flounder out of her
difficulties with France and America, and Colonel Stuart
was patriotically raising a regiment at his own expense.
Boswell never recovered from his juvenile military infatuation; he liked soldiers; they cheered him up and gave him
an opportunity for being good-natured or cordial without
taxing his intelligence. The camp, as a cure for hypochondria, had much to commend it. He was only in London
for a fortnight, and then he followed the new colours to
Chester, where he enjoyed himself gloriously; edified by the
conversation of the Bishop, flirting with the niece of a
Prebendary, and playing a jovial part in the officers' mess.
"I am kept in animated variety," he said. For a time, the
Hypochondriack had found relief. He returned to Scotland
in what he calls, in his confused way, "good insensibility."

In 1780, the year of the so-called Gordon riots, Boswell
did not come to London. His law business was failing, and
he could not afford the expense of a journey, neither could
he prudently arrange for a loan. His daughter Elizabeth
was born in 1780. For part of the year he was moderately
easy in mind, and then his familiar devils came back again.
He described his own condition with considerable skill in
the *London Magazine* for December:

"The Hypochondriack is himself at this moment in a
state of very dismal depression. . . . His distempered
fancy darts sudden livid glaring views athwart time and
space. . . . An extreme degree of irritability makes him

liable to be hurt by every thing that approaches him in any respect. He is perpetually upon the fret; and though he is sensible that this renders him unmanly and pitiful he cannot help shewing it; and his consciousness that it is observed, exasperates him so, that there is great danger of his being harsh in his behaviour to all around him. . . . By religion the Hypochondriack will have his mind fixed upon one invariable object of veneration."

But even religion failed. In February 1781 Boswell sent a querulous letter to Johnson in which he complained of being vexed by the problem of liberty and necessity. Johnson, to whom this was all stuff-and-nonsense, replied: "I hoped you had got rid of all this hypocrisy of misery. What have you to do with Liberty and Necessity? Or what more than hold your tongue about it? Do not doubt that I shall be most heartily glad to see you here again, for I love every part about you but your affectation of distress."

Boswell arrived in London on the 19th of March 1781 and remained there until the 2nd of June. This was one of his longest periods in London during Johnson's lifetime, but his records of Johnson are again relatively scanty, casual and broken, and before the end of the period they had obviously begun to drift away from each other. After the 8th of May there was "a pretty long interval" during which they did not even meet.

This voluntary absence from Johnson, while actually within a short walk of his house, shows on the part of Boswell a most ominous change of attitude, or else an ominous rapidity of moral decay. We have evidence of both.

Thrale, a victim of gluttony, died on the 4th of April. Very shortly after his death, and perhaps in collaboration with Wilkes, Boswell composed an indecent *Ode by Dr. Samuel Johnson to Mrs. Thrale upon their supposed approaching Nuptials*. This almost incredible outrage (actually published in 1788) will have to be considered more fully in a later chapter; it is, in fact, of critical importance in our final estimate of Boswell.

It was during this visit that Boswell appeared at Miss

Monckton's while outrageously drunk, roared stupidly at Johnson to show that he was a match for him, and the next day added to his offence by sending to Miss Monckton a copy of some fatuous verses. But what is even more astounding than the offence is that he should have published this ignominy, ten years later, in the *Life of Johnson*. He left London on the 2nd of June, and was accompanied by Johnson to Mr. Dilly's house at Southill in Bedfordshire, where they spent three days together.

The downward course of Boswell, perceptible to all who knew him, was not an even progress. We have seen how he was occasionally checked or restrained. There were comparatively long periods of slow decline, and then alarming collapses, each of them bringing him to a lower level. Such collapses took place in 1774, 1776 and 1781. He did not possess enough moral energy for any real opposition to his morbid humours, let alone for permanent recovery. His tragedy (if you choose to regard it as such) is not that of a strong will overcome by stronger circumstances, but of a weak mind crumbling and softening through a process of internal corruption. This internal corruption, whatever its pathological or moral nature, was enormously aggravated by intemperance and incontinence.

CHAPTER X

THE NEW LAIRD

THE ownership of land, a thing now discouraged, used to have peculiar attractions for men who were satisfied with a purely accidental form of prestige, and who imagined that human worth could be measured accurately in terms of acres or bricks. This was clearly advantageous to those numerous landowners for whom no other sort of prestige was attainable. Nor was there any hesitation to accept property as a mark of divine favour, and to regard the owner of property as a man with a vested interest in heaven.

In the current views of property and feudalism James Boswell heartily concurred. At the same time, he felt a natural dismay at the idea of being forced to live in the country. In 1780 his aversion to a country life was partly dispelled, and he wrote in the *London Magazine*:

"The Hypochondriack does not mean to limit the happiness of a country life to . . . unprofitable and ignoble indulgence. He has lately returned from having passed some time in the country, where in a sound and placid state of mind he relished a rural life, and divested of prejudice, except, perhaps, what was quite unusual to him, a little particularity in its favour, he considered the subject with a good deal of attention, and was convinced, that there are better enjoyments in the country than he had before supposed."—He was, no doubt, speculating upon the imminent death of his father, and preparing himself for the occupation of Auchinleck.

Soon after his first meeting with Johnson in 1763 he had boasted of the paternal estate which he was to inherit, and Johnson, in a burst of careless enthusiasm or careless verbosity, had observed: "Sir, let me tell you, that to be a Scotch landlord, where you have a number of families dependent upon you, and attached to you, is perhaps as high a situation as humanity can arrive at." Even Boswell, flattered as he was, realised that Johnson was talking nonsense: "His notion of the dignity of a Scotch landlord," he said, "had been formed upon what he had heard of the Highland chiefs."

The idea of possessing the estate of Auchinleck, if it strongly appealed to Boswell in one sense, dismayed him in another. It would mean prestige, but it would also mean responsibility. It would give him, in Scottish society, a new title; it would, on the other hand, complicate his financial affairs and involve him in social obligations of a sort by no means congenial. On the whole, perhaps, the feudal impulses prevailed; the title of laird was worth having, even at the cost of a little inconvenience.

The Hypochondriack (in 1780) gave his exalted views on the subject of being a landed proprietor:

"There is a feeling of dignity and consequence in being master of land above any thing else. It is the natural dominion of man over the earth, granted him by his Almighty Creator, and no artificial dominion is felt like it. . . . He who is master of land sees all around him obedient to his will, not only can he totally change the face of inanimate nature, but can command the animals of each species, and even the human race itself, to multiply or diminish, to continue or to migrate, according to his pleasure."

This liberal concept of natural dominion, apparently extending to compulsory eugenics and the right to banish, and certainly including unlimited power over the landscape, showed that the Hypochondriack was ready to make a proper use of his feudal principles. Even Johnson's imaginary Highland chief was a poor fellow in comparison with masterful young Auchinleck—a man who knew so well the nature of his Creator's mandate.

Boswell's attitude towards his father was that of a frightened child, maintaining with some difficulty the proper level of respectful sentiment. He was conscious of having failed to realise his father's reasonable expectations, and of having given him just cause for complaint. "Honest man!" he said in 1763, "he is now very happy. It is amazing to think how much he has at heart my pursuing the road of civil life." In 1764 he expressed a wish to make his father happy without being "too hard upon himself." In 1767 he said of Lord Auchinleck: "His character is such that he must have his son in a great degree of subjection to him." A little later he wrote: "How unaccountable is it that my father and I should be so ill together! . . . I write to him with warmth, with an honest pride, wishing that he should think of me as I am; but my letters shock him, and every expression in them is interpreted unfavourably. . . . How galling is it to the friend of Paoli to be treated so!" After this, there are periodical exclamations of worthy man! honest man! but in 1775 he said: "I am still very unhappy with my father. We are so totally different that a good understanding is scarcely possible." Later in the same year he complained that he was "totally excluded from parental comfort," and again, that his father made him feel like a timid boy, "which to *Boswell* (comprehending all that my character does, in my own imagination and in that of a wonderful number of mankind) is intollerable." Much as he disliked his stepmother, he had to admit, in 1780, that she treated his children better than their grandfather did, and this in spite of his own tactless attitude.

The failure to keep on good terms with his father was not entirely due to Boswell himself. Lord Auchinleck got on no better with his younger sons, John and David Boswell, the first a lieutenant in the navy, and the second a merchant in Spain, and both, as far as we know, equally obscure and dutiful. Alexander had no more flexibility than a piece of Druidical rock; he was one of those stern men who know exactly what is right, and who live in the unalterable conviction that younger men, and especially their own sons, must be invariably wrong. He was a dreadful old Caledonian gentleman who had acquired learning without culture, and power without grace or courtesy. His Presbyterian stiffness was unrelieved by the fervour or charm or benevolence that Presbyterians may possess like any other people.

And so it cannot be supposed that Boswell felt an overwhelming sorrow when his father died on the 30th of August 1782. Johnson was nearer the truth than he realised when he said: "Your father's death had every circumstance that could enable you to bear it."

Boswell had not been able to afford a visit to London in the spring, and he had anticipated one in the autumn, but now he was prevented by family affairs and by the advice of Johnson. Lord Auchinleck had left him an unencumbered estate with a rent roll worth about £1600 a year. It is extremely doubtful if, on the wisest plan of economy, Boswell could have lived at Auchinleck, kept the place in proper order, entertained his neighbours, retained a house in Edinburgh, paid occasional visits to London, and educated his five children on this income. He had incurred various debts, as much due to unreflecting generosity in advancing money to other people as to raising money for his own needs.

What he did, at any rate up to the end of 1785, when he lived mainly in London, was to spend his time between London, Edinburgh and Auchinleck. After 1786 the direct management of the estate, during the absence of the owner, was handed over to an agent, instructed by Boswell.

Considered as a landlord Boswell appears to his greatest advantage. His drastic notions of feudalism and his confidence in God's plan of subordination were so well tempered by his good-nature that he acted with charity and showed a warm interest in the affairs of his tenants. At the same time, he did not weakly give way in matters involving his legal rights, and he was invariably firm with those who could afford to pay rent but who preferred to avoid doing so. He paid close attention to forestry, to the preservation of highways, and to the management of his colliery or "coalwork." He did not like the idea of "throwing farms together and depopulating the country." His attitude towards the poor and infirm can be gathered from his letters to his agent. For example:

139

"How is old John Wyllie? Give him a crown from me, as a kindly remembrance. I am glad that George Halbert and John Black are in the way to bring up their arrears. I am sure I wish well to my tenants, and to the best of my knowledge would let them have reasonable bargains. . . . I am very sorry for the death of William Lennox. He was a worthy creditable old tenant for whom I had a regard from my earliest years. I hope his son will do well. Poor Hugh Blair must not work too hard. I shall be glad if he continues better. . . . Tell the widow in Weelside to make herself quite easy. . . . Let Adam Currie have another fir tree. . . . I am sorry for David Murdock's heavy losses. Be easy with him. . . . Send John Shaw a load of meal. . . . And let the unfortunate man Thomas Spiers have one, and send him my note."

In the *Life of Johnson* we find that one of Boswell's first actions after inheriting the estate was to bring an old man of eighty-eight "from a lonely cottage to a comfortable habitation within my enclosures, where he has good neighbours near to him." That is enough to display the humanity and the friendly concern of an excellent laird. There is also evidence of his firmness and his plain dealing:

"Orchard's case is as clear as the noonday and I desire that you proceed against him without hesitation. It was exceedingly wrong in James Wear not to reserve his rent out of the £600 he got for his stock. You must not let his rent lye over, for fear of accidents. . . . Mungo Reid must be prosecuted as I formerly wrote, and removed. Mean time, oblige him to pay up all his rent that is due. Let him not be indulged with a half year's rent in his hands. He has behaved very ill. . . . Miller Brown, I am resolved, shall make me a just indemnification for his shameful abuse of my farm."

At times there are gentle remonstrances to the agent himself. "You began your letter 'Good Sir,' which you meant well. 'But 'Sir' is the proper way to a master." Or more severe reproaches: "Last night I received yours of the seventh and am surprised and offended that I have not along with it your current account for last year which I ordered long ago, and have been expecting with impatience."

This new view of Boswell has many surprises. The weaker side of an easy-going disposition is evident in many passages of his life, but the depth and warmth of his discerning humanity is shown for the first time in these estate records. Perhaps the humanity might have been expected; what could scarcely have been expected is the cool, steady and thoughtful attention to business, so evident in these letters, and the admirable common sense and fairness with which problems are handled. A man altogether weak and depraved could never have made such a capable overseer; a hopelessly bad man could never have been such a worthy landlord—and worthy in this respect he certainly was. If there is something here which appears inconsistent with the main lines of the portrait, we can properly maintain that every portrait which is more than superficial must expose inconsistencies; what is unfortunate is that we should regard good qualities or sensible decisions as inconsistent with Boswell's general character, and that we should be so much surprised when we come across them.

Boswell's concern for his estate and his desire to help his tenants or servants appears in the provisions of his will. He granted favourable leases to the owners of several farms. "And I do beseech all the succeeding heirs of entail to be kind to the tenants and not to turn out old possessors to get a little more rent."

Perhaps it is necessary to point out that Boswell's new position, though it certainly brought into relief the best features of his character, did not involve a new recovery or a new reform. When Boswell sent his benevolent instructions or his wise orders to Auchinleck he was all the while tottering down the fatal slope. The wisdom of his advice or judgment was in dismal contrast with the extraordinary folly of his behaviour; the goodness of his heart was tragically outweighed by his miserable lack of control. We see him at his best, therefore, when he is an absentee landlord, managing his estate from a distance by means of letters. The portrait of the good landlord is rather dim and impersonal, rather attenuated by considerations of time and space; but still he is there; the shadowy benevolence is not unreal, the gestures of sympathy are effective, the benefits are substantial, there is no empty simulation.

Probably it would have been a good thing for Boswell if he could have settled on his estate, given up what remained of his legal practice in Edinburgh and resisted the allurement of London. This, at any rate, was the idea of his brother David: "Honest David is perpetually pressing my confining my family to Scotland. . . . My grave brother urges me to quit London and live at my seat in the country; where he thinks that I might be able to save so as gradually to relieve myself." Johnson had said the same thing: "The advice which I sent to him," he told Dr. Taylor, "is to stay at home and busy himself with his own affairs. He has a good estate . . . and he is himself in debt. But if his wife lives, I think he will be prudent." And in a letter to Boswell he said: "The present dreadful confusion of the publick ought to make you wrap yourself up in your hereditary possessions, which, though less than you may wish, are more than you can want; in an hour of religious retirement return thanks to God, who has exempted you from any strong temptation to faction, treachery, plunder and disloyalty. . . . Content yourself with your station. . . . Your estate and the Courts will find you full employment." But this is precisely what he could not agree to: he could not be satisfied with "narrow provinciality"; he would have been "absolutely miserable." The "Spanish brother" had more than a little of old Alexander's ponderous rectitude, he was insurmountably honest, rather dull, unable to sympathise with poor Boswell's eager fluttering towards the brilliance of intellectual society. Mrs. Boswell understood the situation better, and it was undoubtedly because of her understanding that she overcame her prejudice and invited Johnson to Auchinleck soon after Boswell had taken possession of the estate. If Boswell could entertain his brilliant friends in Scotland, all might be well.

But Johnson was now seventy-three, he was beginning to sink, though with manly fortitude, under the weight of years and infirmities. He received the invitation with pleasure, and regretted that he was not well enough for the journey. Yet he was "not without hope of seeing Auchinleck again," and he finished his note to Mrs. Boswell with graceful compliment and with tender injunctions.

In his own series of autobiographical essays, the Hypochondriack recorded a happy, though only a temporary, sensation of relief at the end of 1782:

"I have for so long a time been free of the direful malady from which the title of this periodical paper is taken, that I almost begin to forget that I ever was afflicted with it. . . . All the modes of cure—exercize—medicine—amusement—study—must be tried. . . . And I would now enforce my counsel by the consideration that I have a belief that the malady is sometimes owing to the influence of evil spirits."

At the same time, he refrained from writing to Johnson, or only sent him brief notes. He may have been irritated or disappointed by Johnson's assumption, unmistakably conveyed in his letter of the 7th of September 1782, that he would now enter upon a totally new system of life, with new cares and new employments. Johnson gave him good advice on the subject of economy (which he certainly needed), and less necessary advice on how to treat his retainers: he clearly pictured Boswell settling down at Auchinleck, and relishing the pride of being a respectable landowner. And when Johnson understood that Boswell, on the contrary, was anxious to hurry to London, he quickly and sternly dissuaded him.

Boswell came south again in March 1783, and he reached London on the 20th of the month. Next day he found the Doctor at Mrs. Thrale's house in Argyll Street. Johnson was looking ill, but he cheered up when he saw the new laird. "Sir," he said, "the superiority of a country gentleman over the people upon his estate is very agreeable: and he who says he does not feel it to be agreeable, lies; for it must be agreeable to have a casual superiority over those who are by nature equal with us." Boswell's answer showed at once his own attitude: "Yet, Sir, we see great proprietors of land who prefer living in London." Johnson had to admit that the intellectual superiority which could be enjoyed in London might counterbalance the local superiority of a landlord, and he then turned to the purely financial advantages of owning property.

The conversations of this period are below the level of those in other parts of the *Life*—very far below the level of 1778. This may be partly due to the illness and fretfulness of Johnson, but it is also due to the slackness or indifference of Boswell. There was a sharp explosion of anger on the subject of General Oglethorpe (who was then eighty-six), and a more justifiable explosion when Boswell talked about Johnson in his presence to Mrs. Desmoulins—a piece of clumsy behaviour enough to exasperate the most placid man.

The London visit of 1783 lasted from the 20th of March to the 30th of May. Boswell admits that his records of the interviews with Johnson were very incomplete, and it appears that there were often long intervals between their meetings. For example, he has no record of a meeting between the 1st and the 15th of May. There are few dates in his account of this period, and the talk of Johnson is reproduced mainly in a series of disconnected observations with the merest outline of a social context. Even where the context is given and the conversation is of an intimate kind, it is frequently dull or trivial, as in the dialogue about gardens:

"*Boswell*: 'I wish to have a good walled garden.' *Johnson*: 'I don't think it would be worth the expense to you. . . . I would plant an orchard, and have plenty of such fruit as ripen well in your country. . . . Cherries are an early fruit, you may have them; and you may have the early apples and pears.' *Boswell*: 'We cannot have nonpareils.' *Johnson*: 'Sir, you can no more have nonpareils than you can have grapes.' *Boswell*: 'We may have them, Sir; but they are very bad.'"

One might be tempted to suppose that Boswell and Johnson were becoming less fond of each other. Probably that was not the case, at least where Johnson was concerned. It is more likely that Boswell, himself prematurely ageing and with indications of a progressive mental disorder, was less capable of fixing his attention and too readily disposed to let himself relapse into his old habits of indulgence.

He lived, during this visit, in the house of General Paoli, and he also received much hospitality from the Dilly brothers. He tried to renew a correspondence with John Wilkes, and Wilkes does not appear to have responded with any great enthusiasm. It occurred to Boswell that it would be amusing to see Johnson at dinner in Wilkes's own house, and gratifying to be the successful negotiator of this entertainment. He still looked upon the Doctor as an exhibition. His journalistic mind saw nothing unpleasant in the idea of persuading an old, sick man to put himself in a position that would be curious, historical, unique—and he fancied himself saying, "Oh, yes, I took Johnson to dinner with Jack Wilkes t'other evening." But the dinner did not take place.

He freely called himself the Laird of Auchinleck, and Johnson told him that his boasting reminded him of Mr. Twalmley, who described himself as "the great Twalmley who invented the New Floodgate Iron."

The pride of the landowner had given rise to a new ambition. Boswell had serious thoughts of entering parliament. Johnson, with his quick common sense, at once pointed out that if he got into parliament he would incur fresh and heavy expense. He then told Boswell that it was nonsense to pretend that a man could be genuinely vexed by public affairs, and advised him to clear his mind of cant and to avoid the habit of thinking foolishly. Boswell again talked of living in the country, and Johnson, though without the intention of doing so, demolished one of his secret hopes: "Don't set up for what is called hospitality. . . . If your house be like an inn, nobody cares for you." Boswell replied, that some people could make their houses a home for their guests without putting themselves to inconvenience. "Then, Sir," retorted Johnson peevishly, "home must be the same to the guests, and they need not come."

When Boswell and Johnson parted on the 29th of May, the Doctor made a pathetic and charming little speech: "Were I in distress, there is no man to whom I should sooner come than to you. I should like to come and have a cottage in your park, toddle about, live mostly on milk, and be taken care of by Mrs. Boswell. She and I are good friends now; are we not?"

In less than three weeks after this parting Johnson was alarmed by a paralytic stroke which, though it left his mind clear and active, fatally injured his constitution.

After his return to Scotland, the Laird of Auchinleck determined to make a figure in politics—one of the simplest methods by which a man of mediocre abilities may assert himself. He clamorously joined the party which opposed Fox's India Bill, and he composed and published a *Letter to the People of Scotland on the Present State of the Nation*. He believed, or professed to believe, that any restraint imposed upon the nefarious doings of the East India Company had the appearance, if not the intention, of an attack upon the power and privilege of the Crown. His *Letter*, a piece of boisterous nonsense, is not to be confused (as it sometimes is) with the even more absurd *Letter* of 1785. The conclusion of the first *Letter* shows an equal desire to exhibit political integrity and personal importance:

"I have mentioned former circumstances, perhaps with too much egotism, to show that I am no time-server, and, at this moment, friends to whom I have attached my affection, gratitude, and interest are zealous for the measure which I deem so alarming. Let me add that a dismissal of the Portland Ministry would probably disappoint an object which I have most ardently at heart. But, holding an estate transmitted to me through my ancestors by charters from a series of kings, the importance of a Charter and the prerogative of a King impress my mind with seriousness and with duty."

The frothy confusion of this pamphlet, no doubt written mainly with the idea of circulating the name and the fame of James Boswell, Esquire, may be taken as another ominous proof of mental incoherence; indeed, the puerility of the last sentence quoted above is almost sufficient proof in itself.

Fox's bill was rejected by the Lords on the 17th of December. Parliament had previously voted £50,000 a year for the Prince of Wales and had given him £160,000 for the purpose of liquidating his debts; so the royal prerogatives were most happily and most honourably preserved. Boswell rejoiced: he wrote *Vivat Rex* at the top of a note to Sir Alexander Dick. Perhaps he did not know that a secret committee of the House of Commons had found ample materials for a prosecution against Sir Thomas Rumbold and Governor Warren Hastings.

Either these political activities, or mere procrastination, prevented Boswell from writing to Johnson with anything like regularity, and the old man complained, "You should not make your letters such rarities, when you know, or might know, the uniform state of my health." In the winter of 1783 Boswell retired to Auchinleck, and he had the moderate satisfaction of being elected chairman by his neighbours at two public meetings. He told Johnson about this, and asked him to decide what ought to be done with old horses, having regard both to humanity and economy.

The immediate effect of inheriting the Auchinleck estate was to restore the subsiding buoyancy of Boswell's disposition and to give him a grateful though fortuitous sense of importance, at a time when his chances of being actually important were sadly diminished. The second effect was to bring before him a too vivid realisation of the narrowness of a provincial existence. The ultimate result was a compromise, in which he hoped to use the new dignity of the Laird as a means of advancing in social prestige, without submitting to the inconvenience of being tied down to a country estate. The first aim of this baffled, meandering life, and its only definite or consistent aim, was to achieve recognition. Any loud cry, any frantic assertion of popular principles, might help to give him what he wanted. Any rhodomontade of inflated loyalty might serve his purpose. All the stuttering nonsense about kings and ancestors and royal prerogatives, all the jerky contortions of this tormented egoism, were signs of a mental state in which phantoms of hope and despair danced in perpetual mazes.

Boswell's idea of getting into parliament or of securing a government post was not a new one. He had tried to ingratiate himself with Pitt, and then with Burke; and Burke had actually applied to Conway on his behalf. For some time he had considerable hopes of being assisted by his former school-fellow, Henry Dundas (Viscount Melville), King's Advocate. He prided himself on the patronage of Mountstuart, and then on the more direct patronage of Lonsdale. Now, the owner of no mean property, with a fine manor house and a ruined castle, he saw a larger prospect of political distinction.

There is reason to suppose that his legal practice, by the end of 1783, had shrunk to negligible proportions and implied little more than formal attendances. His *Letter to the People of Scotland* was therefore intended, not only as an advertisement, but as the prelude to a new career. This desire to assert himself, to escape from the mere suspicion of inferiority, appeared to Boswell as a rational form of ambition; though it was not the consciousness of ability but the desire to be conspicuous that drove him forward.

He was forty-three. He had published in his twenty-eighth year a book that gave him considerable celebrity, but he had done little since. All his hopes of rising to eminence at the Scotch Bar had been destroyed. He was the friend of Johnson and Paoli, and he made the most of that; but a man hardly becomes famous through being the friend of other men. Of his earlier companions in London, several were dead and several had grown more distant. His drunkenness and his infidelities had sunk him low in the esteem of respectable persons. His insolence and folly, his ineptitude, made people less anxious to invite him to their houses. The darker forms of mental depression caused him to appear, at times, apathetic or wayward, and tended to mitigate the chief of his attractions—gaiety and good-humour. Although

his children seemed to like him, he was unfitted for the
responsibilities of a parent, and he knew it. His marriage,
through his own fault, was not a happy one: his wife was
ill, reproachful and worried. But now the inheritance of
Auchinleck opened up a fresh, unexplored horizon: he might
yet scramble back to social decency; he might yet be a
"roaring boy," a man of worth; or better still, a man of
political or literary fame.

CHAPTER XI

DEATH OF DOCTOR JOHNSON

IT is occasionally supposed that Johnson managed to keep Boswell reasonably straight, and that after the Doctor's death Boswell at once fell to pieces. That is not entirely correct. The original influence of Johnson was profound, but it was not lasting. There is some excuse for being misled by the artfully uniform tone of reverence in the *Life*, with its recurring notes of personal indebtedness, until we remember the actual circumstances of Boswell's career and the details of his behaviour.

Neither Johnson nor any other man succeeded for long in keeping Boswell reasonably straight or in reducing the fatal impetus of his folly. In his later visits to London, Boswell seems almost to have avoided Johnson and to have taken little trouble in recording his talk. That is not inconsistent with a theory of progressive deterioration on the part of Boswell, but it is entirely inconsistent with any idea of a sustained Johnsonian influence.

The idea of a sudden collapse after the death of Johnson is equally irreconcilable with the facts of the case. The downward movement of Boswell, whatever its variations in velocity, was a continuous movement. Actually, the effect of Johnson's death was to pull him together, at any rate to a certain extent, in order that he might prepare the *Hebrides* for publication and collect the materials for his great biography.

In saying this, we do not imply that Boswell never had a true regard for Johnson. He had such a regard, though it was not proof against the personal desire for assertion and a regrettable tendency to indulge in scurrilous banter. Boswell had no coherence; his affections were fugitive and irregular; he was always tuning himself to the pitch of an occasion, a mood or a personality. The presence of Johnson could raise him to a true state of reverence and wonder; and then he would make sport of him behind his back, show his most private letters to everyone, boast of his familiarity, and violate his confidence. In the same way he could feel, in her presence, the most indubitable affection for his wife; and yet he was capable, not merely of innumerable flirtations but of the lowest and meanest of infidelities. It is impossible, therefore, to build up a static character out of such loose components. All that Johnson had succeeded in doing was to bring about an occasional recognition of social morality, an occasional steadiness.

At the beginning of 1784 Dr. Johnson was in extremely bad health, though in February there was some improvement. Boswell, at his request, wrote for the opinion of Sir Alexander Dick, and obtained the views and prescriptions of three eminent doctors of the Edinburgh school of medicine. He also sent Johnson "a medical packet."

But the chief concerns of Boswell at this time were political. He composed an address to the king from the patriots of Ayr, which was carried by a great majority. He wrote a preliminary election address to the freeholders of the constituency, in which he said that if Colonel Montgomerie did not stand at the next election, he himself intended to come forward as a candidate. "I declare that I should pay the utmost deference to your instructions as my constituents; and as I am now the representative of a family which has held an estate in the county, and maintained a respectable character for almost three centuries, I flatter myself that I shall not be reckoned too presumptuous when I aspire to the high distinction of being your representative in Parliament, and that you will not disapprove of my indulging an ambition that this family shall rather advance than fall off in my time." No doubt he was encouraged by the courtesy of Pitt, who had acknowledged a copy of the *Letter to the People of Scotland* and praised the author for his "zealous and able support given to the cause of the publick."

Towards the middle of March 1784, Boswell set out for London, evidently not prepared for the early dissolution of parliament. He got as far as York, where he had the satisfaction of seeing the Whigs put out of countenance by another address to the king. In the meantime, things were

moving, or being moved, in London. On the 24th of March
the great seal of England was stolen from the house of
Lord Chancellor Thurlow. On the 25th, parliament was
dissolved. News of this reached Boswell at York on the
28th, and he at once hurried back to Scotland, after
sending Johnson a hasty account of his plans. Johnson
replied:

"You could do nothing so proper as to hasten back
when you found the Parliament dissolved. With the
influence which your address must have gained you, it
may reasonably be expected that your presence will be of
importance, and your activity of effect. . . . You are
entering upon a transaction which requires much prudence.
. . . I must entreat you to be scrupulous in the use of
strong liquors. One night's drunkenness may defeat the
labours of forty days well employed."

"Who is this man so busy about addresses?" said Langton.
"The man so busy about addresses," replied the Doctor,
"is neither more nor less than our own Boswell. . . . Whether
to wish him success, his best friends hesitate."

But there was no need to be anxious. Colonel Montgomerie
stood again, and was elected. Boswell, after discreetly
supporting the Colonel, started for London at the end of
April, and arrived there on the 5th of May, a fortnight
before the meeting of the new parliament.

He found Johnson in somewhat better health, although
it was not long since the Doctor had written the most pathetic
of all his letters to Taylor of Ashbourne. In this letter he
said that his life was "very solitary and very cheerless." He
dreaded the approach of death, and shrank with piteous
terror from what he knew to be inevitable. "I have no friend
now living but you and Mr. Hector, that was the friend of
my youth."

In common with his other friends, Boswell probably knew
that Johnson had little chance of living much longer. He
became solicitous and attentive. Instead of being kept away,
as on his previous visit, by laziness or dissipation, he was

frequently with Johnson and kept a more ample account of his meetings.

At the beginning of June the Doctor expressed a desire to visit Oxford, where he could live in the delightful house of Dr. Adams, the Master of Pembroke. Boswell had arranged to hear a Handel festival in Westminster Abbey on the 5th of June, but he accompanied Johnson to Oxford on the 3rd, and then returned to London for his music. He came back to Oxford on the 9th of June.

The ten days which Boswell and Johnson spent in the house of Dr. Adams, from the 9th to the 19th of June, were the happiest, the most serene, of their last days together. Johnson's talk was almost up to the level of his best period. He could be deliciously perverse, as when he said: "I would be a Papist if I could. I have fear enough; but an obstinate rationality prevents me. I shall never be a Papist, unless on the near approach of death, of which I have a very great terrour. I wonder that women are not all Papists." Or he could be prettily gallant, as when the attentive and charming Miss Adams told him that the little pot out of which she had just poured his coffee was the only thing she could call her own, and the Doctor replied: "Don't say so, my dear; I hope you don't reckon my heart as nothing."

Yet the shadow of death rested already upon the mind of Johnson, chilling his warmer fancies and giving to his thoughts a grey sobriety that made them often sad. More than once he was overcome by his dark apprehension. In the whole of the *Life* there is no passage more intensely pathetic or more admirably realistic than the following:

"On Friday, June 11, we talked at breakfast of forms of prayer. *Johnson*: 'I know of no good prayers but those in the Book of Common Prayer.' *Dr. Adams* (in a very earnest manner): 'I wish, Sir, you would compose some family prayers.' *Johnson*: 'I will not compose prayers for you, Sir, because you can do it for yourself. But I have thought of getting together all the books of prayers which I could, selecting those which should appear to me the best, putting out some, inserting others, adding some prayers of my own, and prefixing a discourse on prayer.' We all now gathered about him, and two or three of us at a time joined in pressing him to execute this plan. He seemed to be a little displeased at the manner of our importunity, and in great agitation called out, 'Do not talk thus of what is so awful. I know not what time God will allow me in this world. There are many things which I wish to do.' Some of us persisted, and Dr. Adams said, 'I never was more serious about any thing in my life.' *Johnson*: 'Let me alone, let me alone; I am overpowered.' And then he put his hands before his face, and reclined for some time upon the table."

Again, when Mr. Henderson was having supper with them, Johnson expressed his fear of death. He was afraid, he said, that he might be one of those who were damned. The gentle Dr. Adams, greatly shocked, asked him what he meant by damned, and Johnson cried passionately and harshly, "Sent to *Hell*, Sir, and punished everlastingly." Adams replied, "I don't believe that doctrine." Johnson gloomily maintained that "there was no such thing as infinite goodness physically considered," and he brusquely ended the conversation by saying that he would have no more of it.

But the general tenour of those last Oxford days was calm and harmonious. "There was something exceedingly pleasing in our leading a College life, without restraint, and with superiour elegance." The company in the Master's house consisted of Dr. and Mrs. Adams, both of them pious and placid, Miss Adams, and Mrs. Kennicot, the widow of a celebrated scholar.

Three days after their return to London, Boswell and Johnson dined at the Literary Club. The dinner is memorable as the last occasion on which Johnson visited the Club, and possibly the first occasion on which Boswell met Edmund Malone, who had been elected the year before, and was present that evening. The close friendship between Malone and Boswell, to which English literature is so profoundly indebted, was not formed until the following year.

As on previous occasions, Boswell stayed in the house of General Paoli, who was now in Upper Seymour Street, Portman Square. It was in this house that the friends of Johnson considered a plan for sending him to Italy for the winter.

In this amiable design Boswell took a leading part. He consulted Reynolds on the advisability of writing to the Chancellor, Thurlow, with a view to obtaining an addition to the Doctor's pension, thus enabling him to undertake the journey. It is to be assumed that Johnson would not have accepted money from any other than a purely official source. Reynolds approved of the scheme, and Boswell accordingly wrote to Thurlow on the 24th of June.

The letter to Thurlow is of importance, for it shows Boswell playing a benevolent part with dignity and with proper restraint:

"My Lord,
"Dr. Samuel Johnson, though wonderfully recovered from a complication of dangerous illness, is by no means well, and I have reason to think that his valuable life cannot be preserved long, without the benignant influence of a southern climate.

"It would therefore be of very great moment were he to go to Italy before winter sets in; and I know that he wishes it much. But the objection is that his pension of £300 a year would not be sufficient to defray this expence, and make it convenient for Mr. Sastres, an ingenious and worthy native of that country, and a teacher of Italian here, to accompany him.

"As I am well assured of your Lordship's regard for Dr. Johnson I presume, without his knowledge, so far to indulge my anxious concern for him, as to intrude upon your Lordship with this suggestion, being persuaded that, if a representation of the matter were to be made to his Majesty by proper authority, the royal bounty would be extended in a suitable manner.

"Your Lordship, I cannot doubt, will forgive me for taking this liberty. I even flatter myself you will approve of it. I am to set out for Scotland on Monday morning; so that if your Lordship should have any commands for me, as to this pious negociation, you will be pleased to send them before that time. But Sir Joshua Reynolds, with whom I have consulted, will be here, and will gladly give all attention to it.

"I am, with very great respect,

"My Lord,

"Your Lordship's most obedient

"and most humble servant,

"JAMES BOSWELL."

Thurlow replied sympathetically on the 8th, and Reynolds undertook to carry on the negotiations. Boswell ran off to Johnson with the good news, and arranged to dine with him at Reynolds's the next day, when they could privately discuss all particulars.

Johnson was deeply affected. "This is taking prodigious pains about a man," he said, and the tears came into his eyes. "God bless you all."

The "friendly confidential dinner" with Sir Joshua Reynolds took place on the 30th of June. Dr. Johnson was looking ill, but he was cheered by the prospect of his Italian tour, and listened with pleasure and gratitude to the talk of Boswell and Sir Joshua. They did not doubt that the king would readily consent to a grant from the treasury; they had no reason for anticipating a refusal. The only question was whether there would be an increase of the pension, or a single grant of some considerable sum. The Doctor said that he would rather have his pension doubled than have a grant of a thousand pounds. On an income of £600 he considered that he could pass the rest of his days "in splendour." Such was a philosopher's idea of opulence, and such the measure of his modest anticipation. He told them, with a faltering voice, that one of his physicians, Dr. Brocklesby, had offered him a hundred a year for life. Boswell and Reynolds tried to encourage him by speaking of the delight of seeing classical ground, but he replied quietly: "Nay, I must not expect much of that; when a man goes to Italy merely to feel how he breathes the air, he can enjoy very little."

For the last time they discussed Boswell's particular problem of the advantage or disadvantage of living in the country. Johnson regarded such a life as mental imprisonment. "Sir, it is in the intellectual world as in the physical world: we are told by natural philosophers that a body is at rest in the place that is fit for it; they who are content to live in the country, are *fit* for the country." This irrefutable observation closed the argument. It was followed in a little while by another piece of obvious common sense, when Boswell protested that having too much taste was a restriction upon natural enjoyment: "Nay, Sir; that is a paltry notion. Endeavour to be as perfect as you can in every respect." That is the last fragment of Johnson's conversation, actually heard by Boswell, which is recorded in the *Life*.

Later in the evening, Boswell and Johnson returned to Bolt Court in Sir Joshua's coach. This ride in the coach was the last occasion on which they were together.

There seems to have been in the minds of both men a dismal foreboding. Some of their happiest times had been spent together in coaches, but this was not a happy time. Perhaps we should remember that both were continually afflicted by the darkest forms of pessimism.

When the coach arrived at the entrance to Bolt Court, Johnson invited Boswell to go into the house with him. Boswell declined, feeling that he could not endure a further lowering of spirits. They said good-bye to each other in the coach; Johnson clambered out, and when he was on the pavement he called out "Fare you well," and brusquely turned away. Boswell had seen him, and seen him dimly, for the last time; now he sat alone in the carriage, his mind overshadowed by apprehension, by cloudy sentiment and by tenderness that may have been a little reproachful. The solitary figure of Johnson passed through the court and mounted the steps of his house; his pathetic abruptness had concealed a struggle with emotion, and in the house which he now entered there was no Mr. Levett, no Mrs. Williams, to cheer him with humble companionship.

Boswell stayed in London for another day, hoping for an interview with Thurlow, but the Chancellor was busy and could not see him. On the following day (the 2nd of July) he set out for Scotland.

It is well known that the application to the royal bounty was not successful. The country had no hesitation in pouring £50,000 a year into the pockets of the Prince of Wales, but could not afford £300 for the greatest of all her literary men. Thurlow expressed himself willing personally to lend five or six hundred pounds to Johnson against a mortgage on the pension. Johnson, too manly to admit disappointment, gratefully acknowledged this offer, but said that he no longer contemplated the Italian journey. He afterwards admitted to Reynolds that he had not anticipated the refusal of a grant.

From the 13th of July to the 16th of November, Johnson was away visiting his friends at Oxford, Lichfield, Ashbourne and Birmingham. At first he seemed better, his asthma and dropsy were both relieved, and he could still eat with voracious appetite. He was greatly interested in Mr. Lunardi's balloon which, on the 15th of September, made the first aerial demonstration in Britain by ascending from the Artillery Ground in London, with a pigeon, a dog and a cat. Johnson very justly pointed out that balloons were of little use if they were not dirigible, or unless they could ascend to a height above that of the highest conquered mountain. He saw no future for balloons. By October he was again feeling ill and despondent. "I struggle on as I can. . . . I have made little progress in recovery. I am very weak, and very sleepless: but I live on and hope."

In July, Johnson received from Boswell "a letter filled with dejection and fretfulness."

Boswell had gone back to Edinburgh. He was now pursued by the dreadfully persistent idea that he was not really a success. As a Scotch advocate he had certainly failed, though he still believed that he might do well at the English Bar, and had again and again pestered Johnson for his views on this matter. But there is no process more painful than the slow deflation or shrinkage of a mind once abnormally distended by vain hopes. Boswell had been sustained, though not evenly sustained, by his voluminous, windy enthusiasm and by his belief that eminence was only a matter of time, bound to come sooner or later to a man so happily gifted; and now the enthusiasm was beginning to ebb, and there were dreadful signs of collapse in the fabric of self-esteem. Doubts were growing more hideously substantial; conviction was pressing upon the last defences of egoism. He therefore wrote to Johnson, a dying man, with dreary emphasis upon his own despair.

Johnson rebuked him. He upbraided him, once again, with the affectation of misery: and by doing this he showed that he had never understood the mental complexion of Boswell. "Write to me often," he said, "and write like a man." Later, thinking he had been too harsh, he wrote a milder letter, protesting kindly intention and exhorting to firmness. But the unhappy Boswell had sunk too deep into the slough. He was ill, dissipated, mentally aberrant. He complained, not unjustly, that it was wrong to charge him with affectation, and he wrote no more to Johnson for some time.

The last letter from Johnson to Boswell is reproachful and querulous. He asks why it is that Boswell has not written to him. "Are you sick or are you sullen?" He taxes him again with pretending to be miserable, and knowing all the time that his misery is not real. It is a painful letter, nor is the painful effect lessened by our knowledge that Boswell answered him as kindly as he could, feeling that his kindness was a matter not so much of impulse as of attitude or decorum.

Not long after this, Johnson remarked to a servant who was handing him a letter: "An odd thought strikes me: we shall receive no letters in the grave." He died on the 13th of December at about seven o'clock in the evening.

The name of Boswell does not occur either in the will or in the larger codicil of Johnson. It is but fair to add that the names of Taylor, Hector, Adams, and Burney are also absent. Yet Johnson had expressed on many occasions and to many people, both in speech and writing, an extraordinary affection for Boswell and a very high estimate of his value. The will and codicil are dated respectively the 8th and 9th of December 1784. His negro servant, Francis Barber, a person whose character is not known with any certainty, was the residuary legatee, under the trusteeship of Sir Joshua Reynolds, Sir John Hawkins, and Dr. William Scott.

The death of Dr. Johnson provided Boswell with a first-rate opportunity; it was, in fact, whether he knew it or not, precisely what he had been waiting for. If Johnson could have lived for a few more years, if he had reached the reasonable age of eighty, he would probably have seen Boswell sink before him, wrecked by weak or despairing indulgence or by the loss of all hope. Now, with Johnson out of the way, there was nothing to prevent the publication of the *Tour to the Hebrides* (a book which the Doctor would not have tolerated for a moment) and the immediate search for materials relating to the life of the great man.

In losing Johnson, Boswell gained what was of far greater importance to him—the chance of making free with Johnson's character and the definite prospect of acquiring a literary reputation. Now he was able to put together the splendid mass of dialogue and of biographical detail stored up in his journals. The better part of the *Life of Johnson* existed already, it had only to be sorted in order, and then built up into the form and compass of a book. And the book was to be nothing ordinary; nothing less than the Magnum Opus, not only of Boswell himself but of the century in which he lived. The ambition of a lifetime was to be gloriously realised; he would excel all biographers in the magnitude, the brilliance of his performance; he would be something at last, and something big enough to compensate for every humiliation—the most eminent literary man of his time. How fully he realised this ambition he himself never knew; the measure of triumph that he did actually enjoy mitigated the bitterness of his last years and helped him to endure for a little longer the tragedy of hopeless decline; but even this triumph could not save him.

Soon after he had been informed of Johnson's death, Boswell got to work on his biographical plans. He wrote to men who had known Johnson and who were likely to possess letters of his, or first-hand information concerning him. He put together his materials for the *Tour to the Hebrides*. Even the scheme of practising at the English Bar became a matter of subsidiary importance. For the first time in his life he succeeded in working for a considerable period with resolute concentration. When he told Dr. Percy that he did not expect to recover from the shock of losing his friend, he added the explanation that what he really meant was, that such a man could never be replaced; and he hurried on eagerly to speak of his projected work:

"It is a great consolation to me now, that I was so assiduous in collecting the wisdom and wit of that wonderful man. It is long since I resolved to write his life—I may say, his life and conversation. He was well informed of my intention, and communicated to me a thousand particulars from his earliest years upwards to that dignified intellectual state in which we have beheld him with awe and admiration. . . . The *Life* will be a large work, enriched with letters and other original pieces of Dr. Johnson's composition; and, as I wish to have the most ample collection I can make, it will be some time before it is ready for publication."

If Johnson was well informed of Boswell's intention from an early date in their acquaintance, it is not a little singular that he did not refer to it more directly in his letters and his talk. In this connection, it is interesting to recall one of Mrs. Piozzi's anecdotes, dated the 18th of July 1773:

"And who will be my biographer (said he), do you think? Goldsmith, no doubt, replied I, and he will do it the best among us. The dog would write it best to be sure, replied he; but his particular malice towards me, and general disregard for truth, would make the book useless to all, and injurious to my character. Oh! as to that, said I, we should all fasten upon him, and force him to do you justice; but the worst is, the Doctor does not *know* your life; nor can I tell indeed who does, except Dr. Taylor of Ashbourne. Why Taylor, said he, is better acquainted with my *heart* than any man or woman now alive . . . but Dr. James knows my very early days better than he. After my coming to London to drive about the world a little, you must all go to Jack Hawkesworth for anecdotes. . . . I intend, however, to disappoint the rogues, and either make *you* write the life, with Taylor's intelligence; or, which is better, do it myself, after outliving you all."

Either Mrs. Piozzi had maliciously suppressed the name of Boswell, or the Doctor had never taken him seriously, or for some reason he did not see fit to mention him. Or it may be that Johnson was not "well informed" of Boswell's intention until, about three months later, he read the passage in the Hebrides journal where the intention is openly declared. It is quite clear from Boswell's note on this passage, that he then approved of the scheme. But the tour to the Hebrides did not occur in the early stages of their acquaintance: on the contrary, it marks the half-way stage.

At the beginning of 1785 Boswell zealously began his task of "Johnsonising the land."

CHAPTER XII

DETERIORA SEQUOR

THE man who is engaged in a futile struggle with his own weakness, and who observes his own degradation with piteous cries of despair, may for a time excite our sympathy or impatience. But when the struggle is prolonged, we may be inclined to leave him to himself, and to regard him, if we regard him at all, either with indifference or with a despair equal to his own.

Having said that Boswell's life, socially considered, is a history of continuous deterioration, the history of a lecher and a drunkard, it seems unnecessary to go on amplifying this assertion by producing a mass of nauseating detail. Such detail is not only disagreeable in itself, but also insufferably monotonous. Its importance is not to be disregarded in our estimate of Boswell; indeed it is very material evidence of character and of mental disposition; but the repetition of incidents which do not differ greatly from one another does not assist us in our study of this curious man. It is not necessary to know whether he was more drunk on Tuesday than he was on Thursday, or whether it was Jane or Susan that he was running after on Friday. There is nothing gallant or amusing in the amatory adventures of Boswell; nor is there much variety—and there is certainly no entertainment—in his drunkenness. All that we need do is to remember the gradual submergence of this unhappy being, going down under the weight of doom, and vainly trying to keep himself afloat by vows and resolutions without number.

His literary schemes did not distract Boswell from schemes of a political nature. He composed and published in 1785 another *Letter to the People of Scotland*, this time on the proposal to reduce the number of the Scotch law lords. The *Letter*, like the previous one, is frothy and foolish enough, but it had considerable influence. It gives an intensely characteristic view of the mind of Boswell, with bewildering alternations of vigorous rhetoric and rambling absurdity, strong common sense and pure balderdash. The note of personal assertion is continuously sounded, with or without relevance, like the intrusive braying of a trumpet. For example:

"My old classical companion Wilkes, with whom I pray you to excuse my keeping company, he is so pleasant, did indeed once tell me. . . . I exhort you, my friends and countrymen, in the words of my departed Goldsmith, who gave me many noble truths, and gave me a jewel of the first water, the acquaintance of Sir Joshua Reynolds. . . . Captain Macbride, a cousin of my wife, and the friend of my heart. . . . I love Mr. Lee exceedingly. . . . My amiable and honourable friend Dempster, that *rara avis* of the Scottish breed. . . . My friend, Lord Mountstuart, flattered me once very highly without intending it."

There are several gibes at Henry Dundas, and a vicious attack on Monboddo. Lowther is the man; he is to be "kindly entreated" like a god; he will succour them in adversity and help them to preserve their precious lords of the law. He will also, if he is properly approached, assist James Boswell. There is no doubt as to Boswell's political intentions:

"I myself have reason to hope that many of the real Freeholders of Ayrshire will support me at the election for next Parliament, against which I have declared myself a candidate. Colonel Montgomerie has been chosen by the real Freeholders. May I not have it in my turn! I shall certainly stand upon the interests of the gentlemen of landed property, and if upon fair trial I should not succeed, I have resources enough to prevent me from being disappointed. Perhaps Sir Alexander Fergusson may support me. I have asked his vote and interest in a letter. His answer has neither granted nor refused my application."

Counsellor John Lee is exhorted with terrifying vehemence: "Great God! forgive my thus presumptuously, thus rashly, attempting to forge your thunder, but I conjure you in the name of God and the King, I conjure you to announce in your own lofty language, that there should be a stop put to the conspiracy." So it raves and rambles, joking and blundering, and stuffed from beginning to end with the insane vanity of the author. But reticence and elegance are not to be looked for in an address to the people, and if you want to drive your ideas into the minds of the vulgar you can hardly be too personal or too noisy.

In the matter of mere noise and of personal bragging this *Letter* is actually surpassed by one which Boswell put in the *Edinburgh Advertiser*. In this, after warning his countrymen of the perils of the Bill, he begs them not to be alarmed. He, James Boswell, is defending the liberties of Scotland. He is in the likeness of a lion rampant, not to be defied with impunity. "My friends and countrymen, be not afraid. I am *upon the spot*. I am *upon the watch*. The bill *shall not pass* without a spirited appeal to the justice and honour of the Commons of Great Britain. Collect your minds. Be calm; but be firm. You shall hear from me at large a few days hence." Even if we make due allowance for the current style of political journalism, we cannot help suspecting that no one could have written this nonsense without being in a state of mental instability. Yet, at this time, Boswell must have been preparing for the press that most admirable book of the *Tour to the Hebrides*.

Here we have to take into account a very important factor —the intervention, friendly and solicitous, of Edmund Malone. What we actually owe to this intervention can hardly be estimated.

Malone was a year younger than Boswell. He was the son of an Irish barrister. In 1763 he came to London as a student of the Inner Temple, but he found time to visit the Grecian Coffee-house in the Strand and to hear the conversation of men of letters. He was called to the Irish Bar in 1767. Ten years later he was able to settle in London, and able to live the delightful life of a critic, a scholar, and an

M

author without having to trouble himself about money. In 1780 he prepared an edition of Goldsmith. He was elected to the Literary Club in 1782, and gave admirable dinners to his friends. Malone was a very charming man, whose modesty was not the least of his charms. His fine scholarship was never used for the purpose of ostentation. He was courteous and restrained, though invariably cordial, and always ready to help another in his literary work. This excellent man was highly valued by Johnson, and he became one of the most fervent, though most rational, of Johnson's admirers.

In the spring of 1785 Boswell came to London, bringing with him the manuscript of the *Tour to the Hebrides*. But the entire work was revised, before publication, by Malone. Indeed, it would be correct to say that Malone now became the editor of Boswell.

Not only in the case of the *Hebrides*, but in the infinitely more important task of preparing the materials of the *Life*, Boswell and Malone worked together. The final form of these books does not represent the unaided labour of Boswell. This fact is of the utmost significance, although it does not detract from the unquestionable genius of Boswell in recording the Johnsonian dialogues or in building up that wonderful presentation of character which makes his book the greatest biography in the world. The true significance of Malone's help is that he gave to the materials of Boswell a form, order and coherence, a literary uniformity which Boswell alone could not have achieved. The method of collaboration (for such it clearly was) is not known, but the fact is evident. It has to be remembered that the essential parts of the *Tour* and the *Life* were contained in the journals which Boswell wrote up from day to day, or at short intervals, while Johnson was alive. He had to re-cast his notes in a literary form and to bind them together by a careful system of preface, interpolation or comment. His materials were abundant; the task of arranging them was a matter requiring very great skill and patience, and above all a sound comprehension of method.

For this task of arrangement or presentation Boswell

himself was ill fitted. His thoughts were loose and rambling, and looser and more rambling as he sank to lower levels of melancholy and weakness. His journals, his letters, the crazy effusions which he flung out for the papers, are conclusive evidence. It is incredible that such a man could have handled with competence a vast mass of biographical material, or could have worked with sufficient coolness and steadiness to prepare a book of unusual length.

Malone had seen Boswell's material and had realised its brilliant quality and its tremendous literary importance. He had no wish to thrust himself forward or to bring his name before the public, but he saw that Boswell needed assistance, and he gladly gave him that assistance, not only for his own sake but for the sake of Johnson and the sake of literature. He was therefore an ideal associate. He was a man of leisure, with no interest in literary competition or the scramble for renown. His placid preparation of a new Shakespeare involved no haste or worry. There was plenty of time for him to take up other work if it pleased him to do so. And he was not only skilled in editing; he had the crowning advantage of having known Johnson well and of being intimate with the members of the Johnsonian circle. It is true that he did not revise all the actual proofs of the *Life*, but he certainly edited the manuscript and was responsible—to what extent we cannot precisely determine—for the construction of the book.

The *Tour to the Hebrides* was published in the autumn of 1785 and was immediately, though not phenomenally, successful. A second edition was printed in December. It is to be noted that the substance of the *Tour* was composed in 1773, when the author was thirty-three years old; it shows already the full richness and vigour of Boswell's biographical style, even if it does not contain dialogues comparable to the best of those in the *Life*. The glaring impropriety of certain allusions to living men, such as Sir Alexander Macdonald and Sir John Dalrymple, and the unprecedented candour of personal revelation, excited a good deal of anger and ridicule. That a man should describe his own drunken lapses, his bad manners, his cowardice in the face of peril, even without the excuse of displaying Johnson at the same time, could only be attributed to an incredible degree of superfluous and undiscerning egoism. It was not without reason that Walpole described Boswell as a "comic performer." But the freshness, the sheer vivacity of the book, and its realistic portrayal of Johnson, made it popular. It advertised the forthcoming *Life*, and people speculated, with interest, amusement or apprehension, on what might be found in the larger work. A writer in the *Gentleman's Magazine* in 1803 made a striking comment on the effect of the *Tour*:

> "The publication of his Hebridean Tour . . . exhibiting him as the minute recorder and retailer of whatever careless conversations might have passed between persons of any eminence in his presence, excited among his acquaintances a general alarm, that tended at once to hurt, in some degree, his practice at the bar, and to exclude him from some of those social circles in which he had been before a familiar and welcome guest."

It is interesting to notice how it struck the reviewers.

The *Gentleman's Magazine*, always loyal to Boswell, spoke of "this amusing, instructive and edifying work," and conveyed the erroneous idea that it had been "written with the approbation of Dr. Johnson, and under his inspection." The same notice appeared in the *Scots Magazine*. On the other hand, the *Monthly Review*, a more serious literary periodical, took up a different attitude. The opinion of this review is worth quoting at some length, because it shows a contemporary estimate of Boswell and of Johnson which must have been shared by a very large proportion of the public:

> "The general maxim, that trifles become of serious consequence when connected with men of illustrious names, is very often carried too far by their partial admirers; but when a great man is exhibited in those moments in which he forgets his dignity, we rather blame the historian who records his weaknesses than the hero,

who in common life is no more than a common man. If, however, the hero is pleased to see himself reduced to the level of frail mortality, who will then find fault with the historian? If Dr. Johnson was satisfied to have the foolish speeches he made, and the perverse things he did, recorded with fidelity . . . who will blame Mr. Boswell? A terrific and overbearing haughtiness was a prominent feature in Dr. Johnson's character. His tone of voice, the pompous rowl of his language, and his fierce and uncouth visage, had a repelling quality, which few had the resolution or the presence of mind to withstand. He *petrified* a man of common modesty; and his 'No, Sir!' though it might not convince, was almost sure to confound and to silence. . . . But, though Mr. Boswell hath faithfully recorded all Dr. Johnson's imperfections—his dogmatism, his bigotry, his rudeness, his wayward and childish humours;—yet in the picture which he hath delineated, we discern the features of an acute and comprehensive mind. . . . Much we may question and much we may condemn. But the work before us is not of such a nature as to require a minute and critical examination: and if we began to select false and erroneous maxims, or hasty and bigoted reflections, for animadversion and confutation, we should not know where to make an end."

Johnson's own letters to Mrs. Thrale (who read the manuscript of the original *Journal*) show that he was amused by what he had seen of the record. "One would think the man had been hired to be a spy upon me. He was very diligent, and caught opportunities for writing from time to time." But he never dreamed that Boswell intended to publish this record, nor did he see the final additions; and if he had known of this, he would have denounced the work and the author in terms that even Boswell could never have printed.

Horace Walpole, in a letter to Conway, treated the *Tour* with his usual supercilious contempt: "Have you got Boswell's most absurd enormous book? . . . The more one learns of Johnson, the more preposterous assemblage he appears of strong sense, of the lowest bigotry and prejudices, of pride, brutality, fretfulness, and vanity; and Boswell is the ape of most of his faults without a grain of sense. It is the story of a mountebank and his zany."

Mrs. Boscawen, in a letter to Mrs. Delany, took another view: "We are much entertained with Mr. Boswell's tour to the Hebrides; if your knotting is ever at lesiure to be read to, I think you will be amus'd with this book, which will not require so much attention as lectures on higher subjects, and thus may be proper for an evening hour."

Reynolds's well-known portrait of Boswell, an engraving of which is reproduced as the frontispiece of this book, was painted in 1785, on the understanding that it was to be paid for, either out of the first fees received by Boswell at Westminster, or in any circumstances within five years. It should be compared with the excellent drawing by George Dance, made eight years later, and with the ill-natured sketch by Sir Thomas Lawrence. In each of these portraits the essentially characteristic features are the vigilant though shifty eyes, the long, jutting nose, the pursy lips, the heavy jowl, and the great pendulous mass of rolling fat below the chin. The effort to achieve dignity in the portrait by Reynolds, an effort in which painter and sitter must have participated equally, has only made the face grotesquely serious and has not entirely avoided the suggestion of something which is definitely repulsive.

Boswell's campaign against the Bill to reduce the number of the Scotch law lords was continued while he was in London in 1785. In June he personally presented to George III. an address from his Auchinleck tenantry (that is, an address of his own) protesting against this measure. The Bill was defeated; it is not improbable that Boswell's letters and addresses had a certain effect. But the king, infatuated in youth by the pleasing manners of Bute, was always fond of Scotchmen.

The scheme of settling in London and of trying to pick up work at the English Bar was now to be realised. Boswell returned to Scotland in the autumn of 1785; he was in London again before the end of the year. On the 22nd of

December he wrote to Dr. Adams telling him that he was going back to Scotland to spend Christmas with his wife and children, and that he was returning to London in February, in order that he might "go on with his large Work."

In the Hilary term of 1786 he was called to the Bar. He was therefore in London early in January. His admission was "agreeably celebrated" by classical Wilkes.

The new plan of sober industry which Boswell intended to follow, the new hopes of professional eminence, came to nothing. He described himself as being in "a wavering state." A house was taken for his family, but he still lodged with General Paoli in Portman Square. In March he went on circuit.

The folly of a middle-aged man is treated with savage delight by those who are younger, his weakness becomes a prime source of entertainment, and he is the proper butt for the natural cruelty of youth. Boswell had now the reputation of a buffoon, a silly muddle-headed fellow whose affectation of pomposity was more deliciously amusing than his intentional jokes. He had also, what he unhappily deserved, the reputation of a drunkard who was always getting into mischief. Eldon relates a sorry affair at Lancaster, where, he says, "we found Johnson's friend, Jemmy Boswell, lying on the pavement, inebriated." They merrily collected a guinea fee and sent him, next morning, a brief with instructions to move for a writ of *quare adhæsit pavimento.* The wicked youngsters also composed "observations duly calculated to induce him to think that it required great learning to explain the necessity of granting it." If Eldon is to be believed, the motion for the writ was actually submitted, to the profound astonishment of the learned judge, who exclaimed: "Bless me! I never heard of such a writ. Adheres to the pavement? Pray, gentlemen, *what* is it that adheres to the pavement?"

Psychology, if it has not taught us to be patient with all varieties of behaviour, has at least made them interesting and forgivable. We do not laugh at the gestures of an idiot (unless we are very young or very crude); we may regard the idiot with pity or with curiosity, but we do not encourage him in his antics. The cruel treatment of Boswell by the young barristers, and later by Lonsdale and his friends, and by many others, is consistent enough with the rawness and brutality of an age that often deceives us by its outer shell of elegance or pretension. But the effect of such treatment upon a man slowly recognising his failure can only be described as lamentable. Ambition in excess of capacity, a common state of the disordered mind, brings about a condition which is tragic from every point of view. The tragedy of Boswell is that he was irresistibly impelled to expose himself to what he most feared—humiliation. There were still men like Reynolds who were loyal to him for the sake of Johnson; and others, like Paoli, who were loyal to him for his own sake; but it is unquestionably true, that, by 1786, he was definitely falling in social status. Seeing what was good, he followed what was evil, degrading and foolish. The common-sense view is that he lacked will or balance. But he did not lack the agonising sense of defeat, or the knowledge of a crumbling self-esteem. There were times when he stood outside himself and became the witness of his own confusion. He was never totally insane, he was aware of the conflict, but he was never able to harmonise the clashing elements of his personality or to encounter with hope the advancing powers of darkness.

That such a man can be successful in the practice of the law, or in any profession of a respectable kind, is not to be expected. Boswell had practically no work, and no chance of getting work.

A frank friend said of him in the *Gentleman's Magazine*: "His habits of conviviality, his character for flighty gaiety, incompatible with eminence in business, the lateness of the time in his life at which he made the attempt, and perhaps also his want of perseverance, soon stopped him short in his career of juridical practice in England as before in Scotland." So, in a simple way, the case might be put; but the whole truth lay deeper. Things less condonable than gaiety or conviviality had given him a bad name, and weaknesses more deadly than a lack of perseverance were blasting the last vestiges of hope.

In July 1786 Boswell wrote to Percy: "I am now at the English Bar, of which I long wished to make a fair trial. How long I shall continue will depend upon circumstances." By the end of the year circumstances were anything but favourable. He had run into debt, with little prospect of paying back what he owed, and he was barely able to raise money for his current expenses. He had no work. The experiment of bringing his family to London was not successful; Mrs. Boswell, broken by sickness and anxiety, found it impossible to live there. Boswell could not settle down to his biographical study. He could devise no system of economy, no methodical division of time, that would save him; he could not think of retreating to Auchinleck, a beaten man, forced into the abhorred seclusion of the country, and thus cut away from all that could still make life endurable and occasionally delightful.

His new friend, Malone, probably rescued him from the dangers of extreme despair and turned his attention to the great biography. In 1787 Boswell got to work more steadily on his book. Early in the year Fanny Burney was already expressing her own alarm: "I feel sorry to be named or remembered by that biographical, anecdotical memorandummer, till his book of poor Dr. Johnson's life is finished and published." Other people were equally alarmed or irritated or amused, though perhaps a little relieved by knowing that Boswell had secured the help of Malone.

It would have been good for Boswell if he had kept his mind on his biography. But he was foolishly distracted by his political ambitions. He wanted to have a post of some kind, he wanted to be an official, a dignitary, a man of recognised position; mere laird, mere esquire was not enough; he was, in fact, a place-hunter. This desire for nominal distinction, even for distinction of a petty sort, is a marked symptom in the psychology of failure.

A place-hunter naturally attaches himself to some person with places at his disposal. Boswell attached himself to Lonsdale, a man who is adequately described as a professional politician. Lonsdale was virtually able to put into parliament nine men of his own choosing; he controlled various minor

173

appointments, and he was never hindered by too strict a regard for virtue.

All the vapid insolence of a patron and all the humiliations of a toady are to be found in the relations of Boswell and Lonsdale. The spectacle of this relationship, as Professor Tinker has observed, is both pathetic and disgusting. Lonsdale contemptuously recommended Boswell for a paltry appointment—that of Recorder of Carlisle—and he was accordingly elected. Even Boswell could not pretend that such a post fulfilled his notions of personal splendour, but he took it as a sign of further promotion and a mark of his lordship's esteem: "I shall endeavour," he said, "to deserve his countenance."

Even after a long and lamentable series of broken hopes, Boswell could not believe that he would fail eventually to obtain a splendid appointment. He had, so he imagined, a most happy style of political address. He was, in his own mind, a man capable of tremendous and moving eloquence. He was an old Scots baron, a buttress of monarchy and feudalism, of slavery and subordination, of every glorious Tory ideal. In 1781 Mr. Burke had said to him: "We must do something for you for our own sakes." There had been a positive recommendation to Conway. And ten years after this, Boswell wrote: "It was generally supposed that Mr. Boswell would have had a seat in Parliament; and indeed his not being among the Representatives of the Commons is one of those strange things which occasionally happen in the complex operations of our mixed Government." What an admirable phrase for a disappointed candidate! "Let us not be downhearted, gentlemen: this is the sort of thing that does happen occasionally in the complex operations of our mixed Government!"

Mrs. Boswell could not adapt herself to the circumstances of life in London. She was a most unhappy lady. The conduct of Boswell himself and the state of his affairs allowed no respite from a cruel anxiety; and in addition to this, she must have known, by 1788, that she was mortally ill. Whether she knew it or not, she was rapidly sinking to her death.

Her illness appears to have been a consumption. Boswell, on those occasions when he did think of her, thought of her with tearful solicitude; as he had the intentions of a good father, so he had the intentions of a good husband. Perhaps it was the very sincerity of those intentions which made the case so hopeless; if he had been wantonly harsh or deliberately neglectful there might have been a chance of amendment or recovery; but nothing could be expected from a man whose good intentions were so easily forgotten.

When he wrote to Temple early in 1788, Boswell said: "My wife is, I thank God, much better. But is it not cruel to keep her in this pernicious air when she might be so much better at Auchinleck?" This observation is part of a gossiping postscript; in the next line he is talking of something else. Mrs. Boswell did not get better; she got steadily worse. She was at Auchinleck again in the summer of 1788, and she had only one more year to live.

On the 1st of July 1788 Boswell set out from Auchinleck, on his own horse, to join the Northern Circuit, and on the 12th of the month he was writing to Malone from York. He dined with the Archbishop and was immensely pleased with his Grace's burgundy and with the hospitable manner in which it was circulated.

David Boswell had told him, with brotherly bluntness, that he was only wasting his time and losing his prestige (or what remained of it) by riding about from one assize to another. Still, he would not allow himself to be discouraged. He attended the court with regularity, made notes, and felt that he was acquiring a very useful knowledge of the law. He did not lack a fitful courage, an occasional prompting of real manliness.

At times he was morbidly anxious about his wife's health: "I sometimes upraid myself for leaving her; but tenderness should yield to the active engagements of ambitious enterprise." Tenderness did yield, and still the enterprise was unrewarded. And the worst of it was, that the *Life of Johnson* had been dropped for several months; Boswell had been too busy, or too dissipated, to get on with it.

The cloud of despondency had again settled upon the mind of Boswell early in 1789. He confessed that he was "sadly discouraged"; and yet he was still fascinated by Westminster Hall and still trying to warm his fainting imagination by dreams of splendid fortune as a barrister. "Could I be satisfied with being Baron of Auchinleck, with a good income for a gentleman in Scotland, I might no doubt be independent. But what can be done to deaden the ambition which has ever raged in my veins like a fever? In the country, I should sink into wretched gloom, or at best into listless dullness, and sordid abstraction."

Here is the unmistakable expression of two desires: to achieve something and to avoid something. It is not so much the ambition which is important, as the state of activity which ambition produces. There is hope, but there is also fear; and the fear is that of falling into a state of mental derangement.

That is why the prospect of being deprived of ambition, of losing the plea or pretence of honourable striving, of ceasing to be occupied in a praiseworthy manner, involved the prospect of a most appalling disaster. That is why tenderness had to give way to enterprise, or to the appearance of enterprise. The mental health of this unfortunate man depended upon a fiction that was hardly plausible, the excuse for a pretence. And that is why Boswell followed the judges and plagued his patrons and turned anxiously to this man or that man, hoping for recognition and assurance, and above all for the comforts of employment.

Here, if we judge rightly, is the explanation of his enormous vanity, his gloom, distraction, flickering hope and sickness of despair. It was not only eminence in itself that he desired: it was a testimonial of sanity and of worthiness. A practising barrister cannot be mad, a member of parliament cannot be mad—it is unthinkable; but how can you be sure of a wandering, unsettled creature who is only known as "the celebrated Tourist"?

Before the end of 1778 Boswell had returned to work on the *Life*, but he was also thinking a great deal about his political schemes. The dirty game of party politics was leading to a confused issue in the county of Ayr, and he thought he saw a chance of edging in between the manœuvres of the heavier candidates. Pitt, he said, had done wrong in neglecting him; though why Pitt should have troubled himself with Boswell is not clear. "The excellent Langton says it is disgraceful, it is utter folly, in Pitt not to reward and attach to his administration a man of my popular and pleasant talents, whose merits he has acknowledged in a letter under his own hand." What did the excellent Langton really mean by this?

In the spring of 1789 Boswell (in London) had fits of uneasiness about his wife. The accounts from Auchinleck were disquieting. He almost made up his mind to return to Scotland; and then he decided to write for a full statement from her physician. Her "asthmatick complaints" obliged her to live in the country; but it was also necessary for Boswell to be in London, so that he could get on with his book. Again tenderness had to give way to reason, to enterprise. Nor is it likely that poor Margaret Boswell had any objection to his absence.

The two boys, Alexander and James Boswell, were living with their father and were being educated at the Soho Academy. In March 1789 Alexander was growing restive, and was inclined to oppose his father: it was clearly time to send him to Eton. Veronica (who was sixteen) had to some extent taken her mother's place as lady of the house. It was this devoted, unfortunate girl who attended Boswell in his last years, nursed him in his final illness, and lived only for a little more than four months after his death.

The kindness of General Paoli, who was sixty-four years old in 1789, was of immense value to Boswell and to his young family. The General invited them to dinner, and sent his coach for them; he showed for Boswell a real affection and a real concern, and his return to Corsica in 1791 was an irreparable loss. His new friend, Malone, and his old friends, Langton and Reynolds, helped Boswell and cheered him as best they could.

Temple, the oldest and the most constant of his friends,

rarely met him; the friendship was maintained by the exchange of long letters, full of personal history on the one hand and of comfort or advice on the other.

In the later letters to Temple there is an increasing frequency of reproach or bitterness or despair. On the 5th of March 1789: "I indeed must acknowledge that, owing to the melancholy which ever lurks about me, I am too dissipated and drink too much wine." And on later dates: "I am quite restless and feeble and desponding. . . . I have an *avidity* for death. . . . I deserve all that I suffer. . . . O! my old and most intimate friend! what a shocking state am I now reduced to."

Mrs. Boswell died on the 4th of June 1789. Boswell had received very disquieting accounts of her in the spring, but he had swung, as he always did, from agonies of reproachful tenderness to the bland sophistry of egoism: "Do you not think that the air of the west of England might do my wife good? But I fear she could not be persuaded to leave Auchinleck. How different are she and I. I was the *great man* (as we used to say) at the late drawing room in a suit of imperial blue lined with rose-coloured silk, and ornamented with rich gold-wrought buttons. What a motley scene is life." In April he had gone to Auchinleck, where he found Mrs. Boswell exceedingly ill; she was, in fact, dying. The realisation of this tragedy had plunged him at once into a state of shivering contrition and of watery despair. "A thousand instances of inconsistent conduct"—nay, let us be frank—"frequent scenes of dissolute conduct," rose up in his mind and burnt him with a fiery, stinging remorse. He remembered how, in London, he had noisily invaded her room and woke her up from a precarious and fevered sleep, when he came home after some festivity or revel. Even now, at Auchinleck, trying to soothe and console his wife, or believing that he was trying to do so, he had been frequently drunk; he had fallen off his horse in the dark and severely bruised his shoulder. And then came a message from Lonsdale saying that he was about to start for London— and Boswell left his wife. He had airily written to Temple: "Home is her delight in health and solace in sickness. She has nothing of my roving disposition, who may very possibly be one day in Asia."

News of his wife's fatal illness reached Boswell at the end of May. With his two boys he posted to Auchinleck, travelling day and night, and observing, in the midst of his grief, that the journey was accomplished in exactly sixty-four and a quarter hours. Mrs. Boswell had died before they set out from London, and her death was announced by Euphemia Boswell, who came running out of the house to meet them.

If the mental and emotional states of Boswell could be exhibited by a diagram, such as a calibrated record of temperature or of climatic variations, we should see a most violent rising and falling over and under the line of normality, a wild view of peaks and hollows, of ups and downs, of zigzag and obliquity. The death of his wife sent him staggering to the lowest level of piteous despair. He wrote to Temple, describing the scenes at Auchinleck with a burst of sorrow; and then he went on to tell him about the nineteen carriages at the funeral, and the written character of the deceased which he sent to Mr. Dunn the minister, and which Mr. Dunn repeated "almost verbatim" in his commemorative sermon. After the fall to extreme depression, to the lowest reading on our imaginary diagram, the bouncing alternations began to trace their unaccountable pattern of ups and downs, perhaps with sharper peaks and more prolonged hollows. The grief was not immediately removed, its residue was never removed, but within two months of Mrs. Boswell's death Boswell had gone back to his political plans and was pursuing them with vigour.

He made an astounding appearance at the Lord Mayor's Guildhall dinner in 1790, when he stood up and sang to the tune of *Old Jack*, a ballad of his own writing, a ballad in praise of Pitt under the singular disguise of the *Grocer of London*. This piece of buffoonery, clumsy and exasperating as it was to many, seems to have been tolerated and even to have caused some amusement. It was complacently recorded by Boswell himself in the autobiographical notice which he published in the *European Magazine* in the following year.

Indeed, he complacently published the ballad itself under a title which leaves nothing to speculation: *William Pitt, the Grocer of London. An Excellent Ballad written by James Boswell, Esq., and sung by him at Guildhall on Lord Mayor's Day*, 1790.

But the end of political schemes was in sight. Lonsdale was getting tired of Boswell. A piece of cruel fun at Lowther —the theft of his wig—might have put Boswell on his guard and spared him the final scene of humiliation which took place in the following year.

The *Life of Johnson* became once more the main employment, the principal source of courage and comfort. At the same time, the responsibility of looking after his children was a new source of agitation. Elizabeth, the youngest daughter, was placed in a Chelsea boarding-school. Veronica was lodged temporarily with a Mrs. Buchanan. Euphemia was at school in Edinburgh. In October, Alexander went to Eton, where he was extremely unhappy, and James was a day-boy at the Soho Academy. But James was a problem. He spent most of his time at home with the old housekeeper and the footman. James wanted to go to Eton like his brother, but his father believed it best to keep them separated. Westminster was a possible alternative. "To that there is the objection of danger to his morals, which however is answered by the boys there not being worse than at other schools, and by the first people in the nation continuing to keep their sons there."

In the midst of increasing confusion and a more penetrating sense of discouragement, Boswell tried to concentrate upon his Magnum Opus. He was pathetically delighted when he was treated with civility by the headmaster of Eton. He felt that he was not only presentable, but really of some importance—a social, amusing fellow, known to be engaged upon a great work, and able to quote Latin with good effect. And then came the everlasting reproach, "But I have as yet done nothing essential and permanent for my advantage." He was nearly fifty, and he had not yet proved himself a superior man; he was in danger of proving the exact opposite. He was only a great man by virtue of imperial blue with a rose-coloured lining; he was only playing a part, and there was nothing substantial in his performance. His confidence was rapidly dissolving, and the fear of total disillusionment rose before him like the menace of eternal night. Even the Magnum Opus, his last and largest hope, might be a failure. States of elation alternated with states of despair. A general sensation of grief (translated with facility as mourning for his wife) drove him to the excesses that were becoming habitual. "I have drunk too much wine for some time past. . . . With grief continually at my *heart* I have been endeavouring to seek relief in dissipation and in wine, so that my life for some time past has been unworthy of myself . . . and of all that is valuable in my character and connections."

In 1790 he did succeed in getting through a great deal of work on his book, and the first twenty sheets of it were printed in April. A bitter and humiliating quarrel with Lonsdale put an end to political ambitions, and in June he resigned the recordership of Carlisle.

"Mr. Boswell desires to speak to you, Ma'am."

The idea of Mr. Boswell was never pleasing to Fanny Burney. Now, in the winter of 1790, she was ill, nearly broken by the stupid rigours of court life, and already thinking of resignation. She was on her way to St. George's Chapel at Windsor when she was told that Mr. Boswell had sent her a message. The anecdotical memorandummer! Still, he was amusing, he was odd, he was good-humoured, and he had been the devoted worshipper of dear Dr. Johnson. She met him at the gate of the choir.

"I am happy to find you, Madam," cried Mr. Boswell, making a bow, "for I was told you were lost! closed in the unscalable walls of a royal convent. But let me tell you . . . it won't do! You must come forth, Madam! You must abscond from your princely monastery and come forth. You were not born to be immured, like a tabby cat, in yon august cell! We want you for the world."

And so he rattled on, full of concern at seeing Miss Burney looking so pale, and protested that he would make the Club insist on Dr. Burney taking her away from Windsor. Miss Burney, while he spoke, observed that "his comic-serious face and manner had lost nothing of their wonted singularity."

"My dear Madam, why do you stay?—it won't do, Ma'am! you must resign!—we can put up with it no longer. . . . We shall address Dr. Burney in a body; I am ready to make the harangue myself. We shall fall upon him all at once."

But why had Mr. Boswell come to Windsor? He had come to get the royal assent to the publication of the interview between Johnson and the king in the library. He had also come to see what he could get out of Miss Burney in the way of Johnsonian anecdotes or letters.

"Yes, Madam; you must give me some of your choice little notes of the Doctor's; we have seen him long enough upon stilts; I want to show him in a new light. Grave Sam, and great Sam, and solemn Sam, and learned Sam—all these he has appeared over and over. Now I want to entwine a wreath of graces across his brow; I want to show him as gay Sam, agreeable Sam, pleasant Sam. . . ."

So they walked to the rails of the Queen's Lodge, Boswell chattering like a daw, and poor little Burney getting more and more confused and impatient. From his large pocket he drew with pride a bundle of proof-sheets—the *Life of Johnson* —yes, Ma'am!—the finest book in the world! Do but listen to this conversation—this letter! Is not this elegant? Is not this astonishing? In his own manner—positively his own manner, I assure you!

They were standing at the gate of the Lodge, and Mr. Boswell read aloud with deliberate imitation of the Doctor. No wonder that people began to stop and stare and listen, amazed by this gesticulating and gabbling fellow, whose queer fat face was animated by the singular union of drollery and gravity, and who seemed to think it quite reasonable to keep Miss Burney standing there while he read from his papers. "What do you think of this, Ma'am?—pray listen——"

Mrs. Schwellenberg, the dragon of the palace ladies, appeared at her window. Then—oh, unspeakable confusion!

—the king and queen and the royal family approached from the terrace.

We do not know what echo of Johnsonian thunder pursued Miss Burney as she ran away from the anecdotical gentleman with the proof-sheets.

CHAPTER XIII

ADVERTISEMENT

IN turning from Boswell to his book, and then from his book to Boswell, there may be some excuse for embarrassment, there may be some difficulty in adjusting our concept of the relation between the work and the author. There appears to be something phenomenal, almost miraculous, in the fact of such a book having been written by such a man. We feel the necessity for an explanation of some kind. If there is not a tendency to deprive Boswell of the credit for his work, there certainly is a tendency to regard the work as a thing which Boswell produced in spite of himself and with little of conscious design or of clear intention on his part. For this attitude, still prevalent, Macaulay is no doubt largely responsible.

Macaulay, writing with all the vigour of heedless youth and all the unholy fire of personal animosity, declared that if Boswell had not been a great fool he would never have been a great writer. That is a very curious and a very interesting proposition. It is expressed with such truculent violence that whole generations of readers have accepted it without considering whether it was a reasonable hypothesis or not. Here we have an instance of the paralysing or demoralising effect of a loud assertion. But another proposition may be considered—whether, if Macaulay had not been so young, so brutal, so respectable, so narrow in vision and so exceedingly clever, he would have succeeded in making anyone believe such nonsense.

At the same time, we have to avoid another danger, another kind of assertion which is equally unguarded. In our anxiety to prove that Macaulay was wrong in his literary hypothesis we are apt to forget that he was not entirely wrong in his estimate of Boswell. We may well hesitate before accepting the view of an eminent modern scholar, who describes the *Life* as "the crowning achievement of an artist who for more than twenty-five years had been deliberately disciplining himself for such a task." It is not easy to see Boswell as a conscious artist, preparing a great work by method or deliberation, and there is nothing in his own life which is consistent with ideas of discipline. We may reject the idea of Boswell as a great fool who was lucky enough to write a supremely good book; but we decline to accept, as the only possible alternative, the idea of Boswell as a great literary genius. The internal evidence of his best work— *Corsica*, the *Hebrides* and the *Life*—shows very plainly that he was neither the one nor the other; and this view is confirmed by the *Hypochondriack* essays, the letters, and his private journals. On the other hand, the fool hypothesis would be amply justified by a consideration of the poems, ballads, and occasional verses, and by the absurd political pamphlets, taken by themselves. The genius of Boswell (if we use the word in a somewhat narrow sense) is neither vast nor comprehensive; it may be described as an extraordinary aptitude for characterisation by means of dialogue and by the accumulation of minute particulars, in a style which owes more to fidelity than to care or discernment. When he is not exercising this faculty, when he is trying to be speculative or studiously amusing or profoundly thoughtful, he is dull, barren, tedious, and ready to commit the most direful ineptitudes.

What is the essential inward character of the *Life of Johnson*? Is it the warm-hearted offering of reverence, a monument piously raised to the memory of a friend? Or is it really a work of conscious art, an essay in colossal portraiture? Or, as Macaulay suggested, is it merely a lucky accident, automatically produced by the industry and the pushing pride of a half-witted scribbler? It is, if we are not mistaken, an advertisement.

With all his undoubted respect and affection for the Doctor, Boswell had always treated him as a source of personal advantages. He wanted everyone to understand that it was hardly possible to think of Johnson without thinking of Boswell. By friendship and familiarity he believed that Johnson could raise him to the level of his own eminence, or at least to a level that would keep him in the public view.

As the biographer of Johnson, obviously pre-ordained for the work, he would reap the full benefit of the alliance and he would prove, at last, that he was himself a great man, a man of sound mind, and of sound principles, religious, honourable, just, abounding in wit, knowledge and perspicacity; and not only a great writer, but a respected gentleman.

His aim in writing this biography was therefore intensely personal. He hoped, indeed, that the book would make money for him; but that was a secondary matter. The book was to be the instrument of salvation, it was to give him a rational belief in his own value, and thus to save him from his deepening fear of a mental and moral catastrophe. Liberal applause, a friendly judgment, would even now (so he thought) lift him into an unassailable position of security and happiness. He had not anticipated the personal importance of the book when he began to collect his materials in Johnson's lifetime; that he recognised this importance when he was actually preparing his work for the press is not a matter for doubt. He regarded the Magnum Opus with his customary alternations of hope and despair. The preparation of the work threw him into a strange variety of agitations, some of them pleasurable and others terrifying, but all of them realised with the whole emotional force of his personality. He knew what depended upon the success, or the failure, of his book. He tried to maintain an appearance of confidence, but he could not do so. In 1788 he wrote to Temple:

"I am absolutely certain that *my* mode of biography, which gives not only a *history* of Johnson's *visible* progress through the world, but a *view* of his mind, in his letters and conversations is the most perfect that can be conceived, and will be *more* of a *Life* than any work that has ever yet appeared. . . . I am now in strong, steady spirits, which make me *confident* instead of being in *despondency*."

At the end of 1789 there is a new phase of gloom:

"You cannot imagine what labour, what perplexity, what vexation, I have endured in arranging a prodigious multiplicity of materials. . . . Many a time have I thought of giving it up. . . . Methinks, if I had this *Magnum Opus* launched, the publick has no further claim upon me; for I have promised no more, and I may die in peace or retire into dull obscurity, *reddarque tenebris.* Such is the gloomy *ground* of my mind, that any agreeable perceptions have an uncommon though but a momentary brightness."

An even lower level was reached, and the work was regarded with indifference. Nothing could revive hope.

Malone, always enthusiastic about the *Life,* told Boswell frankly that he was losing the use of his faculties; and Boswell himself admitted a state of invincible torpor. Then, as the time of publication drew nearer, he was gloriously elated. "It will be the most entertaining book that ever appeared. Only think what an offer I have for it—*a cool thousand.*" He revelled in "high expectations both as to fame and profit." He rose above all his cloudy forebodings into the clear sunlight of hope. Chancellor Thurlow filled him with glowing pride by saying that he had read every word of the Hebridean journal.

Suppose the great advertisement were to succeed after all? He would be a famous man, a worthy man, no longer shaken by fears or doubtful of his own merit.

But presently the dark apprehensions flowed back again. He lay once more in the deep hollows of melancholy, uncheered by any light. He brooded over the disappointment of all his hopes, his "towering hopes"; he was tortured by anxiety about his financial affairs; he felt that his children were handicapped by having "so wretched a father." And worst of all, his particular king of terrors threatened him with a new invasion; he realised, in moments of dismally acute reasoning, the perilous condition of his mind. "The *possibility* of a *disturbed imagination* reducing me to the mode of existence in my youth frightens me. Alas! what *real advances* have I made *above* that state?" The book is no longer a means of grace and a hope of glory: "I am at present in such bad spirits that I have every fear concerning it— that I may get no profit, nay, may lose—that the publick

may be disappointed and think that I have done it poorly—
that I may make many enemies, and even have quarrels.
Yet perhaps the very reverse of all this may happen."

In April 1791, about a month before the publication of
the *Life*, he issued one of the most inane of all his crazy
poems: *No Abolition of Slavery, or the Universal Empire of
Love*:

> "Pernicious as th' effect would be,
>   T' abolish negro slavery,
>   Such partial freedom would be vain,
>   Since Love's strong empire must remain."

This alarming piece of nonsense, dedicated "to Miss ———"
is a rhyming love letter combined with a rhyming political
pamphlet. It is difficult to believe that any person other
than a certified imbecile could have written such a thing,
and could then have proceeded to the even greater imbecility
of offering copies to the public at one-and-sixpence each.
But this is not all. When Boswell wrote his memoir for the
European Magazine in 1791—a most peculiar essay in self-
advertisement—he remarked with pride that "he is generally,
believed to be the Authour of a Poem of some length,
entitled *No Abolition of Slavery*." And this wretched performance was gleefully circulated by the very man who was
about to produce one of the most celebrated books in the
world.

In the same month he published in the *Gentleman's
Magazine* an *Ode* to Mr. Charles Dilly, his intimate friend,
his adviser, and the publisher of the *Life*. Although it is the
lightest of trifles, this ode is another example of blind
impertinence and of astonishing puerility:

> "My cordial Friend
>   Still prompt to lend
>   Your cash when I have need on't;
>   We both must bear
>   Our load of care—
>   At least we talk and read on't."

For such performances and for such behaviour there is but one explanation.

It is clear that Boswell had made a complete mess of his money affairs. He lent or borrowed with no sense of responsibility, he bought things without considering whether he could afford them; he lightly pledged himself, and was then appalled by the sudden emergence of liabilities. The *Life of Johnson* was to help him out of these troubles, though even the "cool thousand" would not have been enough. He decided, after much vacillation, to refuse the thousand and to retain his copyright. According to Farington, the first edition gained for the author the sum of £1550, and it is supposed that he had made about £2500 out of the book before his death in 1795.

The great work was published at last on the 16th of May 1791. According to Boswell himself it was "received by the world with extraordinary approbation." The use of such purely conventional language may imply exemption from ordinary ideas of truth. The book was certainly not received with anything like unanimous approval. Many inaccuracies were pointed out by writers to the press, and some of them with considerable weight and asperity.

Our natural delight in reading the *Life of Johnson* is generally untroubled by questions of propriety or of good taste. Contemporary readers were not in the same position. To them, many passages were indelicate and some were inexcusable. Living persons, either by direct reference or by veiled allusion, were treated in a way for which indiscretion is too mild a term. It is enough to recall certain references to Mrs. Thrale, Lady Di Beauclerk, Mrs. Montagu, Wilkes, Dempster, Percy, and Reynolds. Confidence, hospitality and obligation were equally disregarded. Johnson himself, affectionately remembered by all his friends, was often exhibited with a shocking lack of decency and restraint. Certainly Boswell did not spare his own character, but that was part of the advertisement, it was consistent with his usual methods of being interesting and entertaining, it was a splendid proof of originality and entirely his own concern. But what could be said for this anecdotical scribbler who, with odious conceit, wrote so bitterly and so maliciously about the men who were dead, about the men of whose friendship he had boasted and who had shown him unvarying kindness—Beauclerk, Garrick, Tom Davies, and Goldsmith? There must have been many people who would have agreed with Macaulay when he described Boswell as "an unsafe companion who never scrupled to repay the most liberal hospitality by the basest violation of confidence, a man without delicacy, without shame, without sense enough to know when he was hurting the feelings of others or when he was exposing himself to derision."

These violations of decency would have been most apparent to the survivors of the Johnsonian circle, but they were flagrant enough to be offensive both to reviewers and to the general public, who were familiar with most of the names in the book. However, the work had to be judged as a biography, as the portrait of a great man. The portrait had qualities of realism previously unknown in literature—it was, in the most literal sense of the term, a speaking portrait. Here was Johnson, thundering, tremendous, so forcibly drawn that he was almost palpable and visible. Was it the real Johnson?

There were people who said that it was not the real Johnson at all; or at best only a part of him, a lively caricature. To what extent were they right?

Professor Raleigh, in one of his admirable essays on Johnson, has pointed out what is unquestionably true, though not always taken into account: "Never was there a more ignorant fable than the fable which makes Boswell the creator of Johnson's greatness. . . . If Boswell had never lived . . . we should still know more of Johnson than we know of Swift." And he goes on: "We come to closer quarters with Johnson in the best pages of *The Rambler* than in the most brilliant of the conversations recalled by Boswell." Some allowance is to be made here for the point of view of a scholar writing for scholars, but the propositions are undeniable. Large areas of Johnson's personality were never surveyed by Boswell, and he had no means for surveying them. His chief delight was to see Johnson engaged in strenuous intellectual combat or battering some helpless creature with heavy strokes of wit. That he was entirely unaware of Johnson's habit of thinking is abundantly proved, if proof is needed, by the silliness, and sometimes by the unconscious cruelty, of his own questions. But surely no one has ever been in doubt as to the relative intellectual proportions of Boswell and Johnson. If Mrs. Thrale had been a competent writer, and if she had been kinder and more truthful, she could have given us a rich, familiar study of Johnson from a point of view almost unknown to Boswell. Fanny Burney, in a few delightful pages, has preserved the memory of a gay, playful, tender-hearted old man, full of drollery and of whimsical humour, who is certainly not to be found in the *Life of Johnson*. Hannah More shows him in moods of boisterous merriment—"laughter ran so high on all sides that argument was confounded in noise." Murphy spoke of him as "incomparable at buffoonery." Goldsmith, Burke, Reynolds, even Taylor, knew the Doctor's mind far more intimately than Boswell could ever have known it. Leslie Stephen did not hesitate to say: "In following Boswell's guidance we have necessarily seen only one side of Johnson's life; and probably that side which had the least significance for the man himself." Bishop Percy, in a series of damning observations on the *Life*, written about 1805, severely criticised Boswell. "His extravagant accounts," he said, "must be read with caution and abatement." The same critic (who had known Johnson personally) denounced Boswell for having suggested, without any evidence at all, that Johnson had been somewhat dissolute in the days when he kept company with Savage: "This," said Percy, "must be received as a pure invention." These are a few obvious truisms, by no means new to students of the Johnsonian group. A series of less obvious though equally important considerations will be suggested if we trace the impress of Boswell's own character upon his work.

Nothing is more likely to comfort a man who feels inferior than the discovery of his own peculiarities in those who are eminent or respected. This fallacy—it is a double fallacy—is obvious, but the comfort is none the less grateful. Our self-respect is prodigiously increased if we discover that great men are not superior to the common annoyances of life and are seriously disturbed, like ourselves, by noisy dogs or burnt puddings or obstinate collars. We are even better pleased when great men give way to the graver weaknesses of human nature—and that is why biographies are often so comforting, as much to those who write them as to those who read them.

Boswell emphatically desired comfort and reassurance. He therefore put into his book a number of trivial particulars about Johnson which are sometimes obtrusive and sometimes unpleasant. He drew upon the dark stores of his own melancholy and thus intensified the deeper shades of Johnson's character. He morbidly forced upon the Doctor ideas which he knew to be distasteful, in order that he might be relieved by witnessing the painful reactions of a noble mind. He gave undue emphasis to mere banter, to words flung out in the transitory heat of argument or the unguarded moment of irritation. He never knew when Johnson was teasing him. He was perpetually trying to get his own vices condoned, or palliated, by some hint of ambiguity in the moralising of Johnson, and in the most unforgivable of all his lapses he declared that Johnson himself had been guilty of sexual indulgence. It is not so much the imputation which is unforgivable, mean and false though it is, but rather the baseness of the opportunism which could thus find a miserable satisfaction in traducing the memory of the dead. He was eager to show that Johnson treated him with an uncommon degree of cordiality, with affection, confidence and respect. He did not consider in what manner he was repaying him. He gladly recorded the Doctor's occasional severe observations about his other friends—Garrick and Goldsmith in particular. Indeed, he went beyond this: he wanted to show that Johnson esteemed him above any other man, and so conferred upon him the mark of supreme personal value.

This consuming desire to prove his personal value, both as a man and a writer, is, we apprehend, the impulse which gave to the *Life of Johnson* its particular form and style.

With such a directing impulse it is inevitable that the portrait of Johnson should be distorted. Most of us, if we have
literary inclinations, read the *Life* for the first time when
we are very young; and most of us would admit that our
first impression of Dr. Johnson is that of a gloomy, cross,
uncouth, irritable and serious old man, with an indiscriminate
violence in conversation, occasional bursts of titanic hilarity,
and a glorious dexterity in repartee. So Johnson must
actually have appeared to many of his contemporaries;
but he did not so appear to those who knew him well. If
we suppose that Boswell has given us a complete portrait,
or even a portrait containing all the essential features, we
are entirely mistaken. How much we are mistaken can be
proved by a few hours intelligently spent in a good library.

In support of this view, let us take a short passage from
Fanny Burney, written shortly after the publication of the
Life. The king and queen had both been reading Boswell,
and both were a little puzzled:

"The King applied to me for explanations without end.
Every night at this period he entered the Queen's dressing-
room, and delayed her Majesty's proceedings by a length
of discourse with me upon this subject. . . . I regretted
not having strength to read this work to Her Majesty
myself . . . for so much wanted clearing! so little was
understood! However, the Queen frequently condes-
cended to read over passages which perplexed or offended
her; and there was none I had not a fair power to soften
or to justify. Dear and excellent Dr. Johnson! I have
never forgot nor neglected his injunction given me when
he was ill—to stand by him and support him, and not
hear him abused when he was no more, and could not
defend himself! but little—little did I think it would
ever fall to my lot to vindicate him to his King and Queen."

Enough has been said to show that the book was not
everywhere received with "extraordinary approbation," and
that Boswell's portrait of the Doctor was not wholly
acceptable to those who had known him.

Miss Burney told the king that she was glad to find her name barely mentioned: "I ventured to assure him how much I had myself been rejoiced at this circumstance, and with what satisfaction I had reflected upon having very seldom met Mr. Boswell, as I knew there was no other security against all manner of risks in his relations." That is tantamount to saying that Boswell could not be trusted, either to respect confidence or to tell the truth.

Dr. Blagden observed that the book was a new kind of libel, by which it was possible to abuse anyone by attributing the abuse to somebody who was dead.

Horace Walpole, who shrank with equal polite horror from the flat impertinence of Boswell and the rude immensity of Johnson, described the book as "gossiping," and pointed to the gross betrayal of living persons, and complained rightly of "woful longeurs, both about his hero and himself, the *fidus Achates*; about whom one has not the smallest curiosity."

On the whole, the book was immediately, though only moderately, successful. Boswell's book, said Carlyle, had a noiseless birth, compared with Croker's new edition of 1831. The sale of the first edition was at first rapid and then more quietly maintained; a second edition, after long preparation and much delay, was produced in 1793. The third edition was not produced until 1799, and the fourth not until 1804. The sixth edition, prepared by Malone, appeared in 1811, sixteen years after the death of Boswell. As the work circulated more widely it became increasingly popular. it was much talked about, and generally praised. But Boswell himself did not live to see his Magnum Opus recognised as the greatest of all biographies. It rose to pre-eminence by gradual stages, not by the immediate realisation of its literary value.

The *Account of Corsica*, published twenty-three years before the *Life*, had been a rapid popular success, quickly translated for continental readers and giving the author a considerable European reputation. It was not so with the *Life of Johnson*. The first complete translation into a foreign tongue is the Swedish edition, of which the first volume was published only a few years ago—in 1926. A German abridgement was published in 1797, and a Russian abridgement in 1851. Yet *Corsica*, in comparison with the great biography, was a slender performance.

The indiscretions of the *Hebrides*, the open folly of Boswell, his idiotic poems and pamphlets, and above all his unenviable renown as a drunkard, a toady and a babbler told heavily against him and against his book. On the other hand, the fame of Johnson, already becoming a legendary figure of imposing magnitude, made people anxious to know about him and to read his admirable sayings. The most violent prejudice against Boswell could not obscure the startling vigour, richness and vivacity of his Johnsonian dialogues; it was impossible to read them without feeling the joy of a new experience in literature. Such a record of actual conversation was entirely novel; no one had imagined that biography could be made so entertaining. Principles and prejudices are generally overcome by the desire for amusement. But poor Boswell never saw the realisation of his "towering hopes." He may not have been profoundly discouraged—after all, the book was doing tolerably well—and yet he must have known that his work had failed to bring him security, assurance and peace of mind. He was not to be the "great man."

Still, there was always the merciful inward glow of self-satisfaction. In his advertisement to the first edition he contemplated with wonder his own "stretch of mind and prompt assiduity." In the second edition he assumed that only "cold-blooded and morose mortals" could really dislike the book, and the advertisement finishes with references to the "circles of fashion and elegance," and with a fulsome babbling of empty praise. Moreover, in his introductory observations he affirms that Johnson will be seen in his pages "more completely than any other man who has ever yet lived." He knew that his book was a good book, probably a great book, and he was right in believing, as he did, that its real merit lay in the conversations: but not even Malone, the most reliable critic and the most valued friend, could have persuaded him to leave out the insufferably tedious arguments, the dull padding, the fatuous intrusions of the author himself with his prattle about his noble friends or his generous nature or his famous pedigree, the insults and the improprieties and the countless errors of taste or judgment.

General Paoli returned to Corsica in 1791 with the rank of Governor. He resumed with energy his work of reform and development, but there were factions in the island and he was outlawed in 1793. This led to a civil war: on the one side Paoli and his men; on the other the so-called republicans backed by France. Paoli won, assisted by England, but he was recalled by the British Government and again settled in London in 1795, the year of Boswell's death. The absence of this gallant man between 1791 and 1795 deprived Boswell of a constantly benign influence.

The General had done his best to cheer Boswell and to give him a reason for thinking hopefully. Neither Paoli nor any other friend could have done more than alleviate or soothe a state of mental suffering that was no longer controllable, but such alleviation must have been precious indeed.

Boswell still endeavoured to regulate his drinking. He knew that he had broken innumerable pledges, but he made new pledges, trying to reinforce his tottering will by an appeal to conventional or superstitious belief in honour. Yet the vows were not always of a severe kind, nor were they binding for long periods. In the winter of 1790 he swore to John Courtenay that his daily wine allowance should not exceed four good glasses at dinner and a pint after it, and he bound himself not to go beyond those limits before the 1st of March. The allowance—nearly two pints a day—does not suggest a fierce determination to be moderate, though we have to remember that the pure wines of the eighteenth century were very different from the horrible mixtures that we drink to-day. He imposed this regulation on himself in order that he could get on with the Magnum Opus; for although the wilder sorts of writing can be successfully attempted in moments of stupefaction or excitement, sobriety is essential to the biographer.

This particular pledge to Courtenay does seem to have

held, more or less, for the period of stipulated duration. After that period Boswell immediately "went too deep" again. He dined with Michael Angelo Taylor, and then supped with the stewards of the Humane Society, and continued with this merry company until he knew not what hour of the morning.

Reflections upon the state of his mind are frequent in the letters of Boswell at this time (1790–1791). "I have for some weeks had the most woeful return of melancholy, insomuch that I have not only had no relish of any thing, but a continual uneasiness, and all the prospect before me for the rest of life has seemed gloomy and hopeless." "Not only have I had a total distaste of life, but have been perpetually gnawed by a kind of mental fever. It is really shocking that human nature is liable to such inexplicable distress. O my friend! what can I do?" "I am strangely ill, and doubt if even you [Malone] could dispel the demonic influence." "I get bad rest in the night, and then I brood over all my complaints—the *sickly mind* which I have had from my early years—the disappointment of my hopes of success in life—the irrevocable separation between me and that excellent woman who was my cousin, my friend, and my wife—the embarrassment of my affairs—the disadvantage to my children in having so wretched a father—nay, the want of *absolute certainty* of being happy after death, the *sure prospect* of which is *frightful*. No more of this." "I sunk into languour and gloom. . . . I could not escape from myself. . . . In short you may see that I was exceedingly ill. I hoped to be relieved when I got to London; but my depression of spirits has continued; and still though I go into jovial scenes I feel no pleasure in existence except the mere gratification of the senses. O my friend, this is sad!"

It is extremely important to notice that the last passage was written six months after the publication of the *Life*. It shows in the most unmistakable way the failure of his great advertisement, his last effort to gain stability and recognition. It shows, in common with the other passages, the fatal progress of mental disorder, and Boswell's own tragic realisation of that progress.

o   197

In August 1791 there had been a flicker of optimism. Boswell had gone the full round of the Home Circuit, and although he did not get a single brief he enjoyed his experiences. He lightly contemplated matrimonial plans. There was a lady of a certain age, with a certain fortune of £10,000. There was also "a Ranelagh girl, but of excellent principles," whose finances were even more satisfactory. Nor were these plans by any means new: he had thought of marrying again within a year of his wife's death—or at least he had listened to the advice of Temple and had made various enquiries.

He visited Auchinleck in the autumn of 1791, where he was extremely melancholy—in his own literally correct words "exceedingly ill." When he returned to London he kept open chambers in the Temple and he attended at Westminster Hall. "But there is not the least prospect of my having business."

The kindness of Reynolds had found him a small appointment as secretary for foreign correspondence at the Royal Academy. It was an honorary appointment which carried no prestige, but Boswell rightly observed, in his official letter of thanks, that it would provide him with "additional solace for the future years of his life." His English letter was accompanied by letters competently written in French and Italian, to prove, no doubt, that he was equal to his new employment. Any employment was a solace, any appointment, no matter how inconspicuous, was a means of relief to this labouring and heavy mind.

At the beginning of his fifty-second year Boswell could be described as a man who was played out. He attempted no further literary work. His energies as a mere private scribbler were nearly exhausted. Pride, but not hope, still kept afloat the wreckage of a broken personality; and even the pride was no worthy or brave sentiment, it was only the more presentable residue of a sentimental and moral decay.

CHAPTER XIV

SPERO MELIORA

IN spite of our improved knowledge of psychology, there are many people who stick to the old ideas of praise or blame when they are considering a man's behaviour, and positively reject the new convenient ideas of analysis or explanation. Such words as judgment or indictment are still used, even by persons of intelligence, and there are few of us who are so bad or so brave as to escape altogether from a sense of moral responsibility.

Everything, in fact, depends upon this question of being responsible. Those who are concerned (as they suppose) for the well-being of society are naturally perturbed by the apparently mechanistic bias of modern psychological investigation; they feel, and rightly, that the limits of experimental method are not always sufficiently realised. Rather let us be medieval, they would say, than have our principles reduced to mere matters of convenience, our belief to a mere matter of superstition. A wider understanding of the human mind will probably do much to discount both points of view, and in the meantime the sentiment of pity, unquestionably logical, is not without its advantages.

Pity is reasonable enough when we come to the last years of Boswell, and even the stern moralist may hesitate before applying to this mentally broken man the test of responsibility.

The outer circumstances of the miserable history show little variation: sensual pleasures are frantically pursued in order to escape from the crowding fears of madness or some open disgrace. There is less and less restraint in the matter of drinking; and yet to the very end we have the same tearful, exasperating resolutions, the same hopes of a final reform. We seem to be looking at some doomed creature staggering towards perdition—a tragic spectacle, and yet lacking all the noble elements of tragedy. The man is weak, drunken, dissipated; his cheerful bustle is not really cheerful, but only the inversion of despair; he seems to fail everywhere, to be everywhere defeated by his own futility, and always incapable of resistance. The end of this unhappy man is dreadfully consistent with the whole character of his life: even here, where he might have achieved real dignity through suffering, he fails again; there is no sudden girding of the spirit in the last hours of bitterness, no fine redemption of a wasted life by patience or humility. To the very last hour of his existence he was denied the coveted graces of respectability and of social merit. There is no longer any trace of genius or wit. There is nothing admirable or heroic, there is no feature of worthiness. Even contempt is baffled by such a total disintegration; and Boswell is regarded either with pity or with charitable concern.

Paoli had gone back to his island. Reynolds, after some months of painful decline, died on the 23rd of February 1792. Boswell had still the companionship of Dilly and Malone and the venerably satanic Wilkes; but most of his older friends were dead. Sir Alexander Dick, Lord Hailes, and other Scotch gentlemen had passed away; and of all his real or imaginary patrons—Mountstuart, Lonsdale, Burke, Chatham, Dundas or Lisbourne—none was now willing to pay him the slightest attention. There were few survivors of the original Johnsonian circle, and of these only Bennet Langton—"worthy Langton"—chose to remain on friendly terms with Boswell.

The final humiliations were near. People treated Boswell either as one who might claim a certain measure of social tolerance or as a buffoon who could still be entertaining. But there were many who rejected his advances and repudiated his acquaintance. "We are not at home to Mr. Boswell." He was known to be dissolute, foolish, unmannerly, treacherous, and often offensively drunk. He had not the compensating advantages of rank or wealth, and his once agreeable reputation as an eccentric fellow could carry him no further. Such a man was not likely to be well received—indeed, he was not likely to be received at all—in the houses of those who were decent or fashionable.

An anonymous contemporary has thus described the final stages of Boswell's career:

"In the last years of his life, Boswell still continued to frequent the societies which he had been wont to delight. But death carried away, one after another, many of his dearest companions. The fickle multitude of unattached acquaintance deserted him for newer faces and less familiar names. His joke, his song, his sprightly effusions of wit and wisdom, were ready, but did not appear to possess upon all occasions their wonted power of enlivening social joy. . . . His fits of dejection became more frequent, and of longer duration. Convivial society became continually more necessary to him, while his power of enchantment over it continued to decline. Even the excitement of deep drinking in an evening became often desirable to raise his spirits above melancholy depression. Disease, the consequence of long habits of convivial indulgence, prematurely broke the strength of his constitution."

In this extract there is a very significant emphasis upon convivial things. We are told that convivial society became more necessary to Boswell, and that he was ruined by convivial indulgence. There is no paradox here. The writer, like a friend, is trying to make the best of a bad case; and you have to read between the lines. Boswell had gone too far. Nothing could have saved him but the drastic rules of an allopathic morality. He knew this, and he still tried to bind himself by such rules. It is odd, in view of his earlier professions, that he never thought of religion. But the suffering of his mind was only relieved by larger doses of conviviality —that is, by deeper and more desperate indulgence of every kind.

"*Spero meliora*," he wrote at the end of a short letter to Dr. Lettsom. He could still hope, in his rare moments of tranquillity, for better things. And there were still ebullitions of ridiculous though soothing pride. The slightest opportunity for appearing as a man of consequence was eagerly magnified, a purely parochial event became a matter of huge importance.

Mr. Dunn, the minister of Auchinleck, died in October 1792. He had been the first of Boswell's tutors and a very old friend of the family. He wrote a long funerary poem on the virtues of his patron, Lord Auchinleck. When Johnson visited Auchinleck, Mr. Dunn invited him to dinner at the manse, and was foolish enough to talk about fat bishops and drowsy deans until the Doctor said to him: "Sir, you know no more of our church than a Hottentot." Boswell had put this into the *Hebrides* (observing, "I was sorry he brought this upon himself"), but he had always pretended to be fond of "worthy Mr. Dunn." On hearing of his death he had written to his agent: "Worthy Mr. Dunn's death affects me a good deal though he was long infirm. I shall be in no hurry as to providing a successor to him, which is a matter of great moment." On the 26th of February 1793 he wrote to Temple, informing him that he was about to start for Auchinleck in order to appoint a new minister:

"The choice of a minister to a worthy parish is a matter of very great importance; and I cannot be sure of the real wishes of the people without being present. Only think, Temple, how serious a duty I am about to discharge. *I James Boswell, Esq!* You know what vanity that name includes. I have promised to come down on purpose, and *his Honour's* goodness is gratefully acknowledged. Besides I have several matters of consequence to my estate to adjust; and although the journey will no doubt be uncomfortable, and my being *alone* in that house where once I was so happy, be dreary in a woful degree, the consciousness of duty, and being busy will, I hope, support me."

Even now James Boswell, Esq., could puff himself out with real baronial amplitude. The reverence of his poor Auchinleck tenants, pulling off their bonnets or dropping their curtsies to "his Honour," filled him with enormous pride. After all, there must be some reason, even for outward respect. These tacksmen or villagers, dear humble folk, gave him the supremely gratifying sense of being a *master*. Perhaps, if he could only reconcile himself to the idea of living among them, of placidly fulfilling the duties of a laird, he might save himself. Perhaps David was right. Perhaps in these romantic groves, dreaming of old nobility, he would find happiness and all the pleasures of a serene age:

> "—*Quod petis, hic est :*
> *Est Ulubris ; animus si te non deficit aequus.*"

And he was now the laird, choosing a new minister for the parish: no! a chieftain electing a priest for his people. Is not this a position to be envied? Is it not worthy? Let him come back to his own house, the home of his ancestors, and there let him find both dignity and peace.

Quod petis, hic est. Was that true? The house was empty, cold, reproachful. There was nothing convivial here. Well might he cry, as he did to Langton a few months later: "O London! London! there let me be; there let me see my friends; there a fair chance is given for pleasing and being pleased."

Clearly, London was the only place for Boswell; and in making up his mind to stay there he was probably right. He depended more and more upon his convivial distractions. In any circumstances he was a lost man. To put it crudely, but truthfully, he was drinking himself to death; and if that fate was now, as it appears to have been, unavoidable, perhaps it was better to spend the short remainder of his life where he still had the chance of occasional happiness.

His daughter Veronica was twenty-one years old in 1793. She attended her father in the last miserable years of his decline; her devotion was unquestionably the cause of her own death, only a few months after the death of Boswell, in 1795. Veronica Boswell is not well known to us; we can only guess what she must have endured, what agony of mind, what physical suffering must have darkened her brief experience of life. The sins of parents fall heavily and tragically upon their offspring: they have never fallen more heavily and more tragically than upon this unfortunate child.

In the summer of 1793 Boswell had a shock which frightened him into another fit of repentance. He was knocked down in the street when he was drunk, his head was cut and his arms were bruised, and he was robbed of his money. This, he said, was to be a *crisis* in his life. His indulgence in wine had been excessive; but now, even now, he would be "a sober, regular man." Mr. Temple had also frightened him by suggesting that he might be "carried off in a state of intoxication." Such a thought filled him with terror. Nor were the moral and physical effects of this adventure by any means transitory. More than a month later he told a correspondent that he was "not yet free from the consequences of the villainous accident which befell him, being feeble, and not in his right spirits." For a time, he was forced to be sober. An excursion might relieve him and give him a little cheerfulness: he contemplated a visit to the combined armies in Holland and Flanders, he had an ardent curiosity to view the camp at Valenciennes.

Still, from time to time, this undesirable man contemplated marriage. If he could find a proper object, he said, he would "act accordingly." It is fair to suppose that he had in mind the welfare of his children as well as his own comfort; and he was certainly frank enough to believe that the prospect of mutual happiness might be a delusion.

He still tried to keep up the appearance of being busy, and he could still meet his friends without disgracing them. In 1793 he went on circuit, and he visited Langton and his militia camp at Warley. "I beg you may present my best respects to the gentlemen of your regiment," he wrote to Langton afterwards, "whose civilities to me I shall never forget."

And still he flattered himself with visions of official dignity. Pitt had ceased to answer his letters, no one could give him any encouragement; but he wrote hopefully to Dundas in March 1794, suggesting that he might be sent to Corsica as a minister or commissioner, or indeed under any denomination. Paoli and his men, supported by the English forces, were nominally in control of the island: it was a great opportunity. And was he not exceptionally well qualified for such a post? He had been the champion of Corsica for nearly thirty years; he was the intimate friend of Paoli; he knew Italian; he was doubtless remembered by many of the brave islanders. Nor was he wrong in supposing that a commissioner would be appointed: the post was actually given to Sir Gilbert Elliot.

The last published writings of Boswell are typically inane. In 1793 he printed in the *Gentleman's Magazine* a poem on a lock of hair, and in the same year he began in the same magazine his controversy with Miss Seward of Lichfield. The controversy was a futile bickering over matters of no consequence.

Anna Seward, the Lichfield poetess, had supplied Boswell with some anecdotes for the *Life*, and Boswell had not made proper use of them. The chief grievance was over Johnson's verses on the *Sprig of Myrtle*. These verses, according to Mrs. Piozzi, had been composed at the request of a young fellow who "had a sprig of myrtle given him by a girl he courted and asked Johnson to write him some verses which he might give her in return." Miss Seward, however, told a different story: she knew for a positive certainty that the verses had been composed for Miss Lucy Porter. Here was a chance for crowing over Mrs. Piozzi in the *Life*: "Mrs. Piozzi, in her *Anecdotes*, asserts . . . But the lively lady is as inaccurate in this instance as in many others, for Miss Seward writes——" Then came the blow. Johnson's old school-fellow, Mr. Edmund Hector, assured Boswell that the verses had been written for him. Mrs. Piozzi was right; or at any rate Miss Seward was definitely wrong. In the list of *Principal Corrections* (1793) attention was directed to this grave inaccuracy, and a long footnote was added to the subsequent editions of the *Life*. Nor was this all. Soon after the beginning of the controversy Mr. Hector wrote to Boswell and gave him the full and true history of the verses and enclosed the original manuscript: they had been dictated to him by Johnson for the benefit of Mr. Morgan Graves, "the elder brother of a worthy clergyman near Bath." The verses had been composed in 1731, almost two years before Johnson made the acquaintance of the Porter family.

Little remained of Miss Seward in the *Life of Johnson* except an unimportant story about "a wonderful learned pig." Her "ingenious and fanciful reflections" upon the poem which Johnson was supposed to have written at the age of three were treated as mere theories which, though "beautifully imagined," were entirely without foundation.

But this did not prevent Miss Seward from venomously attacking Boswell in the *Magazine*; indeed, this is precisely why she did attack him. She had taken a lot of trouble with her notes for Mr. Boswell; she had "covered several sheets of paper." Several sheets of paper, no matter what she had written upon them, ought to have been received with gratitude. As for the myrtle verses, it was immaterial what Mr. Hector or anyone else said about them; and if Johnson said he wrote them for Mr. Hector, he was not telling the truth, and ought to have been ashamed of himself; he wrote them for Lucy, and he also wrote the epitaph on the duck when he was three years old. She was convinced of these things, and she refused to give up her conviction—and so on.

There is nothing very amusing in these arguments. The letters on both sides were silly and rude. At one time Boswell had called Miss Seward "my charming friend" and had frequently written to her. He had professed to admire her poetry, and was particularly pleased with the *Ode on General Elliott's Return from Gibraltar*—a forgotten masterpiece. But now he agreed with Mr. Hector in calling her "this obstinate woman." He wrote in his clumsy bantering style, a hundred times more offensive than actual roughness. He sported lightly with allusions to the duck and the sprig; he talked about "gentle bosoms" and "fair antagonists," until he made poor Miss Seward positively hysterical. She retorted with complaints of "Mr. Boswell's rage for commemoration" (a fair hit), and proclaimed him "the foe of her whom he has so often called friend."

Boswell's last important literary work was the preparation of the third edition of the *Life*, which he did not live to complete; the edition did not appear until four years after his death. His last separate publication was the *Principal Corrections and Additions to the First Edition of Mr. Boswell's Life of Dr. Johnson*, which appeared simultaneously with the second edition of the *Life* in July 1793.

He was by this time incapable of prolonged work or of

serious effort. He was liable to sudden agitations, gloomy relapses, the symptoms of an uncontrollable and unremitting disorder. His disease—perhaps we should say his complex of diseases—began to gain more rapidly upon the weakening defences of the body and of the mind. Even now he did not fail to keep up some kind of appearances. In his better moments he could still be rational and pleasing, he could speak or write with sense and with humour. He was able to attend the meetings of the Literary Club; he could still enjoy the conversation of Langton or Dilly. But the shadow of the last hope was fading; he was getting beyond all possibility of rescue, or even of relief.

He was at Auchinleck—his last visit—in the autumn of 1794. "I am conscious," he wrote pathetically to his brother David, "that I can expect only temporary alleviation of misery; and some gleams of enjoyment." His daughters were with him, but although they had ten guests on one evening and nine on another, there was no "extraordinary flow of company." His practical interest in the affairs of his estate does not appear to have lessened, but there was no comfort in Auchinleck. "How hard is it that I do not enjoy this fine place." In January 1795 he returned to London. He contemplated another visit to Auchinleck in the following August.

From this point there was a rapid decline of health and spirits. Boswell's last letter to Temple (undated) must have been written early in April. The first sentence is written in his own hand and is almost illegible:

"My dear Temple,
"I would fain write to you with my own hand, but really cannot,—Alas! my friend, what a state is this. My son James is to write for me what remains of this letter, and I am to dictate. The pain which continued for so many weeks was very severe indeed and when it went off I thought myself quite well; but I soon felt a conviction that I was by no means as I should be, being so exceedingly weak, as my miserable attempt to write to you afforded a full proof. All, then, that can be said is that I must wait with patience.

"But O, my friend, how strange is it that at this very time of my illness you and Miss Temple should have been in such a dangerous state. Much reason for thankfulness is there that it has not been worse with you. Pray write or make somebody write frequently. I feel myself a good deal stronger to-day, notwithstanding the scrawl.

"God bless you, my dear Temple.

"I ever am your old and most affectionate friend, here and, I trust, hereafter,

"JAMES BOSWELL."

The signature is written by Boswell himself. His son added a postscript in which he said: "You will find by the foregoing, the whole of which was dictated by my father, that he is ignorant of the dangerous situation in which he was and, I am sorry to say, still continues to be . . . we trust that the nourishment which he is now able to take and his strong constitution will support him through."

A second letter from young James, written a little later, informs Temple that Boswell, after continuing for some time in "a state of extraordinary pain and weakness," had made a partial recovery. He was attended by Dr. Warren, Mr. Earle, Mr. Devaynes and Mr. Kingston. On the 13th of April he was sufficiently recovered to write with his own hand to Edmund Malone.

The final relapse took place about the middle of April. On the 17th Boswell dictated a note to his son, informing Temple that he had been "taken ill with a fever of cold attended with a severe shivering and violent headache, disorder in his stomach and throwing up." He was kept in bed, but still hoped that he would recover.

On the 24th of April he dictated a letter to Warren Hastings, congratulating him on his acquittal. This letter, in the opinion of Professor Tinker, was written by his brother David.

The acute stages of illness, accompanied by a good deal of pain, lasted for nearly five weeks. By the middle of May Boswell could no longer read letters, but even then hope was not abandoned. On the 18th of May, however, it was clear that he was dying. His two boys, his two eldest daughters (Veronica and Euphemia) and his brother David were with him.

He died, not suffering greatly, on the 19th, at two o'clock in the morning. Our authority for the hour is David's letter to Temple: the *Gentleman's Magazine* says three o'clock. "His death," said the genteel recorder, "will be most sincerely regretted by all who really knew him."

Universal regret could not be supposed; true grief would be peculiar to the few intimate friends who had seen what was good in Boswell and had known him in his better days— those "who really knew him." His literary eminence was not recognised; he was only the anecdotical, whimsical biographer who had provided a new sort of entertainment. His foolish escapades, his wild indiscretion, had made the public regard him with uneasiness or with downright dislike. Some thought him mischievous, and others only mad. But his friends had deplored the downfall of one who was so full of good-nature, so curiously and erratically industrious, and so heartily fond of jollification. At the last, the number of those friends was not great, for it needs courage as well as affection to preserve loyalty to a man so degraded.

Two obituary memoirs of Boswell appeared in the discreet pages of the *Gentleman's Magazine*, both of them tepidly eulogistic, but consisting mainly of biographical narrative. In the first of these (probably by Chalmers) the writer says: "I shall not enlarge at great length on his character, because I am sensible how very much things of this kind are apt to be misunderstood. . . . Of his Life I can say little that he has not, in some or other parts of his works, recorded himself." After a brief summary of Boswell's career he goes on: "His enemies are welcome, if they please, to dwell upon his failings. Of these he had not many, and they were injurious to no person. Good-nature was highly predominant in his character. He appeared to entertain sentiments of benevolence to all mankind; and it does not seem to me that he ever did, or could, injure any human being *intentionally*." He then put forward the entirely mistaken idea that Boswell had "imbibed a portion of constitutional melancholy" from

Dr. Johnson. And here is a model of kindly reticence: "Of late years he has often complained of this melancholy; and he flew for relief where, perhaps, it is best to be found, to the society of the learned and the gay. Here, as he confesses, 'he had rather too little than too much prudence'; and, with more attachment to the activity of a rural life, he might, probably, have lengthened his days."

Boswell, in accordance with his own wishes, was buried at Auchinleck, beneath his crest of a hooded hawk and his motto *Vraye Foi*. He was in his fifty-fifth year when he died.

There can be no uncertainty with regard to the causes of his death. He had started life with a tough constitution; but also with a congenital mental weakness, closely related to acute melancholia. Unrestrained sexual indulgence and heavy drinking, desperately continued as the means of relief, increased the disorder of his mind and finally broke down a very stubborn physical resistance. Whether he may fairly be described as insane is a matter for investigation, and we shall be better qualified to judge of this after we have studied the body of collected evidence which is to be presented in the following chapters.

Whatever may be our ultimate opinion of Boswell, it is sufficiently clear that he is not to be regarded as a great man or as a figure of profound significance. His character is by no means a simple one, and it has features of extraordinary interest, though it is never immense, never exalted. If Johnson had not taken a liking to him, it is doubtful if we should have remembered Boswell at all. There is no reason to suppose that if he had not written the *Tour* and the *Life* he would have written something else equally remarkable. Johnson gave him the supreme opportunity. Our chief interest in Boswell must depend in a very large measure upon the fact of his intimacy with Johnson; apart from this intimacy with its related prerogatives there would have been little to bring Boswell to the notice of his contemporaries, and hardly anything to preserve his memory at the present day. The sordid particulars which are revealed by his private journals can only be of legitimate interest if they are studied as data of a purely relative importance. Whether the ample and elaborate presentation of such data can be justified, or whether they ought not to have been preserved in the decent obscurity of private archives, if it was desirable to preserve them at all, are matters for doubt; but we are grateful to Colonel Isham for presenting them in a form that places them for ever beyond the reach of a wide, curious and undiscriminating public.

James Boswell has become associated, in a traditional, popular and proverbial sense, with Dr. Johnson. No one can think of the one without thinking of the other; the two names will be eternally joined together in our social and literary history. And there is a good reason for this. The *Life of Johnson* is a most extraordinary book, and the friendship of Boswell and Johnson is a most extraordinary friendship. But the circumstances of this friendship are too often taken for granted. Boswell is generally supposed to have been a simple, adoring and credulous person, who reverently followed the great man, transcribing with rapture the lightest utterance that fell from his lips, receiving with joy the most brutal abuse or the most annihilating judgment, and solemnly prostrating himself before his tremendous idol: but this, if we are not mistaken, is a totally incorrect view of Johnson's biographer.

CHAPTER XV

JOHNSON'S BOSWELL

AT first sight there is something not easy to explain in Johnson's undoubted affection for Boswell. As long as Macaulay's estimate was accepted there seemed to be no explanation at all, and Macaulay himself carefully avoided the problem: he merely drew pictures of a braying ass and a growling bear.

Certain features of incompatibility are evident enough. Boswell and Johnson differed from each other in age, race, tradition and achievement. It is interesting to note that Boswell, when he died, was only a year older than Johnson was when he first met him. Morally and intellectually they were the very opposites of each other.

Johnson excelled in conversation; while the conversation of Boswell, even as he himself has recorded it, was usually that of a fool. The character of the one was virile and massive, uncompromising and forcible in action, rudely generous and boisterously humane; the character of the other was unstable, nervous, enthusiastic, without moral balance and without any dependable qualities of sincerity. Johnson never had any imagination, and Boswell had an imagination that he could never control. Johnson's idea of conviviality was realised in the liveliness of a tavern debate or in the more rhetorical encounters of the Club; Boswell's idea was to plunge as quickly as possible into the roaring jollification of drunkenness, and then to run after the women of the town. In theory, Johnson must have despised such a character as Boswell's, yet he chose Boswell of all others to be one of his most intimate companions.

But we have to remember that Johnson had an immense number of friends, many of whom knew him far better than Boswell did, and who received, accordingly, a fuller measure of his confidence and esteem. It was the policy of Boswell to prove that Johnson treated him with peculiar distinction. The truth is, that Johnson had a more than ordinary liking for Boswell; but he never placed him on a level with Mrs. Thrale or Burke or Reynolds, or even on a level with Langton and Beauclerk; and the mere thought of a comparison with Garrick or Goldsmith would have been instantly rejected. Although he sometimes wrote to him with gratifying expressions of regard, Johnson never thought it worth his while to write often to Boswell; on the other hand he wrote an extraordinary number of letters to Mrs. Thrale and had a very wide and varied correspondence. Nor must we forget, in reading Johnson's words of regard or affection, that a considerable allowance has to be made for the florid, exorbitant courtesies of the period. The position of Boswell in the life of Johnson, far from being one of unique importance, was only that of one among a chosen circle of friends. How he came to be in that circle at all is a matter of interest.

Some of Boswell's advantages have already been explained. He was, at the time of his first meeting with Johnson, young and amusing. He was a man of good birth. He appreciated scholarship and wit; or at any rate he appeared to do so. His eager volubility, however foolish, was a stimulus to more valuable conversation and a cure for gloom. He did not make Johnson exert his full powers; he gave him opportunities—as Mrs. Thrale did—for playing in the most effective manner with a common theme and for displaying a purely colloquial brilliance. In contrast and in complement to the essentially male character of Johnson, Boswell had feminine qualities of sensibility and responsiveness. And finally he had the merit of being able to stand the full violence of a Johnsonian explosion.

There can be no doubt that Johnson was immediately attracted by Boswell. He had only known him for a little more than two months when he suggested the trip to the Hebrides. He said, "There are few people whom I take so much to, as to you. . . . I should be very unhappy at parting, did I think we were not to meet again." Even if he did not make use of these actual expressions, the amount of time which he devoted to Boswell, and his willingness to spend whole evenings with him, can only be explained in one way.

P   213

Nor can there be any doubt as to the original reverence of Boswell. However much he may have changed, and we believe that he did change, in his attitude towards Johnson, he treated him at first with an almost superstitious degree of respect. His letters prove this conclusively. "I look upon my obtaining the friendship of this great and good man as one of the most important events in my life. . . . His conversation rouses every generous principle, and kindles every laudable desire. . . . I told him that the *Rambler* shall accompany me round Europe, and so be a *Rambler* indeed. He gave me a smile of complacency." With an exaltation of sentiment worthy of a disciple or a lover, Boswell wrote to the great and good man from the tomb of Melancthon: "At this tomb, then, my ever dear and respected friend! I vow to thee an eternal attachment. It shall be my study to do what I can to render your life happy: and if you die before me, I shall endeavour to do honour to your memory; and, elevated by the remembrance of you, persist in noble piety. May God, the Father of all beings, ever bless you!" There is nothing equivocal here; the youth is worshipping the hero in a lucid ecstasy of devotion; he feels that he is ready to suffer or die in his defence. And it will be observed how, with a disciple's true fervour, he desires to bring to other men the blessings of this worship: "O John Wilkes . . . let *Johnson* teach thee the road to rational virtue and noble felicity."

This profound veneration, unquestionably sincere, represented the normal attitude of Boswell for a very considerable period. During the Hebridean tour he wrote in his journal: "Had it not been that I had Dr. Johnson to contemplate, I should have sunk into dejection; but his firmness supported me. I looked at him, as a man whose head is turning giddy at sea looks at a rock, or any fixed object." He frequently realised the blessings of this contemplation, of this comforting sagacity: "Transient clouds darkened my imagination, and in those clouds I saw events from which I shrunk; but a sentence or two of the Rambler's conversation gave me firmness." In 1775 he wrote to Johnson: "I suppose my admiration of you is co-existent with the knowledge of my character." And in 1777: "I do not believe that a more perfect attachment ever existed in the history of mankind."

There is an admirable passage in the Burney Memoirs which gives a view of Boswell at Streatham, probably in 1778. This, it will be remembered, is the year of the great conversations, the year in which the assiduity and the reverence of Boswell rose to their climax. It may be necessary to allow for a slight malicious exaggeration:

"He spoke the Scotch accent strongly, though by no means so as to affect his intelligibility to an English ear. He had an odd, mock solemnity of tone and manner, that he had acquired imperceptibly from constantly thinking of and imitating Dr. Johnson. . . . There was also something slouching in the gait and dress of Mr. Boswell that wore an air, ridiculously enough, of purporting to personify the same model. His clothes were always too large for him; his hair, or wig, was constantly in a state of negligence; and he never for a moment sat still or upright upon a chair. Every look and movement displayed either intentional or involuntary imitation. Yet certainly it was not meant as a caricature, for his heart, almost even to idolatry, was in his reverence of Dr. Johnson."

But the phase of idolatry came to an end. If we closely examine the letters which Boswell sent to Johnson during the six years that followed this climacteric year of 1778 (that is, the letters from 1779 to 1784) we cannot help noticing a more formal and a more perfunctory tone. There is an occasional glow of tenderness, an occasional flicker of the old enthusiasm, but there is a change and a cooling of sentiment. More than once he refrained from writing to Johnson for long periods, feebly pretending that he was lazy, or that he was putting the Doctor's friendship to a trial. In reality, he was becoming indifferent. He was getting tired of Johnson. We have seen how, when he came to London in those years, he was careless in attending the Doctor, careless in recording his conversation, leaving him alone for days together, when he might have called upon him at any time. We have seen how, in moments of drunken arrogance, he rudely affronted Johnson, and boasted of his familiarity. We shall see, in the next chapter, how he wrote a scurrilous poem about Johnson, associating his name indecently with that of Mrs. Thrale. And bearing all this in mind, we realise the difference, the profound difference, between the fervent youth who stood by the tomb of Melancthon and the poor besotted creature who could make an obscene jest at the expense of the man he had professed to venerate above all others.

All that we know of the last published letter of Boswell to Johnson is as follows:

"I trust that you will be liberal enough to make allowance for my differing from you on two points [the Middlesex Election and the American War] when my general principles of government are according to your own heart, and when, at a crisis of doubtful event, I stand forth with honest zeal as an ancient and faithful Briton. My reason for introducing these two points [in the *Letter to the People of Scotland*] was, that as my opinions with regard to them had been declared at the periods when they were least favourable, I might have the credit of a man who is not a worshipper of ministerial power."

We are assured that the letter contained "anxious enquiries as to his health." It was written on the 8th of January 1784: Johnson died on the 13th of December in the same year. Boswell wrote to the Scotch doctors on his behalf in March, and on the 28th of that month he wrote to Johnson from York. In July, after his visit to London, he sent the Doctor a querulous letter, complaining of his own fretfulness and melancholy: Johnson replied with impatience, though he finished on a note of kindliness, and Boswell did not write to him again until November. He excuses himself, in the *Life*, by saying that he was hurt by the perversity of Johnson in accusing him of irrational complaints. The fact remains, that he was not willing to cheer or divert the Doctor by letters which, as he well knew, could have given him both pleasure and entertainment.

It would be most ungenerous to suppose that Boswell treated his dying friend with positive indifference. He wrote to the Scotch doctors on Johnson's behalf, and he also wrote to Chancellor Thurlow. Still, it was at Johnson's own request that he consulted the doctors; and it is permissible to assume that he enjoyed the writing of a letter in which he appeared as the discreet, though official, representative of a great man with a claim upon the royal bounty.

Our sentimental gratitude must not obscure our judgment if we are to form a correct idea of the man who wrote the *Life of Johnson*. Nothing could be more irrational, or more immoral, than to say that a man must be good because he pleases us. He must be clever, he must be amusing, if you will; but that has nothing to do with his personal character or his purely social value. There is nothing to prevent a very bad man from writing a very good book; but however much the book may please us, we should not allow it to confuse our view of the author himself. It is only in minds of touching simplicity that we find the author identified with his work, and given the credit for every virtue that he chooses to describe. The *Life of Johnson* is the most entertaining biography in the world: it is equally clear that parts of it are stiff with prejudice, and that other parts are written with an exclusively personal design. We shall certainly not discover, in Boswell's own account, the whole truth about his relations with Johnson.

There are people who speak of Boswell's "dog-like devotion." This degrading similitude is not appropriate—whatever Boswell may have been, he was no Fido. He was not the good, simple, adoring creature who is occasionally produced by unscrupulous or deluded or ignorant writers at the present day. His youthful worship gave way, in time, to a calculated policy of exploitation, and that was finally succeeded by a phase of impatience and indifference. His ultimate relations with Johnson were determined, in a large measure, by the increasing instability of his mind. The error of most commentators lies in their adherence to the doggy theory, and to the belief that Boswell's attitude remained perfectly constant during the whole period of his acquaintance with Johnson. This is not the case. The mere fact of his progressive mental decay, a thing sufficiently obvious, rules out the possibility of a constant attitude. We need not rely upon hypothesis; there is no lack of evidence.

Before we examine the less amiable qualities of Boswell, it is well to turn to the other side of the picture and to find out, if we can, what Johnson really thought of him.

Of Johnson's true and continued affection for Boswell there can be no doubt whatever. But his affection was not such as a man feels for those whom he meets upon terms of equality. To begin with, Johnson was thirty-one years older than Boswell. He regarded him as men of age and experience, and especially those with no family of their own, frequently regard younger men. Johnson had a capacity for paternal sentiment which he often displayed in his charming attitude towards young people and children—it is evident enough in his relations with Beauclerk, Langton, Malone, Boswell and Mrs. Thrale, and most delightfully evident in his friendship with Fanny Burney. He looked upon Boswell as a person who needed counsel, firm reasoning, and sometimes admonition or reproof. He treated him, in the words of Dr. Burney, "as a schoolboy." Yet he spoke with little exaggeration when he said that he loved him. He loved above all things his liveliness and good-humour. He himself needed to be enlivened, occupied, kept in a state of wholesome mental activity or mild amusement; sooner than be idle or melancholy he would read the *History of Birmingham* while he roasted apples on the hob.

In many ways, Johnson could not have chosen a more suitable companion, though only an occasional companion. Boswell, in spite of his own moods of dejection, was always brisk in company. When Johnson described Edwards to Boswell he gave a reason for liking him which he might have applied to Boswell himself: "Here is a man who has passed through life without experience; yet I would rather have

sions of regard, associated with latent criticism, appear in many of his letters to Boswell. Perhaps the most emphatic declaration is in a letter written early in 1777: "My dear Boswell, do not neglect to write to me; for your kindness is one of the pleasures of my life, which I should be sorry to lose." In a conversation which took place in the same year Boswell reports him as saying: "My regard for you is greater almost than I have words to express; but I do not chuse to be always repeating it; write it down in the first page of your pocket-book, and never doubt of it again." It was on this occasion that Boswell, excited by a musical party at Taylor's, felt that he could have defended Johnson "at the point of the sword." Two years later (in 1779) Johnson told Boswell that he was "a man who made himself welcome wherever he went, and made new friends faster than he could want them." He added: "The oftener you are seen, the more you will be liked"—which was certainly not true in every case. When he was ill or dejected, the appearance of Boswell always cheered him. "You must be as much with me as you can," he said on one occasion. "You have done me good. You cannot think how much better I am since you came in."

It was in 1773 that Johnson brought Boswell into the Literary Club and observed that he had "better faculties than he imagined." From this we may infer that he considered Boswell fit to take his part, or at least to behave without discredit, in meetings of the most highly intellectual society. He did not consider him a man of first-rate abilities, or an author of any particular merit. On the other hand, he never treated his learning with contempt, and seldom refused to examine with close attention his legal arguments.

There were times when Boswell irritated the Doctor to a pitch beyond endurance, and then came an explosion, with "degrading images" or vehement abuse. Such explosions are not to be taken too seriously. The friends of Johnson, even the dearest of them, had to face these bellowing tirades. Indeed, Johnson has left behind him picked examples of colloquial rudeness which are beyond comparison. It is not fair to Boswell to suppose that Johnson treated him more severely than he treated others, or that he took a ferocious delight in making him appear foolish. What is astonishing is that he did not round on him more frequently.

Johnson's less favourable opinions of Boswell are shown in a number of passages. They are not very damaging opinions. For example, when writing to Mrs. Thrale in 1776 he said: "Boswell goes away on Thursday, very well satisfied with his journey. Some great men have promised to obtain him a place, and then a fig for my father and his new wife." Again, he was annoyed by the fears and the agitations of Boswell: "Bozzy, you know, makes a huge bustle about all his own motions, and all mine." And in the course of the tour to the Hebrides, he was displeased with him for the same reason, and reproved him sharply for getting into a fuss: "All boys do it, and you are longer a boy than others."

What chiefly annoyed him in Boswell—and the annoyance was due to his own lack of comprehension—were the complaints of melancholy, which he always believed to be insincere. "What right have you to be melancholy?" he would say: "you have a good position, good friends, a reasonable competence; you have nearly all the advantages, personal and fortuitous, which a man can properly hope to possess; and still you fret yourself with imaginary grievances and imaginary fears." Johnson himself had started life with no fortuitous advantages, he had suffered the most bitter hardship and humiliation, and he could not understand what appeared to him the querulous outcry of a man born to circumstances of comparative ease. He was therefore rough and impatient when Boswell pulled a long face or wrote a despairing letter. He was equally impatient when Boswell talked about solemn things, like death and the future life; or when he impertinently babbled about the mysteries of religion. He was also annoyed by his "troublesome kindness," his thrusting zeal, his incessant questioning. "Boswell's conversation," he said to Thomas Campbell, "consists entirely in asking questions, and it is extremely offensive." Campbell observed: "He seems fond of Boswell, and yet he is always abusing the Scots before him, by way of joke."

Johnson frequently teased Boswell. He told him seriously that he would do well to visit the Great Wall of China, and that if he did so his children would be regarded with uncommon respect. He encouraged him to buy St. Kilda, where they could live in a transportable wooden house. When he told Mrs. Thrale about their visit to the ruined chapel of Inch Kenneth, he put in a sly anecdote: "Boswell, who is very pious, went into it at night to perform his devotions, but came back in haste, for fear of spectres." Again and again he shocked or excited Boswell with some roaring absurdity, and he must have observed its reception with concealed amusement. His colossal jokes about Scotchmen are probably as well known as any of his utterances, and they were nearly all fired off at Boswell. In moments of exasperation he went far beyond the limits of a mere joke, he bellowed abuse, he produced a hot flow of cruel and coarse epithets; but when he saw that Boswell had been too severely punished he was not slow to beg his pardon, to give him a new assurance of loyalty and esteem.

In one of her delightful conversation-pieces, Fanny Burney has given us an idea of how Johnson treated Boswell in company.

Boswell had run over to Streatham, where Johnson was staying, and as he had to get back to town in the afternoon, Mrs. Thrale had prepared a "morning collation" for his benefit. Without considering the possibility of any other arrangement, Boswell prepared to seat himself next to the Doctor. He was told that he was taking Miss Burney's chair. This appears to have stupefied him completely, for, instead of taking his place at the table, he dragged up a chair and placed it immediately behind the back of Johnson.

In this extraordinary position Boswell, caring nothing for his lunch, waited for the sound of Johnson's voice. "The moment that voice burst forth, the attention which it excited in Mr. Boswell amounted almost to pain. His eyes goggled with eagerness; he leant his ear almost on the shoulder of the

Doctor; and his mouth dropped open to catch every syllable that might be uttered; nay, he seemed not only to dread losing a word, but to be anxious not to miss a breathing, as if hoping from it, latently or mystically, some information."

The short sight and the partial deafness of Johnson prevented him from noticing the amusement of the company and the stratagem of Boswell. He assumed, naturally, that his young friend was sitting at the table with the others. But presently the Doctor addressed Boswell, and was astounded to hear the answer come from immediately behind his back. He jerked himself round in his chair:

"What do you do there, Sir? Go to the table, Sir!"

And presently there was another little scene. Boswell thought of something he wanted to show Johnson, and he got up in order to run out of the room and fetch it. The Doctor observed his movement.

"What are you thinking of, Sir? Why do you get up before the cloth is removed? Come back to your place, Sir!" And he rumbled on: "Running about in the middle of meals! One would take you for a Branghton!"

A Branghton? Boswell had not read *Evelina*; he had no idea what the Doctor was talking about.

"A Branghton, Sir? What is a Branghton, Sir?"

"Where have you lived, Sir, and what company have you kept not to know that?"

Boswell, feeling that he was getting the worst of it, and not knowing why, anxiously whispered to Mrs. Thrale: "Pray, Ma'am, what's a Branghton? Do me the favour to tell me. Is it some animal hereabouts?"

In this vivacious account, pointed with delicate feminine malice, we have an extremely characteristic social view of Boswell and Johnson. There is the old man, rumbling and growling, though heavily good-humoured, treating his officious admirer "like a schoolboy." There is Boswell himself, incautiously intrusive and ludicrously serious, fastening himself upon the great man with a complete disregard of company manners and completely unaware of his own preposterous appearance——there he sits, with his goggling eyes and his open mouth, inviting laughter. And the attitude of Boswell, if it is still that of a worshipper, is also that of an opportunist, of a worshipper who is thinking of his own advantage, eagerly collecting, with an eye to future value, every scrap of authentic Johnsonian utterance. It was not reverence alone that placed him in that attentive posture. He was thinking of his "rich stores of anecdote"; he was conscious of his "prompt assiduity."

Johnson's Boswell of 1778, though he is not without reverence, is by no means the simple adoring Boswell of 1763; and the Boswell of 1784 shows another marked variation. The attitude of Johnson to Boswell, on the other hand, is constant: it is the attitude of a kindly, though quick-tempered and occasionally intolerant man towards a relatively young companion.

It is a striking friendship, not dependent upon a close understanding on either side. Intellectually and morally Boswell is not only inferior but greatly inferior, to Johnson. The literary merit of Boswell lies in fidelity of record, in the lesser qualities of the artist: anything like artistic uniformity is broken, in his books, by the heedless inclusion of tedious and irrelevant matter, by stark personal propaganda, and by the most exasperating apologies—apologies which are only introduced when there is no occasion for them. The literary merit of Johnson lies in a hard, architectural magnificence of style, in propriety and perspicacity of thought, and in the resources of a naturally vigorous mind improved by scholarship. Boswell is enthusiastic, responsive; a tune on the fiddle or a skirl of the pipes is enough to fill him to the brim with bubbling sentiment. Johnson is critical, defiant, invincibly sensible though sometimes dull or incredulous; to him music is only a paltry diversion, fit for idle fellows, though less offensive than other noises. Between two persons thus differently constituted there can be no possibility of real comprehension.

The friendship of Johnson and Boswell is therefore marked on the one side by a rather patronising sort of affection, qualified by sentiments of a paternal nature and quite aware of the conveniences of an attentive companion, and on the other by a complexity of changing motive with a steady moral decline. They walked arm-in-arm up the High Street of Edinburgh; but they never walked as equals. Nor have we any reason to be surprised; for if Boswell had not been on a level so far below that of Johnson he could never have written his life so well.

CHAPTER XVI

MACAULAY'S BOSWELL

MAN is a being so contrary by nature that he immediately repels exaggeration in one direction by exaggeration in another, and so manages to avoid a statement of unqualified truth. Positive assertion is countered by flat denial, and nothing is more likely to show up what is good in a man, if there is anything good in him, than a persistently directed stream of abuse. Thus, the genius of Boswell, the touching devotion of Boswell, the innocent gaiety of Boswell, and other ingenious fictions, have been called up to refute the savage rhetoric of Macaulay. Let us recall the principal features of Macaulay's description:

"He was the laughing-stock of the whole of that brilliant society which has owed to him the greater part of its fame. He was always laying himself at the feet of some eminent man, and begging to be spit upon and trampled upon. . . . Servile and impertinent, shallow and pedantic, a bigot and a sot, bloated with family pride, and eternally blustering about the dignity of a born gentleman, yet stooping to be a talebearer, an eavesdropper, a common butt in the taverns of London. . . . Everything which another man would have hidden, everything the publication of which would have made another man hang himself, was matter of gay and clamorous exultation to his weak and diseased mind. . . . All the caprices of his temper, all the illusions of his vanity, all his hypochondriac whimsies, all his castles in the air, he displayed with a cool self-complacency, a perfect unconsciousness that he was making a fool of himself, to which it is impossible to find a parallel in the whole history of mankind. . . . Of the talents which ordinarily raise men to eminence as writers, Boswell had absolutely none. There is not in all his books a single remark of his own on literature, politics, religion, or society, which is not either commonplace or absurd.

... He had, indeed, a quick observation and a retentive memory. These qualities, if he had been a man of sense and virtue, would scarcely of themselves have sufficed to make him conspicuous; but because he was a dunce, a parasite, and a coxcomb, they have made him immortal."

Such rancorous violence might have been caused, in other cases, by notions of retaliation or by the impulse of intense personal hatred. There is an emotional quality in the attack which is not readily explained. Macaulay strikes like a mad boxer, caring nothing for science, and anxious not only to knock out his man but to smash him to pieces. And yet a personal motive can hardly be suspected. It is true that Boswell, in the *Hebrides*, exhibited the Reverend Mr. John M'Aulay (Macaulay's grandfather) and also Mr. Kenneth M'Aulay, the minister of Calder, in a way not altogether favourable, but not in such a way as to justify offence. There must be another reason.

Macaulay was born five years after the death of Boswell. He certainly met persons who had known Boswell in his later years, and he must have been in touch with a living mass of Boswellian tradition. Mrs. Piozzi was still living in 1821 —that is, when Macaulay was twenty-one years old. We know that he frequently met Hannah More during his boyhood. It is important to remember this.

Boswell's private papers were, of course, unknown to Macaulay, and so were the letters to Temple and the greater part of his correspondence with other men. Macaulay's literary impressions of Boswell were derived from his published works and from the publications of his contemporaries. His character of Boswell is based very largely, though not entirely, upon the *Life* and the *Tour*, and upon such details as were accessible in the writings of others. All that he read, all that he heard, built up in his mind an image that filled him with unmitigated fury.

If Macaulay could have read the mass of letters and journals now available, it is unlikely that he would have changed his opinion. He would have probably found in these an ample confirmation of his own views. He would have seen full evidence of the diseased mind, the moral depravity, the folly and drunkenness, the puffing and ruffling of insane vanity. He would not have seen any trace of literary skill: he had seen nothing of the sort in the most entertaining passages of the *Life*.

The paradox of Macaulay is, of course, untenable. Boswell, though never in the academic sense a great writer, and in no sense a great thinker, possessed literary abilities of peculiar brilliance, with a unique gift for presenting real character in dialogue. To go beyond this, and to say that he was a conscious artist is, in our opinion, an equally untenable paradox, and equally unfair to Boswell. No conscious artist could have written such poetry as Boswell took pleasure and pride in writing, or would have interlarded his finest work, as Boswell did, with so much nonsense, vanity, irrelevancy and dullness. No doubt Macaulay is wrong in his literary estimate of Boswell: it does not follow that he is wrong in his personal estimate.

The fact is, that a great deal of what Macaulay has said is unquestionably true. He has not given us the whole truth, and he has included several propositions which are manifestly wrong, but he is not wrong everywhere. The evidence now accessible shows how right he was in some ways and how mistaken in others. Any complete study of Boswell is bound to give due attention to Macaulay's point of view; or, in other words, to examine frankly those aspects of Boswell which appeared to Macaulay to reveal the essence of his character.

We shall begin this examination by taking a piece of evidence of which Macaulay himself was unaware.

Thrale died on the 4th of April 1781. In the following month Boswell composed his *Ode by Dr. Samuel Johnson to Mrs. Thrale upon their supposed approaching Nuptials*. We have already spoken of this astounding ribaldry, in which, no doubt, Wilkes had a share. The authorship of the poem has been proved beyond a doubt by the researches of Professor Pottle. There are clear allusions to the *Ode* in Boswell's letters to Wilkes in 1783, referring to a dinner at Mr. Dilly's in 1781. A number of loose sheets of the *Ode* were discovered at the

Auchinleck sale in 1893. Upon a copy in the Dyce collection at South Kensington is the inscription: "Written by Jas. Boswell, Esq., as he assured me. S. L."—the initials are those of Samuel Lysons the antiquary. There are also allusions to this poem in the *Life of Johnson*.

To have written such a thing, in any circumstances, was bad enough. Boswell had been hospitably entertained by Thrale, and had always pretended to like him. He knew Johnson's affection for "Master," the friend whose face "for fifteen years had never been turned upon him but with respect and benignity." He had read those touching passages in the *Prayers and Meditations* where Johnson speaks of "my dear Friend Thrale," and where he says, "I had constantly prayed with him for some time before his death." And yet the infamy of writing this *Ode* was exceeded by the infamy of publishing it, in 1788, with a scurrilous Preface in which Johnson is described as "a very large man, and by no means well-looking, but rather the contrary; neither was he neat and cleanly in his person and dress."

If Boswell had intended to perpetrate the most abominable outrage on the memory of Johnson, he could have gone no further. But this is not all. Mrs. Thrale had married Piozzi in 1784. The publication of the *Ode* was therefore an insult of the most appalling kind, and one for which there was no legal remedy. The *Ode* is dated 1784, but there is a reference in the Preface (and a very indelicate reference) to Mrs. Piozzi's edition of Johnson's letters, which did not appear until early in 1788.

No one, with this evidence before him, can possibly look on Boswell as a loyal friend. So far from being such a friend, he may well appear as the very opposite. Macaulay, we may think, is probably right after all: here, indeed, is a man "without delicacy, without shame." The *Ode* was not the caprice of a moment, flung away, and perhaps regretted, after it had served to amuse a ribald company. It was carefully preserved, and deliberately circulated, seven years after it was composed, with the addition of a Preface and an Argument. The fact is undeniable. What is the explanation?

Any explanation has to depend upon some theory of the mental and moral abnormality of Boswell. Johnson, when he died, had served his biographer's purpose: there was nothing more to be got out of him. Mrs. Thrale, no doubt for several good reasons, had become one of Boswell's enemies: she was yet to be confronted by the shocking references to her in the *Life of Johnson*. An obscene, pointless joke at the expense of a dead man and a living woman did not strike Boswell as anything really obnoxious, but rather as a piece of elegant satire. He did not put his name on the title-page, but he had no hesitation in letting people know that he had written it. This is not the action of a sane man; for, from whatever point of view it is taken, it is bound to tell against him. We cannot avoid the conclusion that Boswell, after 1780, had ceased to be the loyal friend of Johnson; and it seems clear enough that his decay was due to the reciprocally vicious effects of mental disease and of continuous indulgence.

If the *Ode to Mrs. Thrale* is not to be explained in this way, we have to assume in Boswell a degree of acid malevolence which is not in harmony with our general knowledge of his character. If the *Ode* is a piece of deliberate cruelty, of calculated insult both to the dead and the living, it is the work of a man ten times more wicked than Wilkes at his worst. Fido turns out to be a regular devil. But whatever Boswell may have been, he was certainly not a man who wished to be deliberately cruel and insulting.

Malone speaks of his "politeness, affability and insinuating urbanity of manners." Burke declared that his good-humour was hardly a virtue because he had so much of it by nature. Even Hannah More, who detested him when he was drunk, called him "a very agreeable good-natured man." Fanny Burney, although she deplored his treatment of Johnson, admitted that she could not resist his "great good humour." David Hume described him accurately as "a young gentleman very good-humoured, very agreeable, and very mad." Good-humour, we observe, is the prevailing note.

Walpole criticised him more severely than any other of his contemporaries; he called him a "sot," a "jackanapes," a "zany," and "the quintessence of busybodies"; but he did not accuse him of cruelty or malice. Baretti thought him noisy and impertinent, silly, but not malicious.

His friends thought him gay and amusing, a good fellow, though unhappily weak; his enemies thought him a fool and a roisterer; but no one thought him diabolical. Hume was nearer the truth than he knew when he called him "very mad."

"He has used many people ill," said Macaulay, "but assuredly he has used nobody so ill as himself." That he used himself ill, in every sense of the word, is obviously true. No man ever made himself more ridiculous, or ever exposed himself more incessantly to the contempt of his fellows. He did this in no subtle way. He was openly vain, pompous and impertinent. Temple said to him: "We have heard of many kinds of hobby-horses, but you, Boswell, ride upon yourself." Both in what he said and in what he wrote he displayed an egoism so fantastic that it cannot be reduced to terms of mere eccentricity. In support of this view it is only necessary to quote a few instances.

He said in his letters: "I am the true old Scots baron. . . . Imperfect as I am, I consider myself an excellent fellow in the world as we find it. . . . I comported myself in such a way that I was honoured with the reputation of being a philosopher. . . . I am of a timorous disposition, and my education has done everything to make me the slave of my fears. But I have a soul capable of breaking these vile chains and of making me feel the noble courage of a man." Complaining to Temple of his treatment by his father, he said: "How galling is it to the friend of Paoli to be treated so! . . . Temple, would you not like such a son? Would you not feel a glow of parental joy? I know you would." He delighted to speak of his merit, his dignity, his interesting humours. He was, in his own view, a singular and a very distinguished man. Even in 1792: "I James Boswell Esquire! His Honour!"

In the loose collection of jottings which he called *Boswelliana* he has innumerable complacent descriptions of himself. One of these will be sufficient:

"Boswell compared himself to the ancient Corinthian brass. I am, said he, a composition of an infinite variety of ingredients. I have been formed by a vast number of scenes of the most different natures, and I question if any uniform education could have produced a character so agreeable."

No doubt many men, perhaps most men, secretly think of themselves in such a way. But only a man who is mentally disjointed will commit those ideas, cheerfully and openly, to speech and writing. And only a man who is mentally disjointed will commit wantonly those flagrant misdemeanours, those appalling treacheries and indiscretions, that Boswell committed at every stage of his life.

Consider, for a moment, the nature of those treacheries, particularly in the case of people with whom Boswell had been on terms of cordial friendship.

When he published his *Letter to the People of Scotland* (1785), he made the following reference to his friend Monboddo:

"Is a count of ten the same with a count of fifteen? Is a two-legged animal the same with a four-legged animal? I know nobody who will gravely defend that proposition, except one grotesque philosopher, whom ludicrous fable represents as going about avowing his hunger, and wagging his tail, fain to become a cannibal and eat his deceased brethren."

The *Life* is full of such instances, nor is it possible to account for most of them by supposing any kind of personal dislike. Indeed, he is often extremely offensive to those for whom he professed the warmest regard, such as Reynolds, Percy, and Wilkes. He does not hesitate to print a letter from Johnson in which the Doctor says: "Reynolds has taken too much to strong liquor, and seems to delight in his new character." The addition of a note (perhaps insisted upon by Malone) in which he calls this "a fanciful description" does not greatly improve matters.

A more shocking example of this behaviour is shown by his treatment of Tom Davies, the friendly and simple man to whom he owed his introduction to Johnson. He rarely speaks of Tom Davies without a sneer, and he quotes with delight the saying of Beauclerk, "that he could not conceive a more humiliating situation than to be clapped on the back by Tom Davies." Beauclerk himself is spoken of as "one who had the character of being loose, both in his principles and practice . . . gay, dissipated." Hume, the friend of his youth, he referred to with pious horror as "an infidel writer" who should not be treated with "smooth civility." He drew Johnson maliciously to talk about Garrick, in order that he might show Garrick from what appeared to be an unfavourable point of view. The most virulent remarks of Johnson about living people were set down without the smallest regard for decency. Take Johnson's character of the Reverend Mr. Seward of Lichfield, as recorded by Boswell:

"Sir, his ambition is to be a fine talker; so he goes to Buxton, and such places, where he may find companies to listen to him. And, Sir, he is a valetudinarian, one of those who are always mending themselves. I do not know a more disagreeable character than a valetudinarian, who thinks he may do any thing that is for his ease, and indulges himself in the grossest freedoms: Sir, he brings himself to the state of a hog in a stye."

Again, Johnson is reported to have said of Mr. Harris ("Hermes" Harris, the Salisbury philosopher): "Harris is a sound sullen scholar; he does not like interlopers. Harris, however, is a prig, and a bad prig." In the course of the *Tour* we are told how the Doctor referred to Mr. Harris as "a coxcomb."

This sort of thing is bad enough; but to have set down all the harsh things that Johnson said of his friends, all his explosive and careless utterances, is infinitely worse. Taylor of Ashbourne, the old friend of Johnson and the obliging host of Boswell, came in for his portion of censure; and

234

Boswell gratuitously observes that he only once heard him say anything witty.

In regard to the particular friends of Boswell himself, the climax of indecorum is reached by a well-known passage in the *Hebrides*, where Johnson is represented as saying: "It is wonderful to think that all the force of government was qreuired to prevent Wilkes from being chosen the chief magistrate of London, though the liverymen knew he would rob their shops—knew he would debauch their daughters."

Boswell had nothing to gain by offences of this kind: they merely degrade his own character, and that of Johnson in many cases, without being witty or amusing or pertinent. On the other hand, he ran the risk of losing a great deal, and of incurring those very opinions that he was most anxious to avoid. A conscious artist would not have behaved in this way, because there is not artistry in such records; a man with a normally regulated mind would not have behaved in this way, because he would be in danger of defeating his own purposes.

Petty malice alone cannot explain the majority of these lapses, though it may be adduced in the treatment of Mrs. Thrale. And in this instance we feel that Macaulay is fully justified in many particulars of his denunciation.

In 1782 Boswell wrote to Mrs. Thrale from Edinburgh, acknowledging a letter from her, and saying that he had kissed her signature "with fervency." He said: "My dear Madam, from the day that I first had the pleasure to meet you, when I jumpt into your coach, not I hope from impudence, but from that agreeable kind of attraction which makes one forget ceremony, I have invariably thought of you with admiration and gratitude." This effusion is clearly due to his desire to open a correspondence by means of which he can receive news and anecdotes relating to "our illustrious Imlac." Let us remember that it was written not long after the composition (not the publication) of the scurrilous *Ode*. It was not many years since he had sat in Thrale's house, listening to the illustrious Imlac and exchanging with Mrs. Thrale glances which showed their "congenial admiration and affection" for the great man.

In 1786 Mrs. Thrale (then Mrs. Piozzi) published her *Anecdotes of Johnson*, and in 1788 her collection of Johnson's letters. The *Anecdotes* may not be scrupulously veracious, but they are entertaining, and the little book certainly helps us to know Johnson. The *Letters*, of course, are extremely valuable: they are the best examples of the free and happy style in which Johnson could write to his friends.

These publications, coming out some time before Boswell's *Life of Johnson*, did not exhibit Boswell as a figure of any importance. In the *Anecdotes* he makes only one appearance, referred to as "Mr. B——," and then as the butt of a sharp retort from Johnson on the subject of drinking. In the *Letters* there are several allusions which must have caused Boswell a certain degree of annoyance. He retorted, in the *Life*, not only by unduly severe and superfluous criticisms of the Piozzi *Anecdotes* on every possible occasion, but also by the most indelicate references to Mrs. Thrale herself.

When the Doctor showed Boswell his drawing-room, "very genteely fitted up," he is supposed to have said: "Mrs. Thrale sneered, when I talked of having asked you and your lady to live at my house. I was obliged to tell her, that you would be in as respectable a situation in my house as in hers. Sir, the insolence of wealth will creep out." And Boswell replied: "She has a little both of the insolence of wealth, and the conceit of parts." But this is comparatively mild.

On Sunday, the 16th of May 1784, Johnson talked of Mrs. Thrale, we are told, "with much concern," and he is represented as saying: "Sir, she has done every thing wrong since Thrale's bridle was off her neck." He was going on, says Boswell, "to mention some circumstances which have since been the subject of public discussion, when he was interrupted by the arrival of Dr. Douglas." And even this is nothing to the report of Johnson's observations on the marriage of Mrs. Thrale to Piozzi.

But the crowning insult of the *Life* is the insult to the

memory of Johnson himself. The passages in question are very well known:

> "His conduct after he came to London, and had associated with Savage and others, was not so strictly virtuous, in one respect, as when he was a younger man. It was well known, that his amorous inclinations were uncommonly strong and impetuous. He owned to many of his friends that he used to take women of the town to taverns, and hear them relate their history. In short, it must not be concealed, that like many other good and pious men, among whom we may place the apostle Paul upon his own authority, Johnson was not free from propensities which were ever 'warring against the law of his mind,' and that in his combats with them he was sometimes overcome."

Here, indeed, is Macaulay's Boswell at his worst. In the first place the statement is entirely unfounded. According to Percy, Johnson did talk to women of the town, and his own amusing stories of Bet Flint and of others frankly and openly confirms this: his intention was "to hear them relate their history," and when a sceptical friend questioned him, "Johnson expressed the highest indignation that any other motive could ever be suspected." In the second place, whether it was true or not, the inclusion of such a statement indicated the lowest possible level of bad taste, as well as being totally irrelevant. Coming from Boswell himself, a persistent lecher, the whole thing is a piece of sickening hypocrisy. There can be little doubt that he was anxious to extenuate his own deplorable failings, no matter how privately and obliquely, by wagging a moral forefinger over the supposed lapses of Johnson.

Macaulay's assertion that Boswell had no shame, no sense and no delicacy appears to be well founded. Is it also true that he was a pompous fool, a common butt, a man bloated with ridiculous pride, a coxcomb and a parasite? Charity may well intervene, protesting that no such man could have enjoyed the social popularity of Boswell.

No such man could have been so well received by those who were eminent, learned or witty. Think of the people who dined with him; think of Johnson, Paoli, Reynolds and all the others. That is true: but think also of the decline of Boswell's popularity, especially after the death of Johnson; remember how only the bravest or the kindest or the most loyal of his friends could endure him or cheer him in the last wretched years of his life. Is Macaulay right, or is he wrong?

Letting a man speak for himself is generally supposed to be consistent with fairness. Boswell spoke and wrote of himself with unquenchable enthusiasm, and with a facility that was only interrupted by periods of physical derangement. He was painfully anxious to impress on all who knew him, and on the public as far as he could reach it, the lineaments of his own character. He wrote voluminous journals, hundreds of letters, innumerable notes and references. Personal assertion comes up through every one of his books and pamphlets. If the editor had not cut him short, he would probably have continued the *Hypochondriack* essays indefinitely. His deplorable poetry is excessively personal. There is no getting away from this garrulous man who is always talking or writing or singing about himself, always putting himself on paper or in print, or forcing people to hear his long descriptions of trouble or triumph. It would be ungrateful to resist this importunity.

Macaulay has described Boswell as a man of the feeblest intellect, whose original remarks were not above the capacity of a boy of fifteen. This is an exaggeration. He was not a man of strong intellect, and his original remarks are not above the capacity of an intelligent boy, but Macaulay would have been nearer the truth if he had said eighteen instead of fifteen. There is a passage in the Hypochondriack's essay on War, for example, which is not by any means contemptible; and there are scattered reflections in his books which are occasionally sensible enough, though never striking. But then, the qualities that make Boswell so entertaining are not those of an intellectual man or of a man with original views. The question of his intellect or of his capacity for thinking is neither here nor there; it matters no more to us than his capacity for arithmetic. Macaulay is not wrong; but this particular assertion is of little importance.

So much, then, for the intellectual side of Boswell. A lack of originality in speculation does not prevent a man from being good company or from exercising all the resources of a playful wit. Boswell himself desired to be convivial and sprightly, to cut a good figure among "the gay, the learned and the elegant."

He certainly considered himself to be vastly amusing. He wrote down choice fragments of his own conversation, he recorded an immense number of what seemed to him the best examples of his aphoristic fancy. It was not in repartee that he believed himself to excel, but in maxim or metaphor, in rapid allusion or in subtle conceit. If Macaulay is right, Boswell deceived himself most egregiously; instead of being amusing, he was only fatuous or absurd or miserably idiotic.

Again we are led to the conclusion that, in this particular also, Macaulay is undoubtedly right. No one has recorded a single good thing of Boswell's, and he himself has recorded none, with the exception of that facetious remark on the bridge at Blenheim. His fatuity in pursuing and worrying to death the metaphors of Johnson is enough to prove that he was destitute of what is known as humour. Many of the Doctor's most enlivening flippancies were thus brought down and trampled upon by Boswell. His own part in the Johnsonian conversations is nearly always lamentable, however much it may contribute to the organised reality of the whole.

But suppose we adopt the "conscious artist" theory, and assume that Boswell sacrificed himself gladly to the brilliance of Johnson? At that rate, we must turn to what he put down in his archives as the chosen, precious examples of his own wit. We need only give two specimens:

"Boswell and Erskine were one day sauntering in Leicester Fields and talking of the famous scheme of squaring the circle. 'Come, come,' said Boswell, 'let us circle the square, and that will be as good.' So these two

poets took a walk round the square, laughing very heartily
at the conceit."——"Lady Di Beauclerk said to me (Boswell)
she understood Mrs. V—— was an idiot. I said I was
told so too; but when I was introduced to her did not find
it to be true. 'Or perhaps,' said I, 'her being less an idiot
than I imagined her to be may have made me think she
was not an idiot at all.' 'I think,' said Lady Di, 'she is
bad enough, if that be all that a lawyer has to say for her,
that she is only less an idiot than he imagined.' Said I,
'There are different kinds of idiots as of dogs, water idiots
and land idiots, and so on.' 'I think,' said Lady Di, 'that
is worth writing down.'"

Macaulay scores again, for surely no one but a fool could
have uttered and complacently recorded, such hollow
inanities. There are hundreds of other examples, equally
exasperating and equally futile.

Then we are told that Boswell prostrated himself before
men of rank, that he was a toady, a lick-spittle, a place-
hunter, a snob, and a parasite. And again he is condemned
by his own words. Whenever he gets a chance he addresses
noblemen in terms of servile flattery. Chatham, he says,
"has filled many of his best hours with that noble admiration
which a disinterested soul can enjoy in the bower of philosophy"—rhetoric which is both fulsome and without
meaning. The admission of such vulgar fellows as Gibbon
and Adam Smith to the Literary Club fills him with horror:
the Club, he declares, has lost its "select merit." He says of
Gibbon, "He is an ugly, affected, disgusting fellow and
poisons our literary club to me." He loves to refer mysteri-
ously to "great personages" and "important quarters," with
liberal use of italics and of capitals, although he was never
familiar with the first and seldom admitted to the second.
When he wishes to excuse his own lack of taste, he shelters
himself "under the authority of a very fashionable baronet
in the brilliant world," as though nothing more need be
said. The sermons of Mr. Carr were bound to be good,
because Lord Mansfield had said so. He agreed with
Johnson, that if you were invited to dine on the same day

with the first Duke and the first genius in England, you would not know which to choose. Everything has to be sacrificed, if necessary, to the dignity of rank: "It is, no doubt, to be wished, that a proper degree of attention should be shown by great men to their early friends. But if either from obtuse insensibility to difference of situation, or presumptuous forwardness, which will not submit even to an exteriour observance of it, the dignity of a high place cannot be preserved . . . encroachment must be repelled, and the kinder feelings sacrificed." Snobbery can no go further. The dignity of place must be upheld, even at the cost of humanity and friendship: a resolution so extreme is almost religious, almost heroic. The first duty of man is to respect the glorious principle of subordination.

Again and again Boswell is content—nay, eager—to exhibit himself as a toady. "Talking of the danger of being mortified by rejection, when making approaches to the acquaintance of the great, I observed, 'I am, however, generally for trying.'"

He is also desirous of parading, at every opportunity, the nobility of his descent. He draws your attention, by text or footnote, to the important fact that the blood of Bruce flows in his veins, that he is a true Scots gentleman, that his grandmother was Veronica Countess of Kincardine, that the pride of ancient blood is his "predominant passion," that he was (occasionally) treated with the reverence due to his birth, that his mind was "ever impressed with admiration for persons of high birth," that he was anxious to promote "the continuation of feudal authority," that he was an elegant fellow, quite familiar with duchesses, and so on. And here we are confining ourselves, almost entirely, to the information which he was pleased and proud to set before the public at large.

And yet this born gentleman could behave with treachery and rudeness; he could play all the tricks of a mischievous ape, and show all the social insensibility of a raw buffoon. He thought it very amusing to make Lady Lochbuy ask Johnson if he would have some cold sheep's head, and then to laugh at the Doctor's anger and the poor lady's confusion: what he actually says on this occasion is, "I sat quietly by and enjoyed my success." He thought it was quite proper to run about telling people what other people had said about them.

His jackdaw chatter committed him to the wildest impudences and the most foolish dilemmas. It is quite true that he was often a butt, an eavesdropper and a laughing-stock. But the point of vital importance in all this is to remember that he openly published, as proper themes for glory and congratulation, and as the means of advancing his prestige, innumerable examples of his folly and misde-meanour. The man who can do such a thing is obviously a man lacking in mental balance.

Macaulay had a strong case, but he made too much of it. He was carried away by the terrific impulse of hatred, which we do not pretend to explain, and he made Boswell so com-pletely imbecile that neither he nor anyone else could under-stand how this imbecile had written a great book. The sheer vehemence of his fury drove Macaulay to the acceptance of a paradox which even the famous boy of fifteen can easily refute. Boswell, no doubt, was a fool; but if he was nothing more than Macaulay's idiot he could no more have written the *Life of Johnson*, or even the *Hypochondriack* papers, than he could have jumped over the dome of St. Paul's.

The Boswell of Lord Macaulay represents, not by any means the totality of Boswell himself, but certainly a number of his most obvious features. It is like one of those vicious caricatures, those masterly caricatures by Gilray or Bunbury, in which a brutal exuberance of detail gives you the most unfavourable and yet the most unmistakable picture of the victim. The special, diabolical merit of a caricature is that it does give an immediate and memorable impression of personality. If you have ever seen one of Gilray's cruel etchings of George III., you will never again think of George III. without being reminded of Gilray's virulent though amusing satire. So it is with Macaulay and Boswell. If you have read Macaulay's description, you will be affected, to a greater or lesser extent, by his burning animosity. There are two dangers here: one is, that you may accept Macaulay's view of Boswell as a complete portrait, whereas it is palpably very incomplete indeed; and the other is that, in your anxiety to avoid prejudice where it is so apparent and to show your superiority to antiquated notions, you will fail to see that Macaulay has described certain aspects of Boswell with deadly accuracy.

CHAPTER XVII

AUTOBIOGRAPHY

THERE are several popular illusions concerning autobiography. One is, that a man becomes truthful the moment he sits down to write about himself. Another is, that he wishes to be equally truthful about others. And a third is, that autobiography is writing of a special and privileged character, almost of a sacred character.

Naturally there is a difference between writing intended for publication and writing which is intended only for private perusal with a view to relieving the mind of the writer or preserving his deeds and memory in family archives. Whether private papers ought to be made public in any form (unless they are historically important) is open to question. But we assume that a man is more likely to reveal himself in his private journals than he is in a work designed for the press.

These considerations are only partially true in the case of Boswell. When he wrote for himself he merely accumulated detail upon detail of a character already displayed in his books and letters. His frankness—if that is the proper word—his garrulity and lack of restraint led him to expose himself to his friends and the world with unexampled and unedifying freedom. Little is to be gained, if anything is to be gained, by a minute knowledge of squalid amours and of a drunkard's fall. By reading page after page of sickening particulars, with no illumination of wit or brilliance of expression, no subtle note of character, no interesting reference to contemporary life, we may well be dejected and inclined to wonder what serious purpose can justify the printing of such pages. It is enough to know that Boswell's private life did not differ from that of other weak and vicious men; and if weak and vicious men put their lives into journals, and those journals are published, it is difficult to see who is the better for it.

Our chief concern, both with the journals and with the published work, is to discover how Boswell saw himself and how he wished others to see him. It is only by studying the hopes and illusions of a man that we are able to arrive at a full knowledge of his character.

Nothing is more characteristic of Boswell than his anxiety to push himself before the public. He would have delighted in the resources of modern publicity and he would certainly have availed himself joyfully of all the forms of trumpeting advertisement. As it was, he did his best. It is said that he wrote for the papers under at least forty-five pseudonyms, and it is not possible to trace every paragraph that he either composed or inspired. He wrote, in nearly every case, about himself. The notes about James Boswell, Esq., which occur so frequently in the *London Chronicle*, were all written by James Boswell, Esq. He was a pioneer of publicity methods. Whatever he could do to work up interest in himself and his books he did, with a blatancy of self-assurance almost beyond the more vulgar and more aggressive methods of to-day.

It is for this reason that students of Boswell have called him "incredible." He is not incredible if you consider him as a mentally disordered man trying to stabilise his character by setting up a pattern of what he wished to be in reality; trying to fix upon the popular mind as well as upon his own, firm notions of his excellence, his eminence, his good breeding, worthiness and romantic genius.

To coincide with the publication of the *Life*, he printed in the *European Magazine* an extraordinary memoir of himself. Ingenious amplification of this memoir was at one time the usual practice of those who wrote biographical notes on Boswell.

The most peculiar thing about the memoir is the combination of simplicity with arrogance. The author wants to appear as the singular and accomplished man, the scholar and the wit, who has completed that stupendous work, the *Life of Samuel Johnson*. In order to do this he gaily displays himself as the Cub at Newmarket and the King of the Soapers. He is, according to himself, still recognisable

as the King of the Soapers. He is still in love with half a
score of ladies, and he can still exhibit "that egotism and
self-applause . . . yet, it would seem, with a conscious smile."
And he quotes his ridiculous lines:

> "Boswell is modest enough,
> Himself not *quite* Phoebus he thinks."

He goes on with an account of his career which would
certainly have been "incredible" in the case of any other
man. He does not hesitate to tell us about the silly prologue
he composed for Mr. Ross to speak at the opening of the
Theatre Royal in Edinburgh, and how the effect of this
prologue was "aided by friends properly planted in different
parts of the theatre." He describes his courtship and
marriage with eager confidence; but the high level of
absurdity is reached when he deals with the period immediately following the death of his wife:

> "He however did not resign himself to unavailing grief,
> but endeavoured to dissipate his melancholy by occupation
> and amusement in the metropolis, in which he enjoys
> perhaps as extensive and varied an acquaintance as any
> man of his time. We find him at least extremely gay,
> and occasionally exercising his poetical talents. At the
> last Lord Mayor's Day's festal board he sang with great
> applause a State Ballad of his own composition, entitled
> *The Grocer of London*, in praise of Mr. Pitt's conduct in
> the dispute with Spain. . . . He is generally believed to
> be the Authour of a Poem of some length, entitled *No
> Abolition of Slavery; or the Universal Empire of Love*. . . .
> But his attention to the business of Westminster Hall
> has been chiefly interrupted by his great literary work. . . .
> *The Life of Dr Johnson*, which he has at last published . . .
> and which has been received by the world with extra-
> ordinary approbation."

Here is a man doing all that he can to defeat his own
purpose; a fool prating of his folly and proclaiming his lack

of taste; mentioning, almost in the same breath, a poem so bad that it might have been written by a defective child, and then—*The Life of Johnson*. Only the ghastly inconsequence of a wandering mind can account for such a memoir, and for the zealous concern with which it was forced upon the attention of the literary public.

Boswell himself knew that he was mad: or, if that is too sharp and shocking a word, knew that he was mentally abnormal. There are many passages in his journals and letters where he refers to this melancholy knowledge, and many passages in all his writings where he conveys this knowledge without intending to do so. He was aware of inherent qualities that prevented him from ever being what he desired to be; he knew that he was followed, wherever he went, by the black dog of his fears. Perhaps he would have been happier if he had been more completely mad, instead of oscillating, as he did, between the regions of lunacy and lucidity. His illusions and his ambitions were never totally destroyed, and as their substance became less, their attentuated phantasmal presence became more insistent and more terrifying. Consider, now, what he was and what he intended to be.

He gives us a little picture of himself in the *Hebrides*: "Think," he says, "of a gentleman of ancient blood, the pride of which was his predominant passion. . . . His inclination was to be a soldier; but his father, a respectable judge, had pressed him into the profession of the law. He had travelled a good deal, and seen many varieties of human life. He had thought more than anybody supposed, and had a pretty good stock of general learning and knowledge. . . . He had rather too little, than too much, prudence; and, his imagination being lively, he often said things of which the effect was very different from the intention." In the same book he says: "I am, I flatter myself, completely a citizen of the world. In my travels through Holland, Germany, Switzerland, Italy, Corsica, France, I never felt myself from home; and I sincerely love 'every kindred and tongue and people and nation.'"

He wanted to be a liberal man and a good man. "I would,

in due time, be a *Nestor*, an elder of the people." And he said to Johnson when they were at Southill together: "My dear Sir, I would fain be a good man; and I am very good now. I fear God and honour and King; I wish to do no ill, and to be benevolent to all mankind." The reply of Johnson showed an extraordinary degree of insight: "Do not, Sir, accustom yourself to *impressions*. There is a middle state of mind between conviction and hypocrisy, of which many are unconscious." In saying this, the Doctor described, no doubt with greater accuracy than he was aware of, the middle state of Boswell.

He made no secret of his attitude towards great men, and it seemed to him a reasonable attitude. When he was with Johnson at Dunvegan he was harshly snubbed by Colonel Macleod. They were talking about Sweden, and Boswell said it would be a fine thing if they went there and had a talk with the king. "I doubt, Sir," said Johnson, "if he would speak to us." "I am sure," said Macleod, "that Mr. Boswell would speak to *him*." Boswell, having recorded all this, takes advantage of the opening: "Let me offer a short defence of that propensity in my disposition, to which this gentleman alluded. It has procured me much happiness. I hope it does not deserve so hard a name as either forwardness or impudence. If I know myself, it is nothing more than an eagerness to share the society of men distinguished either by their rank or their talents, and a diligence to attain what I desire." He was immensely pleased when Johnson, confirming him in his respect for ancient families and their habitations, assured Lady Macleod, "with a strong voice and most determined manner"—"Madam, rather than quit the old rock, Boswell would live in the pit; he would make his bed in the dungeon."

Of his own dignity as a laird he speaks frequently: "I reminded him (Johnson) that the Laird of Auchinleck had an elegant house, in front of which he could ride ten miles forward upon his own territories, upon which he had upward of six hundred people attached to him; that the family seat was rich in natural romantick beauties. . . . That when all this was considered, I should certainly pass a part of the year at home, and enjoy it the more from variety, and from bringing with me a share of the intellectual stores of the metropolis." Again Johnson gave evidence of his acute vision: he smiled at Boswell and said he "hoped it might be as he supposed."

In theory he was a feudalist of the romantic order, with rigid views upon subordination. He was a variant of that curious biological freak, the true conservative. Nothing, in his opinion, ought ever to be changed. "I am averse to change any old custom whatsoever," he says in one of the *Hypochondriack* essays, "even the most minute, having a certain pleasure in what has been long practised, and imagining that no new contrivance would do as well. . . . Innovations in the laws and constitutions of a country are ever to be dreaded." Upon every possible occasion he added the title of Esquire to his name—a title to which, unlike our modern users, he had every right, but which he certainly contrived to make ridiculous. He realised, no doubt, that conservatism is the best of all formulas for a born Boswell. Once, when he was talking to Dr. Johnson about the respect due to "old families," the Doctor observed: "Sir, you have a right to that kind of respect, and are arguing for yourself" —which was quite true.

On the subject of his relations with women his printed references are comparatively reserved, though his references to drinking are surprisingly frank. He freely quotes a friend who spoke of himself and Boswell as "men who live laxly in the world," and who were inconsistent when they shunned an infidel one day and got drunk the next day. He sets down at great length, and in many places, his arguments in favour of wine. He is cheered by learning from Johnson that "Isaac Hawkins Browne drank freely for thirty years," and then wrote a poem called *De Animi Immortalitate*. He insists upon all the world knowing of his drunken carousals in the Hebrides and of his drunken insolence to ladies and to Johnson himself. Yet he could moralise about this failing, or soothe himself with plausible sophistry. Take, for example, the engaging candour of his reflections after the revel at Corrichatachin:

"I felt myself comfortable enough in the afternoon. I then thought that my last night's riot was no more than such a social excess as may happen without much moral blame; and recollected that some physicians maintained, that a fever produced by it was, upon the whole, good for health: so different are our reflections on the same subject, at different periods; and such the excuses with which we palliate what we know to be wrong."

As a youth he was already aware of the perils of mere frivolity. "My great object is to attain a proper conduct in life." He tried to think, even at the age of twenty-three, that he was "at bottom a sober and grave man." When he wrote to Zelide, he conjured her in the most passionate style, to reduce her vivacity, to renounce the pursuit of imaginary pleasures, and he assured her of his own solemn devotion to the Christian faith. These counsels are due neither to a lover's jealousy nor to the pertinacity of a prig: they are in keeping with the serious ideal of behaviour that Boswell actually desired to personify.

He also wanted to be a man of culture. He wanted to appreciate the genuine æsthetic value of antiquities, of noble ruins, of lovely pictures. He wanted to know something about music: flute or fiddle, it mattered not if he could only become reasonably proficient. He was anxious to be a scholar, or at least to have the appearance of being a scholar. When he decided to go without dinner, sooner than lose the privilege of hearing Johnson talk, he was pleased to find that his "intellectual inclinations" had predominated.

Generally speaking, his intellectual inclinations did not predominate. His accounts of women in his private journals are those of a wallowing sensualist, with no relieving circumstance of gaiety or adventure or singularity—except, possibly, an escapade with Mrs. Rudd, celebrated in his maudlin poem of *Lurgan Clanbrassil*. There are touches of real sentiment and of real esteem in his allusions to his wife: he was never passionately in love with her, and the sight of the pretty Irish lady at Stratford instantly drove her out of his mind. He calls himself jocosely "an old Patriarch,"

and tries to make Temple (of all men!) condone his views on
"Asiatick multiplicity." After a very brief period of reform,
he ran as wild as ever. In describing one of his many
endeavours to make Johnson excuse adultery even on the
part of a woman, he wrote that deplorable passage in which
every contemporary reader could see the portrait of Lady
Diana Beauclerk:

> "While wewere alone [in Thrale's house] I endeavoured
> as well as I could to apologise for a lady who had been
> divorced from her husband by Act of Parliament. I said,
> that he had used her very ill, had behaved brutally to her,
> and that she could not continue to live with him without
> having her delicacy contaminated; that all affection for
> him was thus destroyed; that the essence of conjugal union
> being gone, there remained only a cold form, a mere civil
> obligation; that she was in the prime of life, with qualities
> to produce happiness; that these ought not to be lost; and,
> that the gentleman on whose account she was divorced
> had gained her heart while thus unhappily situated.
> Seduced, perhaps, by the charms of the lady in question,
> I thus attempted to palliate what I was sensible could
> not be justified; for when I had finished my harangue,
> my venerable friend gave me a proper check: 'My
> dear Sir, never accustom your mind to mingle virtue
> and vice. The woman's a whore, and there's an end
> on't.'"

As a fragment of autobiography, nothing could be more
illuminating. It would not be easy to combine, in a paragraph of the same length, so many different sorts of indelicacy.
At the same time, there is no malevolence of intention.
There is a moral, though brutally pointed, in the tail of the
story: the venerable friend gives him a proper check.
Beauclerk was dead when the *Life* was published; but Lady
Diana was alive, and so were scores of people who had known
her as Lady Bolingbroke.

And yet this crazy fellow, so garrulous and so mon-
strously indiscreet, had a way of making himself popular.

He was eminently a sociable man. Upon those who did not know him, and who met him for the first time, he generally made a good impression. He could not be alone with any man for two minutes without chattering to him, or with any woman without making love to her. It was an engaging disposition.

He was not one of those grim fellows who sat in the corner of the coach with their hats pulled over their eyes and their chins deeply sunk in woollen mufflers. He was all for a hob-nobbing and a tittle-tattle and a jolly indulgence of his pattering loquacity. That is why he was such a good travelling companion. In casual encounters he was charming: the proper man to meet in the parlour of an inn, here to-day and gone to-morrow, leaving behind him the memory of a droll, bantering fellow, a bit too fond of a bottle or a girl, but exceedingly pleasant.

"I have thought," he wrote to Temple, "of making a good acquaintance in each town upon the road. No man has been more successful in making acquaintance easily than I have been. I even bring people quickly to a degree of cordiality. I am a quick fire; but I know not if I last sufficiently." At another time he gave a striking instance of this: "I got into the fly at Buckden, and had a very good journey. An agreeable young widow nursed me and supported my lame foot on her knee. Am I not fortunate in having something about me that interests most people at first sight in my favour?"

In likening himself to a "quick fire" he was right. He knew that he was inconstant, always liable to changes of sentiment or affection.

He was aware of his change in regard to Johnson, though perhaps not aware of its real meaning. On the 20th of March 1778 he wrote in his journal: "I missed that aweful reverence with which I used to contemplate Mr. Samuel Johnson, in the complex magnitude of his literary, moral, and religious character. I have a wonderful superstitious love of *mystery*; when, perhaps, the truth is, that it is owing to the cloudy darkness of my own mind. I should be glad that I am more advanced in my progress of being, so that I can view Dr.

Johnson with a steadier and clearer eye. My dissatisfaction to-night was foolish. Would it not be foolish to regret that we shall have less mystery in a future state?"

In a little more than a year's time after he had written this, he was teasing Johnson, and himself, with his foolish experiment of keeping silence. He then discovered that Johnson's solicitude was "very flattering." He did not realise that he was actually being disturbed by the decay of a vital illusion, that he was actually getting tired of the Doctor.

"I am doubtful if it was right to make the experiment," he said, "though I have gained by it." He was wrong. He had not gained by it: he was trying, by a desperate artifice, to revive the old affection and the old mysterious reverence, but he had failed.

A deepening melancholy, a sense of inadequacy became more evident in the letters and other writings of the last fifteen years of his life. From his earliest days he had been aware of a morbid bias; at times, he said, he was a most unhappy dog, just rumbling along, dejected, apathetic, incapable of the least effort. And then a sudden bright effervescence of hope would sparkle up through the dark sediment of gloom, and he would again dream of eminence, of applause, and the glorious fulfilment of ambition. But, from about 1780 onwards, there are touches of mournful humility. "Often do I upraid and look down upon myself when, in contemplation of the heights of learning to which men may attain, I view my own inferiority, and think how much many others . . . are above me." In 1786, having realised that he could hope for no success at the English Bar, there is a more persistent note of despair in his writings. Pride was never quite extinguished, there were even revivals of ambition, new dreams of dignity, new visions of renown; but the last years were years of increasing darkness.

Perhaps it may appear strange that Boswell, who had so often expressed himself as a pious man, never received any substantial comfort or any enduring hope from religion. Yet he frequently walked into churches for the purpose of "adoring his god," he loved the observance of public worship and the placid solemnity of his Easter celebrations with Johnson is well known to readers of the *Life*.

It will be remembered how, on the Hebridean excursion, he carried *Ogden on Prayer* in his pocket, often reading this book aloud and often forcing it upon the Doctor. It will also be remembered how, near the close of Johnson's life, he joined with Dr. Adams in pestering him to compose a volume of prayers for the family.

There are many passages in the *Life* where he quotes the solemn meditations of Johnson or speaks reverently of his pious exercises. His general attitude, whenever he shows it, is that of a highly respectable churchman, treating religious infidelity as the most horrible evidence of a depraved character. In his youth he had been attracted by Roman Catholicism, and he had many conversations with Johnson on the subject of Catholic dogmas. He told Johnson, not long after they had met for the first time, that he had been "misled into a certain degree of infidelity," but was eventually "fully satisfied of the truth of the Christian revelation, though not clear as to every point considered to be orthodox." He argued about death and predestination until the Doctor told him to hold his tongue. He affirmed his belief that the supreme article of the Christian faith was the doctrine of immortality. On a certain Easter Day he earnestly told Johnson that he wanted to have all the arguments for Christianity always available in his mind, so that he might avoid being uneasy when his faith was attacked. In 1779 he informed the Doctor that he found it "divinely cheering" to think of the English cathedral at Carlisle, "so near to Auchinleck"—although it was more than eighty miles away. In 1781 he wrote a serious passage on the duty of communicants, and, although his own acts of devotion were only occasional, there is no reason to doubt the perfect sincerity of his religious impulse whenever it happened to show itself. The idea of "people with no religion at all" distressed him. If there are not many references to Christian teaching in his books and essays and private papers, the references, when they do occur, are such as might have been written by the most eminently religious man.

There are two essays on religion in the *Hypochondriack* series, in which exemplary principles of piety and toleration are demurely though clearly exhibited:

> "Supposing that religion were altogether a fiction, it is so grand a work of the imagination that the very ambition of a noble mind must desire to preserve it. . . . That there are many good Christians papists, and many good Christians methodists, I have no manner of doubt. . . . Surely the comfort which a religious man has in distress must be allowed to make his situation more desirable than that of an unbeliever; and in this view alone which of the two characters is best entitled to think itself superior to the other is obvious to the eye of wisdom."

Of course it is easy to say that Boswell's life was not that of a religious man, but rather the exact opposite. This need not be true. It is quite possible for a weak or dissolute man to be extremely religious when he happens to think about religion, or when he is brought into the sphere of direct religious activities. So it was in the case of Boswell. He looked at religion from two different points of view, the social and the emotional. The church was the permanent appanage of respectability, it represented the spiritual side of his atavistic propensities, it was the union of feudalism and of ancient privilege with divinity, it contained the holy registers of noble descent. On the purely emotional side the church (any church) represented a source of hope and encouragement, a theatre for the display of the more creditable aspirations. There need be no hypocrisy in either point of view, there is not the slightest evidence of religious hypocrisy in Boswell.

But still, his faith in Christianity had no effective influence upon his general behaviour, and no power to soothe or control the disorder of his mind. His vows in regard to drinking, for example, were not religious vows: they were nearly always conventional pledges of honour made to his personal friends. Perhaps the direct personal influence of a religious man, such as Temple, might have comforted him. As it was, he could find in Christianity nothing more than a casual emotion, a transient relief, and a guarantee of gentility.

CHAPTER XVIII

PERSPECTIVE

WE have studied Boswell in his relations with Johnson, we have seen him from Macaulay's point of view, and we have tried to find out what he thought of himself. In this manner, we have examined the testimony of many witnesses. Certain conclusions have no doubt presented themselves, certain ideas or suspicions have taken a more definite form. The ultimate assessment of character—if such a thing is possible—lies outside the true province of biography, and could only be attempted by means of a frigidly scientific analysis of mental components and of personal permutations. But surely it is the duty of the biographer to arrange or summarise his evidence in such a way that it may be quickly available for the more delicate procedures of the analyst. It is doubtful if bias can be totally excluded from this arrangement, but the attempt has to be made, the loose details have to be fitted together in a final stereographic view.

Boswell thought of himself, in happier moments, as a man of delightful originality, wise among philosophers, cheerful with good fellows, brilliant among wits, a citizen of the world, a gentleman worthily representing an ancient house and certainly deserving a place in the government, a writer of uncommon genius, a gay companion, a splendid lover, impulsive and romantic, and yet afflicted with dark humours, a strange man, a man of mystery, the most puzzling, the most interesting, the most remarkable man that ever lived. Other people thought very differently of him. Those who liked him praised his good-humour and allowed that he was entertaining. No one, except Johnson, ever praised him in terms that were not qualified by some derogatory addition. Even his capacity for amusing is reduced to that of a mere buffoon. Cowper said, "Boswell was an entertaining companion when he had drunk his bottle, but not before." It is impossible to produce, on behalf of James Boswell, anything like a substantial body of contemporary comment which is entirely favourable or even reassuring.

It may be doubted, perhaps, whether the life and character of Boswell are of sufficient interest to deserve an elaborate or voluminous presentation. He is not a thinker, he is not a figure of historical importance, he is not a master of literary style. His merit, for us as for his contemporaries, is that of an entertainer. In no sense can we reckon him as one of the really significant men of his period.

All this may be true; and yet it is equally true that Boswell is profoundly interesting. He is interesting because of his unique position in literature, and because of his legendary association with Dr. Johnson. He is interesting because of the apparent difficulties in the way of getting a true register between the social and the personal view, and also between futility on the one hand and a more than ordinary competence on the other. In believing himself to be a singular man he was not mistaken. He did not appear to others as he appeared to himself, except in this matter of singularity. He had many of the qualities that make a man offensive, or even intolerable. And yet he was admitted to the most brilliant and the most exclusive society; he was the friend, or at least the associate, of the most distinguished men.

The explanation of this character will depend, we believe, upon the study of its mental abnormalities, keeping in view the probability of a definite mental disease. We intend, in conclusion, to present the reader with some of the more obvious materials for such a study.

All the writings of Boswell, his journals and letters and his published books, provide evidence of an exaggerated sensibility, often approaching a state of erethism. A touching story or a noble sentiment will bring the tears to his eyes. Let him but hear the skirling pipes and he is ready to grasp a claymore and rush to battle. There are times when his adoration of Johnson reaches the level of ecstasy. He was penetrated by Johnson in the earlier days of his infatuation: he went to the length of imitating him habitually, of copying his loose clothes and fidgety manners. His letters are full of twitterings and flutterings—O Temple! O Jack Wilkes! Alas, my friend! O my dear friend! What a fellow am I! What a state is this! The combined influences of placid weather, Sunday peace, worship in a country church, and the presence of the Doctor in a grave, serene mood fairly melt him in a gush of piety and affection. There is a complete surrender, almost a womanly surrender, to the impressions of the moment.

Take this passage from the *Hebrides*, in which he describes the effect of McQueen's account of his experiences with the Highland army in 1745:

"As he narrated the particulars of that ill-advised, but brave attempt, I could not refrain from tears. There is a certain association of ideas in my mind upon that subject, by which I am strangely affected. The very Highland names, or the sound of a bagpipe, will stir my blood, and fill me with a mixture of melancholy and respect for courage; with pity for an unfortunate and superstitious regard for antiquity, and thoughtless inclination for war; in short, with a crowd of sensations with which sober rationality has nothing to do."

When Johnson spoke of the people rising against an abuse of power, Boswell immediately felt "his blood stirred to a pitch of fancied resistance." He would certainly have followed any leader who could thus rouse his emotions. After talking to Captain Cook, he "catched the enthusiasm of curiosity and adventure, and felt a strong inclination to go with him on his next voyage." Johnson drily observed that a man could learn little from such voyages, and Boswell replied: "But one is carried away with the general grand and indistinct notion of *A Voyage Round the World*." No reply could have been more characteristic. He was being continually carried away (though never carried far) by these grand indistinct notions. He listened to Johnson talking about travel in foreign countries, and expressing a powerful and perverse admiration for the Great Wall of China. Boswell at once "catched the enthusiasm," as he did when listening to Cook, and he said: "I really believe, Sir, that I should go and see the Wall of China had I not children, of whom it is my duty to take care."

Again and again you will find the evidence of a quickly responding element of pure fantasy. He is ready to imagine himself in a character or a situation "with which sober rationality has nothing to do." "I am continually *conscious*," he wrote to Temple, "continually *looking back* and *looking forward* and wondering how I shall feel in situations which I contemplate in fancy." He is abnormally sensitive to impressions of a romantic nature; he is like an instrument so adjusted as to respond to all emotional frequencies, but the response is automatic, undiscriminating, and without control.

At Fort George, the mere sound of a drum beating for dinner is enough to make Boswell "fancy himself a military man," and the childish fancy pleases him. When he is being rowed past the black shores of Skye by a crew of wild, singing Highlanders, he gets "an impression of being upon an American river." On the occasion of another Hebridean voyage, he "imagines that he could go with ease to America or the East Indies"—until he is reduced by sickness. The sight of the ladies' maids at Inveraray makes him feel that "he could be a knight-errant for them."

He is always playing up to some entirely romantic idea of personality. He struts on the parade ground at Potsdam with a blue Scotch bonnet on his head, hoping that people will say, "Who is that extraordinary fellow, and what on earth is he wearing?" and that someone will answer, "It is James Boswell of Auchinleck, Esquire, a young Scots gentleman of noble blood, now on his travels." Before visiting Rousseau and Voltaire he keyed himself up to the appropriate mood, he studied his dress, his manners, every stage of his approach; and he sent before him letters which he considered marvels of delicacy and wit, so that Rousseau and Voltaire might also be keyed up to the appropriate mood. Everywhere, and at all times of his life, even in the last miserable years, it is the same story.

In Corsica, he becomes as much of a Corsican as possible:

when he is in a monastery he soon feels "as if he had been a friar for seven years." To get on Paoli's horse is to be Paoli for the moment: "I allowed myself to indulge a momentary pride in this parade, as I was curious to experience what could really be the pleasure of state and distinction with which mankind are so strangely intoxicated." All that is necessary in order to realise this pleasure is a horse with furniture of red velvet, and an escort of half-a-dozen foot-guards. Again, when the jolly Corsicans are trying to sing "Hearts of Oak," our versatile Boswell fancies himself "to be a recruiting sea officer," with his Corsican chorus "aboard the British fleet."

These examples of sensibility and imagination are enough to prove something more than a mere harmless peculiarity of mind. What they do prove is a purely infantile quality of make-believe, not extended to the level of conscious art, and a very precarious mental balance. It is necessary to insist upon the infantile quality and upon the absence of anything like a true poetic, or even a true romantic, bias. The response is emphatically not that of a poet, but it certainly is the response of a childish mind. If this quality was a symptom of mental disorder, or at least of inadequate mental development, it was not by any means without compensating advantages. It gave Boswell a feminine air of responsiveness which, coupled with a gushing good-humour, must have been a principal reason for such popularity as he did obtain. It made him eager to adapt himself, or to abandon himself, to people or places or societies. It served the purposes of argument or appeal; and it prevented his friends from taking him too seriously. Nothing is more significant than the fact that Boswell's relations with women, at least his intimate relations, were exclusively sexual. He never obtained, and he never sought, the friendship of a woman. And it is abundantly clear that women generally avoided him and despised him. His reputation for drunken-ness and lewdness cannot have accounted for this entirely: it was due to a more subtle discernment of his mental character, which was essentially not the character of a normal man. There is nothing which excites more readily the aversion and the horror of women than a suggestion of insanity, for there is nothing which tends more to confuse or disintegrate the sexual distinctions.

On the other hand, mental instability is likely enough to make a man amusing and attractive to other men; particularly when it involves, as it did in the case of Boswell, qualities not commonly associated with masculine types. He was obviously attractive and amusing, but here again it is important to remember that the attitude of other men towards him was almost invariably a guarded or qualified attitude. Men of natural benevolence, like Johnson, Paoli and Reynolds, treated him with patronising care; they tried to protect him or advise him; they never thought of him as one who was really independent or responsible in the ordinary sense. The attitude of Johnson, in particular, was clearly emotional. So in all his relations with the men he knew there was a blending of patronage and conviviality: there was very rarely a deep sentiment of real friendship. The most important friendship of his life was undoubtedly his friendship with Temple, and this was largely maintained by the tepid medium of letter-writing.

The feminine side of Boswell is curiously and vividly illustrated by his delight in watching executions. The hanging of men, women and children was a London spectacle in which many others took delight; and the immense crowds which flocked so eagerly to Tyburn were composed largely of women.

"Of all publick spectacles," said Boswell, "that of a capital execution draws the greatest number of spectators. And I must confess that I myself am never absent from any of them." Sometimes he rode in the hearse or the carriage with a condemned man, closely observing him. When he first attended these dismal scenes he was deeply shocked, but presently he viewed them "with great composure"— they were only "matters of curious speculation, relieved of their dreary ideas." They were fine opportunities for the gentle exercise of sensibility; and they cost nothing. In this he resembled another effeminate man, with an even greater passion for corpses, hangings and burials—George Selwyn.

In the course of this book we have come across many of Boswell's own references to the state of his mind. He was aware of his disorder. There was nothing imaginary in his pictures of mental gloom and of rioting fancies. We have seen how he tried, by various unavailing devices, to "fix" himself; how he turned from one scheme to another; at what crazy angles he deviated from his path in order to pursue some new illusion.

The actual dread of insanity, the fear of the "black dog," is painfully exhibited in scores of passages. "I am conscious of my distempered mind." In 1789 he said to Temple: "Years of life seem insupportable. . . . Every prospect that I turn my mind's eye upon is dreary. *Why* should I struggle? I certainly am *constitutionally* unfit for any employment." And again: "Malone says I have not the use of my faculties. They have been torpid for some time, except in conversation. I hope to recover them." There is no need for a minute or extended analysis of such evidence, which is clear to the most amateur psychologist: it points in one direction and its meaning is unmistakable.

In those curious *Hypochondriack* essays, highly important in the biography and the bibliography of Boswell, he often touches upon aspects of his mental troubles. Of these allusions the most singular are those which describe the effect of words or speculations upon his mind. He wrote in 1779: "To speculate for instruction, or for amusement, is wise; but to distend our faculties by ineffectual stretches is both unwise and painful."

Again in 1782: "Words, the representations, or rather signs of ideas and notions, though habitual to all of us, are, when abstractly considered, exceedingly wonderful; in so much, that by endeavouring to think of them with a spirit of intense enquiry, I have been affected even with giddiness and a kind of stupor, the consequence of having one's faculties stretched in vain."

And again in 1783: "To think eagerly of the nature of Time itself, simply considered, is enough to turn one's brain."

There are many passages in the *Life* where he stresses the

melancholy of Johnson, and he certainly did this with the idea of suggesting a comforting parallel with his own case. Johnson, he says, was (like his biographer) a hypochondriac; but he was not degraded by this; his mind was entire. "Insanity was the object of his most dismal apprehension; and he fancied himself seized by it, or approaching to it, at the very time when he was giving proofs of a more than ordinary soundness and vigour of judgment." This is a purely gratuitous theory. He also refers to "the oppression and distraction of a disease which very few have felt to its full extent," and there are frequent dark allusions to the supposed mental uneasiness of Johnson, his terrors and his mournful sense of moral imperfection. Here, as Dr. Birkbeck Hill pointed out many years ago, Boswell is exaggerating the infirmity of Johnson for his own advantage.

Mental disequilibrium is accompanied by eccentricity of behaviour, and by a failure to make those adaptations which are required by normal social intercourse. Of all this the life of Boswell affords continuous evidence. His behaviour was often eccentric to an almost unbelievable degree, and there was never a man who blundered more frequently. Over and over again, by his failure to recognise ordinary social contingencies, he wandered off his bearings—not knowing that he had done so, and eagerly recording and publishing the evidence against himself. Extreme sensibility to emotional and dramatic values was associated with extreme blindness to general opinion; an association which is commonly found in cases of megalomania.

Symptoms of megalomania, indeed, are to be found in all the phases of Boswell, in all the actions of his life and in all his writings. His wretched oscillations, his moral staggering, his total inability to fix himself, were caused by a top-heavy, unsteady load of egoism, a burden of enormous conceit.

But this, in its turn, was modified by a partial recognition of his own state. Had it not been for this load of inordinate pride he would have been blown unresisting into the limbo of pure lunacy. There was nothing that he dreaded more than a forcible reduction of pride. For this reason he tried, by all possible means, to justify his conceit of himself; for this reason he exploited Johnson, living or dead, with all the resources at his command; and for this reason he composed his grand biography. Nor is there any difficulty if we remember this constant reference to the ego, in explaining how it was that he never knew when he was being futile or irritating or absurd. He kept in view an idealised version or vision of himself, and he believed in the special merit of all that he did or said. "There is," he wrote, "a benignant principle in human nature which disposes men in general to have an irresistible predilection for themselves, and all that is connected with them as participating of themselves."

Nothing short of a distempered egoism could have led him to set down for the public such records of talk and action as may be found in his books. It is enough to recall the part which he played, and which he was proud to play, in the Johnsonian dialogues. Take, at random, his actual sentences in one of these dialogues:

"Foote has a great deal of humour.—He has a singular talent of exhibiting character.—Did not he think of exhibiting you, Sir?—Pray, Sir, is not Foote an infidel? —I suppose, Sir, he has thought superficially, and seized the first notions which occurred to his mind.—What do you think of Dr. Young's *Night Thoughts*, Sir?—Is there not less religion in the nation now, Sir, then there was formerly? For instance, there used to be a chaplain in every great family, which we do not find now.—But, Sir, the mind must be employed, and we grow weary when idle."

These lines, let it be observed, which are picked at hazard from the *Life*, show Boswell at his best: he is not driving the Doctor into a rage, or spoiling the talk by his own floundering buffoonery. And even at his best he is dull, wearisome or futile, rambling vaguely from one thing to another. He was content to set down as a chosen example of his wit such a feeble thing as the following:

"My wife was angry at a silk cloak for Veronica being ill-made, and said it could not be *altered*. 'Then,' said I, it must be a *Persian* cloak,' alluding to the silk called Persian and the unalterable *Persian* laws."

Sanity is not among the necessary qualifications of a writer, nor is mere literary competence a thing which depends upon high intellectual standards. Boswell could certainly write; he was a competent writer with special abilities; but he is not one of the great masters of literature.

His motives in writing have already been suggested: he wrote copiously, in letters, and in private journals for his immediate relief, and he wrote books, pamphlets and essays in order to obtain the vital comfort of public praise and of public renown. His private papers, handed over to Colonel Isham by the living representative of the Auchinleck family, form an enormous bulk of exceedingly varied materials, some of them entirely worthless, others of the highest biographical importance, and others which merely amplify, in no pleasant manner, the aspects of Boswell which are made sufficiently clear in his letters to Temple. In one sense, the importance of these papers is their prodigious number. They show that Boswell must have spent no small part of his life in the practice of private journalism. The bulk of what he published is far greater than is commonly supposed: he wrote, under pseudonyms, a vast number of notes and articles for the Edinburgh and London papers. The industry and zeal of Professor Pottle have unearthed nearly two hundred of these newspaper items from the *London Chronicle* alone. But the bulk of what he wrote for his own "archives" is probably greater than the whole bulk of his published work. When we remember his idleness, his drunkenness and distractions, it is clear that he must have written with extraordinary facility.

From his boyhood to the last year of his life Boswell never let slip an opportunity for getting into print. What he actually printed was not his chief concern. In his periodical essays, he employed, without shame, the most paltry devices of the journalist. He borrowed without acknowledgment; he copied Greek and Latin tags from other writers, without knowing whether they were correct or not, and so he transferred to his own copy innumerable mistakes. He did not hesitate to reveal his technique for the benefit of his readers: "It is not very difficult," he said, "to avoid direct quotation, by changing the form of a sentiment." In all his various essays there is hardly a single idea which can be termed original, or even a borrowed idea which is neatly presented. He is only felicitous when he is recording what he has observed with his own eyes, or heard with his own ears—when he is transcribing from direct experience. Such felicity is naturally cultivated by the keeping of a private journal.

The literary excellence of Boswell is undoubtedly in his narrative. This particular excellence is to be found in many parts of his journals, where he is describing his jaunts or tours or wayside conversations. As long as he is observing and recording he is delightful; but there is no writer more insufferably dull when he tries to reflect or moralise. Let him once fall into the hollows of his pompous manner and he is flat, sterile, disheartening. No one can deny that there are hundreds of pages in the *Life of Johnson* which cannot be read without irritation or bewilderment. It is indeed the most striking proof of the admirable qualities of this book, that we are able to endure the blundering intrusions of the importunate Scotch gentleman, with his vexing footnotes, his foolish confidential whispers and his poor meandering gossip.

But if he excels in his rendering of dialogue, he is not less admirable in his lively portraits of men. He could not attempt, with any degree of confidence, the portrait of a woman. He could reproduce, with vigour and with joy, a bold character, a striking gesture, a curious appearance; the more subtle shades or graces eluded him. Men who were gentle or reserved in company, such as Reynolds or Burke, do not leap to life in his pages like those who were obstreperous and picturesque—men like Goldsmith and Garrick and Wilkes. A deep knowledge of human nature was beyond him; he did not possess the power to comprehend the essential qualities of the mind.

His portrait of Johnson, visible and vociferating, is perhaps the most wonderful objective portrait in literature. Yet the picture, with all its marvels of relief and illusion, is a picture with clear dimensional boundaries, it is objective in the proper sense of the term. This quality of pictorial vigour is often found in the smaller portraits, as in those of the priest in Corsica, of Langton, of Dr. Taylor, of Monboddo and scores of others. Take, as a particularly good example, the portrait of Malcolm Macleod:

"He was now sixty-two years of age, hale, and well proportioned,—with a manly countenance, tanned by the weather, yet having a ruddiness on his cheeks, over a great part of which his rough beard extended. His eye was quick and lively, yet his look was not fierce, but he appeared at once firm and good-humoured. He wore a pair of brogues,—Tartan hose which came up only near to his knees, and left them bare,—a purple camblet kilt, —a black waistcoat,—a short green cloth bound with gold cord,—a yellowish bushy wig,—a large blue bonnet with a gold thread button."

Half of this description, you will notice, is devoted to the dress of Macleod. It is a breathless description, running along with a series of dashes, as though he is determined to hold your attention while you listen to these interesting particulars; or as though he was quickly jotting down the details of the costume in the presence of Macleod himself. It is a typical Boswellian portrait—a full-length miniature, brightly painted. If you had seen Macleod walking up to the farm at Corrichatachin, so, no doubt, he would have appeared to you, a very complete Highlander with a purple kilt swinging above his bare knees. The dress is recognised, properly, as highly important; all the touches of colour are in the right place.

Even in a single sentence Boswell is able to give all that need be known of a character: "Lochbuy proved to

be only a bluff, comely, noisy old gentleman, proud of his
hereditary consequence, and a very hearty and hospitable
landlord."

It is in such descriptions that Boswell is most happy.
When he is looking about him with that good-humoured air
of his, forgetting all his fears and anxieties, he feels the zest
of life and the joy of companionship. People who could
make him gay appealed to him most, for he was continually
seeking distraction. He liked bustling fellows, fellows with
careless vivacity. Players and soldiers were always congenial
to him. Dresses and uniforms were his particular delight—
clothes are the representation or defence of character, they
help to fix you, or to lift you above the dreadful hum-drum
of the commonplace. This attitude towards dress, clearly
the attitude of Boswell, is yet one more instance of a feminine
point of view.

He wanted to be natural, and yet he wanted to be
extraordinary. His extreme egoism was actually the defence
of a man who is desperately trying to escape from the crowd
of besieging fears in his own mind. Boswell knew that he
was being hunted down by devils and black dogs and all the
horrors of melancholia. He tried to escape, but he never did
escape. All his blatancy, all his ridiculous pride, all his
wild excesses were due to this recurring panic. In his actions,
his writings, in the attitude of his contemporaries, in silence
as well as in assertion, there is unmistakable evidence of the
fact that he was insane; not insane to a dangerous or marked
degree, but certainly on the wrong side of the border-line.
It is important to recollect that he was the first child of
cousins-german, that one of his own children, Euphemia,
was mentally deranged, and that his brother John, the
second son of Lord Auchinleck, was taciturn to a degree
bordering upon actual insanity.

If we are right, it was not drink that made Boswell insane;
it was congenital insanity that drove him to drink and every
wild indulgence; and those indulgences at last destroyed him.
The biographical data cannot lead to any other conclusion.

Biography used to be a vehicle for noble sentiment or

profitable moralising. The good biographer brought his work to a close with gentle harmonies of approval or with pious valediction. Now we are more accustomed to reviews of neuroses and complexes and all the rest of the psychological paraphernalia. Those who are not yet tired of playing at psycho-analysis will find in the history of Boswell most promising materials for their pastime. The moralist will not be so well satisfied. Perhaps the ordinary person, who is neither moral nor scientific, will not be ashamed of trying to think kindly of Boswell and of pointing to the better side of his unfortunate disposition. His work brings to innumerable thousands the comfort, relief and delight that he himself sought in vain. How and why he wrote this work need not concern us any longer; mere gratitude, mere decency will make us compassionate, will incline us to regard Boswell, if not with tenderness, at least with pity.

His conscious impulses were those of a kind man. He readily interceded, less than two years before his death, on behalf of three convicts who had escaped from Botany Bay and who were kept languishing in Newgate. His kindness to the tenantry of Auchinleck, especially to those who were old or sick, is amply displayed in his letters and papers. He tried, honestly enough, to give good advice to young men. He lent or gave money to those in distress as freely as he borrowed it for his own needs. If he was a little ostentatious in hospitality, no man ever took a warmer social delight in entertaining. Even those who disliked him (Mrs. Thrale, Hannah More and Fanny Burney, for example) admitted the charm of his good-humour and his drollery.

It may be said that his failings outweigh his limited stock of minor virtues; that his treatment of his wife can only be termed execrable; that his treacheries were not lessened, but rather aggravated, by the flashy appearance of good-nature. If this is true, we can still defend him by showing that he was not a man of a composed mind, he was not morally responsible. An ideally bad man is incapable of remorse; but poor Boswell felt remorse of the most searching and most agonising description.

The story of this unfortunate man—for so he was—is the story of one who was doomed by a nameless, incurable and persistent malady of the mind. If there is a moral here, it is a purely eugenic moral in favour of exogamous marriages.

INDEX

DATE DUE